MW00957922

Publisher: Blitzen, LLC

Copyright © February 8, 2022 Paul Caimi

One Minute to Serenity

365 Daily Strategies to Navigate Life in the 21st Century

Paul Caimi JD, LCDC

Contents

Appendix

Why use this book?

Here's something we all want! Serenity. The problem is we try to get it in the WRONG way, and most of our attempts lead to misery. What do we do wrong? We try to get serenity through power, materialism, security, hard work, vanity, vacations, the attainment of goals, winning, and futile attempts at controlling people, places, and things. But, even when we attain these things, we discover that we are still not fulfilled – still not serene. This book provides an answer to the puzzle of serenity. It is especially for you if you keep failing to find lasting serenity. It gives you a method that has worked for hundreds of thousands of people worldwide.

The Author's background at a glimpse:

Lost, bankrupt, and miserable, I finally flipped my car over in a drunken haze. Suspended upside down by my seat belt, I realized that I was sorely mistaken about what would bring me serenity. This crisis started my journey from a handcuffed, shame-filled failure to a successful lawyer, therapist, and app developer.

I had all the advantages growing up...safe neighborhoods, wants fulfilled, two loving parents. But I had a problem. I always felt something was missing in my life. I never felt at peace. I always felt as if I had to live up to others' expectations. I compared myself to others, was jealous, resentful, and a sore sport. I never accepted anything about myself. I had the classic Napoleonic complex and was narcissistic - an egomaniac with an inferiority crisis. Even as a child, I was driven to attain status and live the perfect American dream even though, like my hero Holden Caulfield, I inwardly felt that people who sought the American dream were phony. I loved no one and considered people as obstacles to my desires.

At 16 years old, I stole a six pack of beer from the grocery store where I worked and drank it alone on a deserted golf course near my home. That six pack changed my life. For a moment, I felt peace. From that day on, I tried to duplicate that moment the only way I knew how: by drinking, but that magical feeling would not come back. I would study, try to build my list of accomplishments in a panic driven, desperate desire to be admitted to Harvard, and drink alcohol to cope with my stress. After finally being admitted to Harvard, I drank daily, and dreamed of becoming a movie star. I believed that stardom would bring me peace - that fame, fortune, and sex would give me that feeling I had felt for that brief moment back on the golf course when I first got drunk. After a year in Hollywood, stardom seemed hopeless, and I continued to drink never able to find that magical feeling until my last drunk when I flipped over my car. Since then (for 33 years as of the date of this book), I have stayed sober by practicing serenity principles. I have been able to recover from alcoholism, raise a family, be faithful to my wife, attain financial security, keep good health, maintain serenity, and be almost as loyal to my dog as he is to me. All of this is due to the principles - the daily process - I discuss in this book. **If they can work for me, and for the hundreds of thousands who have used them in my app, they can work for you.**

How to use this book

Read a message each morning.
This should take about a minute.
If you have a serenity threatening
issue, go to "Troubled?" for a
relevant, helpful message.

Check the appendix for concepts
referred to in the messages.

January 1

Let Go Before Making Scratch Marks On It

"Acceptance is usually more a matter of fatigue than anything else."
- David Foster Wallace.

Today I know it's OK to accept life on life's terms without endless struggling, well before I am worn out and fatigued...that I can let go of trying to direct everyone and everything. I am allowed to relax and let others live their lives. All of this over controlling used to make me want to escape life through bad habits like raging, over sleeping, isolating or withdrawing into myself. Today I am grateful I can let go and live by a new philosophy. If I need to take care of something, I face the challenge, act reasonably, but I don't expect everything to go my way.

TO DO: Today I will remember to let go of what I can't control, act reasonably to face challenges, but not make my serenity* dependent on outcomes. I will make enjoying the adventure more important than the outcome.

*see appendix, page 424, for a definition of serenity

January 2

Oak Tree Breaks, Willow Tree Bends

Be like the willow tree not the oak tree. The willow tree adapts to life and bounces back to stand tall when the winds stop blowing. The oak tree snaps when the winds of life strengthen. In recovery, we do what we can to change ourselves to adapt to life rather than always trying to change life which can often be an impossible task. This concept is especially helpful if I become shocked, overwhelmed, or if I need to compromise when making a decision.

TO DO: Today I will think and act like the willow tree because I know to stay serene I need to adapt to life rather than expect life to adapt to me.

January 3

I Fail but I Am Not a Failure

There is a big difference between recognizing that I do acts that fail and labeling myself as a failure. For example, I may say something that seems wrong, but that does not mean I am an evil person. I may make mistakes at work but that does not mean I am a bad employee. Nevertheless, if I keep suffering bad consequences as a result of my actions, it may be helpful for me to admit I need help.

TO DO: Today I will be careful about labeling myself. I will not be hard on myself, be discouraged or ashamed. I refuse to label myself a failure just because I do something that failed. In fact, I will congratulate myself for trying, attempt to learn from my mistakes, and be open to change.

January 4

"Ain't No Saint Without a Past,
Ain't No Sinner Without a Future."

- Saint Augustine

Don't give up hope, even if you have done worse things than you can imagine. It doesn't matter where you've been. It's where you are going that counts. You have potential for greatness. James had spent years in prison for drug trafficking. There he began his recovery from his addiction. When released he continued to go to recovery meetings and worked a great daily program. He became a great lawyer. Whenever I treated an addicted patient who had been imprisoned, I would ask James to talk to the patient. Because he had also been incarcerated, my patients were always inspired by James.

Where do you need to forgive yourself? What can you do today to take a small step to improve? What kind of a person would you like to be?

TO DO: Today, I will remember not to give up faith in attaining greatness. I will measure greatness not by what I get, but by what I give, by what I can contribute to the solution without overcontrolling others or making my happiness dependent on results. By hitting bottom, I can reach the top. I will not be afraid or ashamed. I will not be depressed. I will not be hopeless no matter how low I may have fallen. I will look to this day with hope and faith!

January 5

I Can't Dance With Arrogance

Sometimes it's hard for me to quell my arrogance and narcissism because they seem to give me a rush of power that temporarily gives me strength to press on. I've come to believe that this rush is erroneous personal programming because I actually perform better when I am calmly doing what I need to do in the moment. For example, when I make a bad shot during a tie breaker in tennis, rather than self-flagellating or conversely telling myself I am great in order to motivate myself, I tend to play better if I just quickly analyze what I may have done incorrectly and adjust. Taking my imbalanced ego out of it keeps me from quitting, getting intimidated or becoming overconfident. What keeps you hanging on to your arrogance?

TO DO: Today, I will be aware of my arrogance and narcissism. If I feel manic or depressed, I will pause and meditate on being even keeled. I will calmly deal with problems without making the problems a reflection of how great or bad I am. I will remember that the World is not all about me, and that I can't dance with arrogance.

January 6

Stinking Thinking is Serenity Shrinking

Sometimes I need to repeat throughout the day: "Stinking thinking is serenity shrinking." Today, I knew stinking thinking had started because I kept wondering why something I definitely could not control had to be the way I wanted it to be. I was thinking about how my sister was in prison due to her addiction. I was worrying about how my daughter was flying on an airplane and whether or not she would be safe. I got out of stinking thinking by consciously saying to myself that my thoughts were not productive. I then substituted the stinking thinking with GRATEFUL THINKING. Another stinking thought is thinking IF I GET WHAT I WANT I WILL BE HAPPY. Nothing can be further from the truth. I got the Mexican vacation and the children threw up, the plane was delayed, and the accommodations were overlooking the dark jungle instead of the sunny beach. I finally passed the bar exam, and then I was confronted with all the stresses of being a lawyer: the angry clients, the demanding partners, the obnoxious judges. Until I was able to practice serenity principles during the vacation and while practicing law, I was miserable. In fact, every time I've gotten what I wanted, it has ended up making me want more or something else. Even if things have worked out, there have been commensurate difficulties along the way. The key to happiness is not getting what I want. It is removing the want and simply working toward a goal by doing the next reasonable thing according to effective serenity principles.

TO DO: Today I will not worry about things that are beyond my control. I will also be grateful for what I have rather than wanting more. I will remember that wants cause stress and that acceptance causes peace. I will repeat to myself, "STINKING THINKING IS SERENITY SHRINKING."

January 7

Your Crisis is a Miracle Waiting to Happen

So you've hit bottom and you don't know what to do. You've lost all your money. You've lost your wife. You struck out when the game was on the line. You feel like you made a stupid decision. You are waking up and have to go to a job you hate. You can't make it through the morning without crying in despair. Or, you just feel as if life is pointless, that you have no real future.

TO DO: Whatever your crisis, try applying the four steps*. (1) Accept and adapt, (2) be grateful for what you have, (3) connect to HELP for your particular issue, and (4) try to identify and change a self-defeating behavior. Miracles will happen! One day you will realize that your crisis will be the beginning of a triumph you could never have predicted.

*see appendix, page 425, for a description of the four steps

January 8

Mindfulness is Like Walking on a Safe Tightrope

What would you be thinking if you were walking on a tightrope? Would you be worried about how to pay for your children's education? Would you be hating your neighbor because he can't control his barking dog? Or would you be completely focused on the HERE AND NOW? Mindfulness can be done anytime, anywhere. If you are worried, resentful, or fearful, mindfulness will lead you back in the right direction.

TO DO: Try approaching each moment today as if you are walking on a tightrope. Every time your mind wanders, refocus on each step so you can walk safely and peacefully. And remember, if you relax and breathe easy, you can't fall off of this tightrope...it is actually a very safe place.

January 9

Sometimes My Higher Power Calms the Storm, Other Times My Higher Power Calms Me Until the Storm Passes

When troubles come, we are never alone. We may not be able to control the storm but we can always turn to our Higher Power* to give us peace. Our Higher Power might be, but does not have to be a religious God; our Higher Power can be anything that restores us to sanity that does not interfere with our ability to function. Everything changes and our Higher Power helps us survive and thrive if we accept change. The more we try to control things we can't, the more we turn away from our Higher Power's peace. Especially when overwhelmed or stressed, our Higher Power calms the storm.

TO DO: Today I will know that my Higher Power will help me deal with any storm if I follow my Higher Power's guidance. Such guidance might be asking another person for help, journaling, eating something healthy, exercising, dealing appropriately with a feeling, remembering to be grateful, being flexible, having perspective, letting go of controlling others, or perhaps just being still and meditating on love.

*see appendix, page 437, for a description of Higher Power

January 10

If My Higher Power Is My Co-Pilot, I Am Going to Crash

It's Saturday morning. Hooray! Nothing is going to get in the way of what I want to do. I roll out of bed and see my dog has pooped on the floor. I grimace as I clean it up. Then, I check my emails, and I have to do some work. On and on, things happen that are not in my plans for this Saturday morning. I am clearly not in charge of my own destiny. I look back on my life and it is clear that I have never been in charge. Yet, this illusion keeps making me frustrated, disappointed and angry. I tell myself that I truly need to remember that I am not running the show and that I need to stay flexible and follow, not fight, where my Higher Power (the process that keeps me serene) leads me. My Higher Power is the power to accept and adjust, to live with love and unselfishness. All of a sudden the bad feelings disappear. I remember that even though I have to clean up dog poop, I am blessed to have a dog. Eventually I am joyfully surprised as I see beautiful children surfing in the ocean (which I interpret as a little gift from my pilot that was not in my plans). When I accept and adapt well to life's difficulties rather than retreat into denial and resentfully react, I am following my pilot's will and I stay serene.

TO DO: Today, I will avoid being overwhelmed and confused as I remember who is running the show. I will remember that taking control from my pilot makes me crash.

January 11

The Big Red Stop Sign

I used to lash out at others even though such behavior only alienated them. I used to think that ruminating over something I could not change, like a bad call in a tennis match, was somehow going to improve a lost outcome. But all it did was distract me and make me resentful. I used to think that trying to be perfect was an asset, but all it did was make me feel worse when I inevitably was not perfect. I used to think that worrying would somehow help me, but all it did was make me more fearful. I used to think selfishness, impatience, dishonesty and other character defects actually helped me. But all they did was make me anxious, depressed and then drunk. Part of my problem was my mistaken belief that these character defects (angry outbursts, ruminating, worrying. perfectionism, etc.) had some value in getting my way. The beginning of change for me was realizing that they are NEVER effective in any way.

TO DO: Today I will remember that character defects don't help me or anyone else. I will be aware of my feelings, and if a feeling is threatening to make me "act out" in a self-defeating way, I will remember that "acting out" is a character defect, and my character defects do not have any redeeming value. I will then envision a RED STOP SIGN, take three deep breaths, and enjoy the freedom that results from not turning a challenging feeling into a character defect.

January 12

"Always in Motion Is the Future."
– Yoda

Yoda understands serenity. He knows that to try to control the future is like trying to catch a feather in a hurricane. Attempting to control what we cannot is a set up for misery. You do not have a crystal ball. You cannot control the future so stop obsessing on it.

TO DO: Bring your mind back to the NOW. Stretch your hands open and repeat to yourself, "Let go! Let go!" Try this technique throughout this day if you start worrying about what might happen to you or if any wasteful thoughts enter your mind.

January 13

Don't Beat Yourself up Over Mistakes

You are going to make mistakes; so it's unreasonable to worry about
making them. Trying to be perfect is a character defect. Trying to
learn from mistakes is of course helpful, but sometimes you might
even make the same mistake again even though you thought you
were doing the best you could. Sometimes it is even hard to assess
whether you made a mistake because you are looking at what
happened in hindsight and "hindsight is 20/20." Sometimes time
makes what seemed like a mistake not a mistake. But whatever
the outcome, remember NOT TO BEAT YOURSELF UP OVER
MISTAKES. I used to treat myself very unfairly and get very
depressed just because I made mistakes. How do you treat yourself
when you foul up?

TO DO: Today I will not beat myself up for making mistakes. I will
also not fret over whether I am making the correct decision. Rather,
I will try to remember similar situations and consider whether any of
the mistakes I made apply to my present decision. I will have faith
that if I am practicing good principles like love, purity, honesty and
unselfishness (the four absolutes), I am acting reasonably in this
moment.

January 14

Unselfishness Is Self-Caring

I am usually upset when something I don't like is happening to me. A tool to take my focus off of me is to be unselfish. Doing something for someone else, even a smile at a stranger, takes my focus off of my problems and relieves my bad feelings. Self-caring involves unselfishness, compassion, love, and good acts. Selfishness is greed, resentment, fear, and bad acts. Self-caring makes me feel good. Selfishness makes me feel bad.

TO DO: Today, I choose to be self-caring by being unselfish. I choose to feel good so I will do good acts and not worry about what happens to me. If I fall into selfishness, I will immediately do something kind for someone else.

January 15

The Big Picture

Each day we are bombarded with problems and decisions. That is the nature of life. A key to serenity is not allowing the little problems lead to frustration. A powerful coping skill is to focus on the Big Picture. The Big Picture is that our life is trending better so long as we practice the Four Steps of Serenity. The little problems pale in importance when compared to the general success we are experiencing. The little problems will eventually be solved, resolve or simply dissolve. We will feel like we made some good decisions and some not so good decisions. We will win some and we will lose some. They are all minutia because they cannot threaten the Big Picture.

TO DO: As problems and decisions arise today, I will not become frustrated because I will keep my focus on the Big Picture. The Big Picture is that the more I practice the four steps, my life gradually improves regardless of the outcome of the stream of minutia (little problems and decisions). I will not ruin the Big Picture by turning little problems into trouble by relapsing emotionally.

January 16

Life Can Look Good or Bad Depending on Which Window I Open

It's not what is, it's what we perceive that's important. If I perceive the tree bark as being a beautiful sculpture created by a loving eternal power beyond human explanation, I experience a peaceful, hopeful feeling. If I perceive the same tree bark as a manifestation of an apparently unending winter of dull, colorless gloom, I experience a nihilistic nightmare.

I don't want to relapse into negative thinking. I don't want to be stressed, overwhelmed, sad, or worried. I don't want to act out in a way that is symptomatic of my negativity. So long as I follow a nurturing program that includes the four steps and a balanced lifestyle, I perceive life as being manageable. If I do not follow a self-caring program, I lose the choice of a positive perception.

TO DO: Today I'm going to open the window which makes me see life is good. I open this window by practicing a nurturing program which consists of taking care of my Five Natures*: my body, my mind, my emotions, my social self, and my spirit. I will plan my day to devote time to staying connected to each nature. For example, I will exercise and eat correctly to improve my body. I will do something intellectually stimulating (perhaps read a challenging book) to stimulate my mind. I will perhaps watch a funny movie to stimulate my emotions. I will arrange some time to be with a friend. And I will practice spiritual principles like compassion, understanding and kindness to stimulate my spirit.

*see appendix, page 438, for a description of the Five Natures

January 17

Determination Without Works is Dead

Much like faith without works is dead, determination without works is dead. Determination means you are highly motivated. But unless you follow up that motivation with action, the motivation wanes. And as the motivation wanes, we fall back into habits which used to threaten our serenity. In my counseling practice, I have seen countless motivated, determined, confident, "I will never ever use again" alcoholics and addicts relapse because they never did the necessary work such as continued therapy, meetings, readings, helping others, cognitive restructuring, making amends, and eliminating self will run riot.

TO DO: Today, support your determination with continued serenity nurturing. Ask yourself if you are daily devoting time to each of your Five Natures (physical, mental, social, emotional, and spiritual). Are you neglecting any spiritual activities like helping others? (Helping others can be as small as wearing a kind face.) Do you need to physically exercise, stimulate your mind, feed your emotions, meet with a friend?

January 18

You Never Know What Happiness Is Until You Know What It Isn't

I finally have a better idea of what happiness is now that I am practicing effective serenity principles. Previously, I had no idea that I could be fulfilled by enjoying a sunset, a song, a conversation and then a morning free from fear. I placed too much emphasis on material things and accomplishments. I neglected taking care of my Five Natures: mind, body, emotions, social, and soul. I now value healthy relationships more than money. I enjoy experiences more than things. I can let go of results while reasonably striving for healthy goals. Perhaps, best of all, I am not so mean to myself.

TO DO: Today I will remember to be grateful for learning what happiness isn't. I will think kind thoughts when I think about me. I will be self forgiving. I will try not to measure myself in material terms, and keep devoting some time to taking care of my Five Natures.

January 19

Unscathed?

Who amongst us gets through this unscathed? Anyone? Anyone never had a personal tragedy? Is tragedy reserved for the terminally unique?

Probably not.

Can tragedy become an opportunity? Is tragedy an attitude? Respond to being an addict by helping another addict. Respond to being poor by helping the poor. Respond to aging by helping the aged. Respond to your grief by helping the aggrieved. Respond to resentment with understanding, fear with faith, and self-hatred with self-forgiveness. At first, my alcoholism was the worst thing that ever happened to me. Today, it has become the best thing because it has forced me to take care of my Five Natures and to practice the four steps to serenity. Everything has gradually gotten better, and I have been able to ride out the ups and downs of life without getting drunk.

TO DO: Hopelessness turns to hope when I find devote myself to the serenity process. Today I will focus on finding and living that program. A part of that program will include realizing the power of humility and asking for help.

January 20

Striving to Be Average

Humility is not weakness. It is a healthy, modest view of one's own importance. Humility tends to balance out the TOO HIGH OR TOO LOW opinions we have about ourselves. These EXTREMES can sacrifice our peace of mind. Sometimes it can be a challenge for us to just relax and be average, but we must remember being average can be a good thing. Before I got into true serenity practice, everything was such a drama. I was either a glorious winner or a pathetic failure. You were either a beloved friend or a hated enemy. Little problems which occur to everyone were catastrophes when they occurred to me. So I isolated to deal with them. Throughout recovery, I have been taught to be humble. I have learned the process of keeping life in perspective. I am keeping it real. Life is so much better this way.

TO DO: Today I will be on guard for my EXTREME thinking and behaviors. I will remember that I am an imperfect human and that it is OK just to be average and balanced. If I start to lose my humility, I will breathe deeply and relax. I will review the 30 Serenity Killers* in this book and see if I am sabotaging my peace of mind. I will then devote some time to taking care of my mind, body, emotions, spirit, and social self.

*see appendix, page 449, for a description of the 30 Serenity Killers

January 21

Common Sense is Realizing What's Worth Trying to Change and What Isn't

At the risk of being egotistical, and knowing that one should not mess with perfection, I would like to suggest adding a sentence to the Serenity Prayer. The serenity prayer says, "God grant me the serenity to accept the things I cannot change, the courage to change the things I can, and the wisdom to know the difference." I would like to add a sentence that says..."and the commonsense to realize what's worth changing and what isn't." So often, I can influence something, but the consequences and the nuisance value are self-defeating. Sometimes even things I think I can change are better left alone. I have to remember that I am not responsible for fixing everything and everybody...that everybody has their own Higher Power and I am certainly not it.

TO DO: Today I pray that my Higher Power gives me the commonsense to know what's worth trying to change and what is not - and that I have the self-restraint to let go.

January 22

Problems Never End,
But Solutions Never End Either

Stay positive. If your brain keeps thinking "My God, as soon as one problem ends, another starts!" Or if your brain cries, "This problem will never end!" substitute those negative thoughts with "Problems do end! Just not on my schedule." Problems resolve or dissolve. There is always a solution. Often, the solution is simple: acceptance.

TO DO: Substitute negative thoughts with positive thinking. Sit up straight and put your shoulders back! Refuse to be impatient or worried. For every problem, there is a solution. Sometimes the solution is that there is nothing more we can do. In such cases, the solution is acceptance. Often the solution is not what we immediately wanted. Often things don't turn out the way we think is best, so try not to judge outcomes. Just keep doing the next reasonable thing according to the four absolutes: love, unselfishness, purity, and honesty. Make your life about the journey, not the end of the journey.

January 23

Be in This World but Not of It

We can create our reality according to what we emphasize. So our reality can be peaceful if we emphasize peace as we live our lives. Peace does not depend on external conditions. Being in peace does not mean the absence of problems. Peace comes from within, and its presence puts us in the privileged position to make assertive, reasonable decisions.

For me, the obstacles to peace were anxiety, guilt, and shame. These obstacles NEVER solved my problems. On the contrary, they took away my focus and put me in a precarious situation, unable to solve anything and even creating new trouble.

TO DO: Don't get down for too long if something happens that throws you out of whack. Remember that we are spiritual beings within a human frame. The body breaks but not our spirit. Nothing and no one can break our spirit. Take a few moments today to breathe and meditate on the word Peace deep within your soul. Relax and then do one thing at a time peacefully. You don't have to escape from life. Rather you can find solutions by accepting and adapting. What defines you is not what happens to you, but how you deal with it.

January 24

We Don't Think Less of Ourselves,
We Think About Ourselves Less

Healthy self-image is our goal today. I have therefore tried to eliminate self- measuring according to outcomes. The adventure is more important than the outcome. Before I practiced serenity principles, it was all about self-measuring. I was either worthless or grandiose. It was all about what I was getting for me. Today, I can be self-caring without being selfish. I think about what I can do for others.

TO DO: Today, I will be kind to myself and others because we deserve it. I will see a big red stop sign in my mind if I feel humiliated, ashamed, sad or fearful - and instead of beating myself up, I will imagine giving myself a big hug. I will refuse to think less of myself just because I make a mistake or fail in some way. Today will not be about how the World treats me, but how I treat the World with my goal to do the next reasonable thing unimpeded by my character defects.

January 25

"There is a principle which is a bar against all information, which is proof against all arguments, and which cannot fail to keep a man in everlasting ignorance - that principle is contempt prior to investigation."

-Herber Spencer

Prejudice against others causes harm, but prejudice against trying new ways to overcome self-defeating behaviors may be the most harmful prejudice of all. Particularly if you are overwhelmed or discouraged, the first step to recovery is HONESTLY admitting that something may be wrong with you and that the World is not all to blame. The second step is being OPEN-MINDED to others' suggestions about how to get help. The third step is simply being WILLING to try to follow those suggestions. The acronym for this process of healing is HOW: Honesty, Open-mindedness, and Willingness.

TO DO: Today, instead of blaming the world, I will seek new strategies to deal with the World. I will be open to trying a new way to walk the journey of life.

January 26

Keep Your Feet Moving

Things are not going to go as planned. The laptop battery is going to drain too fast. The report you received will be incomplete. The repairman will be late. You will have three issues emailed to you at once. Don't despair. They have an old saying in hockey: "Keep your feet moving." This saying advises us to STAY IN THE MOMENT AND ACT REASONABLY. So don't think about what's happening to you. Don't judge it. Don't lament. Don't editorialize about life's inherent deficiencies and inequities. Just work your way through it by keeping your feet moving.

TO DO: Think like a hockey player. Expect the unexpected, keep your feet moving, and you won't fall down on the ice.

January 27

Make It All Fun

Monopoly takes concentration, calm, resilience, the ability to handle frustration, the ability to handle setbacks; indeed, it can make one extremely angry. In fact, it can be extremely stressful. Yet, people play Monopoly for recreation. The secret of enjoying life is to face problems with a light-hearted attitude. Try to make chores fun. Make believe you are just playing a game. This is not too far fetched an idea because each chore and problem will either resolve or dissolve and it might only help to face them with a cheerful attitude.

TO DO: Today I will imagine my problems as just games. I will be confident that although I may not get what I want, I will get what I need.

January 28

Don't Give Them Free Rent in Your Brain

If you are angry or resentful at someone or something, you are giving them free rent in your brain. They are not thinking about you. They are not giving you free rent. Obsessing over how you are going to get even - worrying about what they think about you - wondering how they should act in a certain way: these are just a few examples of how we give others free rent in our brain. Usually this kind of "stinking thinking" leads us to feeling depressed.

TO DO: If I find I am obsessing over someone else, I will consciously tell myself to just stop it. If I hate someone, I will forgive them in my heart. If I resent someone, I will pray that they heal. I will think of something to be grateful for in this moment. Then I will make a decision to turn my life and will over to the care of my Higher Power (good spiritual principles) and I will live my life according to those good spiritual principles.

January 29

Do You Have Unrealistic Expectations?

A major trigger for my loss of serenity was disappointment, feeling like a loser. I sabotaged myself by creating unrealistic expectations which caused me to feel like a failure when I did not reach them. I lived by the motto, "Shoot for the stars and if you land on the moon you'll be great." But I was never satisfied whether or not I landed on the stars or the moon. I always seemed to want more. The principle of humility has taught me that it's absolutely okay that I'm just a regular human being and that I have to stop conditioning my happiness on the attainment of expectations. There are many things that can happen in my life that are far beyond my control, and I have learned that reducing expectations - and just trying to do the next reasonable thing - is often best for my peace of mind.

TO DO: Today, I will not tell myself I am a loser no matter what. I choose not to be humiliated, disappointed, or stressed. I will make the journey more important than the results. I may make plans, but not outcomes.

January 30

Surviving Riptides

So I'm floating peacefully and playing in the waves just off the beach in the great Atlantic Ocean when suddenly I am being pulled by the sea out into the deep. My heart pounds. I know I am caught in a riptide. I think about the lady from Minnesota who drowned in a riptide last year. I know it is pointless to swim directly toward shore. The riptide is too strong to swim against it. So I try to swim sideways to get out of it, but I am still being swept out. I see a fisherman on shore and my wife and dog playing peacefully on the beach, on solid ground. I can see they don't know how helpless I feel, that anything's wrong. What an embarrassing way to die I think. I stretch one foot down as low as I can praying to feel the sandy floor. But there is nothing. I try swimming sideways some more and then stretch my foot down again and my toes feel the ocean floor. I try to pull myself toward shore with my foot. Finally, I am able to walk and get to shore. I am still panic stricken and panting. My wife hadn't noticed anything. I look down the beach and see my friend, a wise old surfer studying the surf. Reaching him, I say, "Guess what, I got caught..."

He completes my sentence by saying..."In the riptide. I saw the whole thing." He says, "When you are in a riptide you just relax your breathing and gently float with it. You just let it take you out because soon it will dissipate and you can then easily swim back to shore. You don't put your foot down on the ocean floor because that is the way you get bit by sharks because there are a lot of them and that is where they feed. Sharks are bottom feeders. The only time surfers get bitten is when they accidentally step on a shark." He adds, "Experienced surfers actually swim into the riptide because they use it to easily get out to where the better surfing waves are." He says, "Like life, you can turn this problem into an ally."Pointing toward the sea, he adds "You can actually see riptides by noticing where the boils are in the surf...See there's one." He finally smiles and says, "Next time I want you to find the riptide and swim right into it and let it take you till it dissipates."

TO DO: Breathe, relax, and do the right action in this moment. Even best laid plans can be interrupted by sudden emergencies or surprises. Today I will not panic. I will do what is necessary but not overdo. I am not going to struggle against forces that are stronger than I am. I cannot control the riptides. I am going to relax, breathe and float with them. I am not going to be impatient, anxious, or fearful. I will not panic or struggle, but just float, confidently knowing they will dissipate. I am going to remember that the World has sharks and that they tend to attack desperate people rather than calm people. I am going to enjoy each riptide and gently swim back to shore when it releases me. I will remember that I can't fight the power of the great ocean. I will welcome the riptide and may even figure out how to use it to help my symbiotic relationship with Life. I may therefore choose to fearlessly swim right into problems for the riptides of life are unavoidable and the only thing that can hurt me is the fear.

January 31

Who Cares?

Not to sound cold but so many of our problems are just petty. We worry about whether we are liked. We obsess over size medium or size large. We resent someone who didn't smile at us. We stress over running out of ketchup. We feel humiliated or ashamed because our car is not as new and shiny as our neighbor's. Meanwhile, people starve, get shot, lose children, get cancer.

TO DO: Today, I will say, "Who cares?" when I fret over pettiness. Whenever I am scared, nervous, sad or depressed, I will exercise that wonderful serenity tool called PERSPECTIVE.

February 1

Are You a Wounded Healer?

"Nobody escapes being wounded. We all are wounded people, whether physically, emotionally, mentally, or spiritually. The main question is not 'How can we hide our wounds?' so we don't have to be embarrassed, but 'How can we put our woundedness in the service of others?' When our wounds cease to be a source of shame, and become a source of healing, we have become wounded healers."
- Henri Nouwen

TO DO: Right now I choose to be a wounded healer. I will not be ashamed of who I am. I will not be sad or angry for being a unique individual even though, like all human beings, I may have not lived a perfect life. Instead I will use my experience, strength, and hope to heal others.

February 2

The Most Dangerous Animal

I live on an island with many dangerous animals. I had an alligator attack me. The ocean has sharks, jellyfish, and stingrays. There's a bobcat in the woods next door. Raccoons scratched my dog. There are foxes, coyotes, many kinds of snakes, and strange toads whose venom can kill you. I won't even mention the bugs. But far more dangerous and threatening than any of these animals are the humans. We humans drive drunk and kill each other with our cars. We rob from each other. We steal each other's loved ones. We treat each other with anger and words that sting like daggers. And who is the most dangerous human? Me. My own character defects, my ego, my inability to deal with the frustrations of the daily little things that go awry. My selfishness, my fear, my self-flagellation: these are the things that can consume me, cause the most heartache, and create the most trouble in my life. I used to deal with them by isolating and procrastinating. Today I try to live consciously by keeping perspective, being grateful, and staying flexible. I don't blame the World or myself. I just try to change how I respond to the World.

TO DO: Today, I will pay attention to how I am responding to life's challenges. I will not be afraid to ask for guidance when I feel I am struggling with a self- defeating behavior. I will try doing an action which is opposite to a bad feeling. For example, if I am worrying about what might happen to me, I will seek to help someone else. If I am feeling self-pity, I will think a grateful thought. If I am thinking that something has to work out a certain way, I will remember to be flexible. Most importantly, if I am treating myself with contempt, I will remember that I love and care about myself.

February 3

The 600 lb. Gorilla

How do you change? How do you resist the temptation to return to your bad habit? Answer: think about how you wasted so much money over the years...how you damaged relationships...lost time. Think about how you tried to exercise willpower to change, but still failed to control your bad habit. Decide to try a new way to change so that you can regain the self-esteem your bad habit stole from you.

TO DO: Think of your worst habit as a 600 pound gorilla that you could never beat up by yourself, that is pounding the living daylights out of you, that is killing you. If you just "cry uncle," the gorilla will get off of you. In other words, surrender to win. Once you realize that fighting alone (through will power) won't work, you will free yourself to get help. Help can come in many forms like simply asking someone you trust for advice. But the first step is simply to admit that you can't control the 600 pound gorilla alone and that it is making your life unmanageable.

February 4

How Can I Resist Temptation?

Some time ago I was asked how can you resist the temptation to return to your bad habit? Answer: At first I thought it would be very difficult to resist. Then I did a retrospective of my life, and to my amazement, I answered: It was not easy to change, but it was much harder to manage the lies, the suffering, the remorse, the self-pity, the need for approval of all, the fear of tomorrow, the martyrdom of yesterday, dealing with an infinite emptiness, which I thought was solitude, when in fact it was the absence of myself... To manage all this was very difficult and tiring. I resisted temptation only for today to try to become a better version of myself – to regain my self-esteem.

TO DO: Today I will remember the horrible consequences of my bad habit without shame but as an antidote to returning to it. I will cherish the fact that I am slowly becoming my true self again by avoiding my bad habit. I will not hesitate to discuss any craving I have to return to my bad habit with someone else who understands. I will have faith that any pain will be replaced by a wonderful Peace.

February 5

Suffering? Become a Lake

A wise old man asked a sad young man to put a handful of salt in a glass of water and drink. "How does it taste?" asked the Master. "Bad," said the apprentice. The Master smiled and asked the young man to take another handful of salt and toss it in a lake. The two walked in silence to the lake, and the young man threw the salt in. Then the wise man said, "Drink some of the water from the lake."

As the water ran down the young man's chin, the old man asked, "And now, how does it taste?" "Very good!" said the apprentice. "Do you taste the salt?" asked the Sage. "No!" exclaimed the apprentice. The wise man then sat down next to the young man and said, "When you feel pain, increase your sense of everything in your life, and give more value to what you have than to what you have lost."

Pain is inevitable, but the suffering (the emphasis and priority you spend on pain) is optional. Thus, the end of suffering is to stop being a glass and to become a lake.

TO DO: Each time I feel pain today, I will think of five things for which I am grateful. I will thus make it my practice to emphasize what I have rather than what I lack.

February 6

Which Wolf Do You Feed?

The Fable of the Two Wolves (of the Cherokee Indians)

One day a young Cherokee Indian came up to his grandfather for advice. Moments before, one of his friends had committed an injustice against the young man, and in his anger the Indian decided to seek the wise counsel of that old man.

The old Indian looked deep into his grandson's eyes and said, "I too, my grandson, sometimes feel great hatred of those who commit injustice without feeling any regret for what they did. But hatred erodes those who feel it, and never hurts the enemy. It's like taking poison, wishing the enemy to die. "

The young man continued to stare, surprised, and his grandfather continued:

"Several times I struggled against these feelings. It's as if there were two wolves inside me. One of them is good and does not hurt.

He lives in harmony with everyone around him and is not offended. He only struggles when he has to, and in a straight line."

"But the other wolf ... This is full of anger. The most insignificant thing is capable of causing him a terrible fit of rage. He fights with everyone, all the time, for no reason. His anger and hatred are very great, and so he does not measure the consequences of his acts. It is a futile rage, because anger will not change anything. Sometimes it is difficult to live with these two wolves inside me, for they both try to dominate my spirit."

"The boy looked intently into his grandfather's eyes and asked, "And which one wins?"

To which the grandfather smiled and replied softly, "The one I feed."

TO DO: Today I will feed the good wolf by giving myself and others positive messages, by being warm hearted, by forgiving, by being grateful, by trying to help others, by exercising understanding rather than resentment, love rather than hate, kindness rather than self-righteous indignation, faith rather than fear, acceptance rather than denial, open-mindedness rather than prejudice.

February 7

Who Knows?
The Farmer's Son: Fortune or Misfortune?

CLASSIC WISDOM TALE: "One day in late summer, an old farmer was working in his field with his old sick horse. The farmer felt compassion for the horse and desired to lift its burden. So he let his horse loose to go the mountains and live out the rest of its life.

Soon after, neighbors from the nearby village visited, offering their condolences and said, "What a shame. Now your only horse is gone. How unfortunate you are! You must be very sad. How will you live, work the land, and prosper?" The farmer replied: "Who knows? We shall see".Two days later the old horse came back now rejuvenated after meandering in the mountainsides while eating the wild grasses. He came back with twelve new younger and healthy horses which followed the old horse into the corral.

Word got out in the village of the old farmer's good fortune and it wasn't long before people stopped by to congratulate the farmer on his good luck. "How fortunate you are!" they exclaimed. You must be very happy!" Again, the farmer softly said, "Who knows? We shall see."

At daybreak on the next morning, the farmer's only son set off to attempt to train the new wild horses, but the farmer's son was thrown to the ground and broke his leg. One by one villagers arrived during the day to bemoan the farmer's latest misfortune. "Oh, what a tragedy! Your son won't be able to help you farm with a broken leg. You'll have to do all the work yourself, How will you survive? You must be very sad." they said. Calmly going about his usual business the farmer answered, "Who knows? We shall see."

Several days later a war broke out. The Emperor's men arrived in the village demanding that young men come with them to be conscripted into the Emperor's army. As it happened the farmer's son was deemed unfit because of his broken leg. "What very good fortune you have!!" the villagers exclaimed as their own young sons were marched away. "You must be very happy." "Who knows? We shall see," replied the old farmer as he headed off to work his field alone.

As time went on the broken leg healed but the son was left with a slight limp. Again the neighbors came to pay their condolences. "Oh what bad luck. Too bad for you"! But the old farmer simply replied; "Who knows? We shall see."

As it turned out the other young village boys had died in the war and the old farmer and his son were the only able bodied men capable of working the village lands. The old farmer became wealthy and was very generous to the villagers. They said: "Oh how fortunate we are!" to which the old farmer replied, "Who knows? We shall see." TO DO: Today I won't be quick to judge a situation as good or bad. I will sim- ply try to do the next right thing, guided by positive concepts like love, unselfishness, purity, and honesty rather than by harmful reactive concepts like anger, greed, selfishness, fear and dishonesty. Doing so is important to my peace of mind in an ever changing world.

February 8

We Are Called

We who struggle with peace of mind must not view this struggle as an affliction but rather an opportunity. For we have been graced with no choice but to follow a better way or endlessly suffer from our affliction. Such is the highest calling. Each human is put on earth, lives and dies. Many unafflicted seem to live a rather banal, meaningless existence. But some have been called to help others. We who struggle are these chosen people. Our calling begins with our crisis. Our crisis leaves us lost in the desert, shocked, unable to use any of our previously treasured resources to survive. So all that's left is to cry out for help. All that's left is to follow a new way of living. And we are saved. We ultimately discover that we have not been afflicted but graced and empowered. So let us not mourn our affliction but be grateful for the opportunity to live a life of true meaning.

So, in the words of Alan Ginsburg, "You who saw it all, or flashes and fragments, take from us some example, to try and get yourselves together, to clean up your act, find your community, pick up on some sort of redemption of your own consciousness, become more mindful of your own friends, your own work, your own proper meditation, your own proper art, your own beauty, and go out and make it for your own eternity."

Love, Light, Wisdom and Live the Miracle

TO DO: Today I will look at difficulties as a calling not an affliction. I refuse to be ashamed, depressed, or worried. Instead, I will use my serenity practice to help others, to follow and manifest the miracle that has saved me.

February 9

You Cannot Change Them,
You Can Only Change Yourself

A friend wrote to me saying, "My main source of frustration is I have these people in my life, and I cannot change them without risking becoming physically ill, without violating my own morality, and without hurting them. For example, I have been married for 23 years and my sex life is boring and I would cheat but I don't want to get aids, and I also don't want to lie to my wife or risk hurting her. Another example: I have a brother who won't stop using drugs and he always asks me for loans which of course he never repays." Another example: "I have these elderly parents who need care but I don't have time, or money to give them all of the support they need. I feel guilty when I am not helping them. They also verbally hint at how much they did for me and the frustrations I caused them because I was not the ideal son. How do I deal with these people?"

TO DO: You cannot change them, you can only change yourself. Regarding your boring sex life, you may have to simply be grateful for the positives that she has given your life and focus on that rather than the negatives. UNSELFISHNESS may help with regard to sexual matters. Regarding your brother, you should stop ENABLING. You should convince yourself that continuing to loan him money is only weakening him. You should learn the power of saying NO. You should remember that you are helping him deal with his problem by saying "NO." Regarding your parents, you should edit your life reasonably knowing that you need BALANCE. You should make sure you take care of other responsibilities to yourself like fun, work for money, basic survival. You remember that you must give yourself oxygen before you give it to them. You should LOSE your GUILT feelings by asking a Higher Power to remove them (like sharing them with a friend, thinking the opposite, etc.).

IN ALL OF THESE CASES, YOU ARE NOT TRYING TO CHANGE THEM, YOU ARE ONLY TRYING TO CHANGE YOUR ATTITUDES, THOUGHTS AND ACTIONS. You are learning to say no, setting priorities, creating limits and boundaries without trashing the relationship if possible, editing your life by setting priorities which include healthy self-management, seeing others' positives, staying calm so you don't choose a wrong solution, having a sense of humor, being grateful for what you have, exercising perspective, realizing they and you are not perfect. Interestingly, you don't look for justice. You don't defend your rights. You don't allow yourself to take the victim mentality. You don't worry about what these people can do to you by letting go of those thoughts and realizing it is more important for you to change yourself. ONE OF THE GREATEST TEMPTATIONS AND GREATEST ILLUSIONS IS THINKING YOU CAN CHANGE THEM. TRYING TO CHANGE THEM USUALLY ONLY RESULTS IN THEIR RESISTANCE AND RESENTMENT OF YOU. Follow through trying to change them to its bitter end: frustration and misery. Loving detachment is key. You can love them, without your controlling them or their controlling you.

February 10

Ask Not Whether Life Is Treating You Well, but Whether You Are Treating Life Well

It is a typical introductory sentiment to say "Hello, I hope life is treating you well..." However, being in recovery, when someone wished me this sentiment this morning, I thought that it was far more important for me to treat life well rather than being concerned about how life was treating me. Today I can only do that which is in my control. I cannot control how life treats me, but I can control how well I treat life. Treating life well today includes being kind to others and substituting negative thoughts with positive thoughts. Treating life well means that I'm doing that which is necessary to remain serene regardless of how life treats me.

TO DO: Today I will treat life well by practicing the four serenity principles: by accepting and adapting rather than denying reality and trying to escape. I will be grateful for needs met in this moment, I will seek HELP (a higher effective loving power). I will focus on self improvement rather than improving others. I will do this especially when things don't seem to be going my way. I have already made a good start by reading this daily message.

February 11

So Grateful to Practice Serenity Today!

Sometimes it is so hard to be serene in the face of life's common difficulties. First, I transferred money from one account to another and when I checked it online, it looked like money was missing. When I waited on the phone for about an hour and finally got a Bank representative, the representative gave me the wrong information and directed me somewhere else. After three hours, I was finally able to make progress on the situation even though I still had to wait for a final answer about where the missing money went. Second, someone tried to scam me. I received an email saying that they wanted to feature me on a television show because I have a great product. I thought it was a public-interest show and there would be no charge. However, after scheduling a time to talk to the person, I realized that the person was just trying to sell me advertising. She said the minimum cost would be $5,500. After that, my boss told me to do something I disagreed with.

So how did I maintain my serenity (let alone my sanity)? First, I owned my feelings. I allowed myself to feel angry, disappointed and hurt. I felt stupid for almost getting ripped off by the scam. I felt humiliated by my boss. I felt abused by the bank. I then applied the Four Serenity Principles. I knew that it was time to stop controlling these situations. I let go of having an immediate outcome. I realized that life always had unexpected situations. I therefore accepted and adapted. I then realized that all of my needs were fulfilled and it was my wants that were frustrating me. I thus became grateful. I got some advice from a friend, and exercised patience. I also took care of my body by exercising, eating correctly and then resting. I then used perspective to realize that my problems were not life threatening, and I then even tried to help someone else.

This process corrected my thinking. I did not exercise all-or-nothing thinking. I was able to say to myself that this too shall pass. I was able to avoid being resentful at the clerk, the sales person, and my boss by exercising "understanding" that they had stresses of their own. I was able to avoid magnifying the situation by remembering that these were not big deals that would end my life. I was able to exercise perspective by thinking that there are other people who have cancer, or a multitude of things that are worse than my problems. I was able to say to myself that I am thankful to have a job. I was able to say I was thankful to have a product that others wanted to advertise. I was able to say to myself that I was thankful even to have money at bank accounts. I made a commitment to be flexible with my work plan so that I could take care of the financial issue. I was able to avoid personalization in that I did not see myself as the cause of the negative external events. So I did not blame myself. Finally, I did not adopt a victim stance where I adopted an attitude that the situations and problems were hopeless and impossible to solve. I took small steps to deal with each one. SO, this is victory for me today. What I used to view as a bad day was a great day. I was able to starve my bad wolf and feed my good wolf.

TO DO: When frustrations occur today, try using the four serenity principles. It's not what happens, it's how you respond to what happens that counts.

February 12

There Is No Night So Dark
That There Is No New Sunrise

Each day is a unique opportunity to start fresh! I can start my day over at any time by recommitting to making serenity the priority. I accept that I cannot change the past, but I also accept that if I change how I respond to challenging people and situations, I can make my life significantly better. There is hope!
Today is where we get the power to change!

TO DO: Today, I will not let my failures discourage me. Rather, I will turn them into success by using them as a motivation to change. I will start this process by looking at the 30 Serenity Killers at the beginning of this book and determine what I may need to guard against to avoid jeopardizing my serenity. I will then apply the Four Steps of Serenity to any challenges that arise. I will commit to this new way of life because despite having been in the darkness, I am now moving toward peace and light!

February 13

Serenity Means Letting Go!

Last night, the internet went out during the third quarter of the football game involving the team I love. In the old days, I would have been enraged, frustrated, miserable. I would have cursed while on hold with my internet service provider. But last night, I calmly unplugged and replugged the router. Unfortunately the internet still did not work. I then called customer service and listened to their music for about ten minutes before giving up and going to sleep. But I went to sleep peacefully even though the internet was still broken. This serenity occurred because I applied the four steps to the situation.

1. I accepted that I could not control the broken internet having exhausted reasonable efforts, and I adapted by letting go and getting some rest.

2. I remembered that even though my desire was not fulfilled, my immediate needs were fulfilled.

3. I connected with my Higher Self by breathing peacefully rather than frantically.

4. I focused on simply being patient, thereby fixing myself rather than being resentful.

This morning, I woke up feeling great! I wasn't particularly worried one way or another whether the internet was working. Nevertheless, when I looked at the router, both green lights were on and after checking all the devices, they were all working again. Had it not been working, I would have taken reasonable measures to try again, but in this case I did not need to. Letting go had worked. More than getting my way by having the internet work, I am grateful today that I can get a good night's sleep without things going my way.

TO DO: Today, let go of controlling results. Try memorizing and applying the four steps. Open your hands and breathe when conflict comes. Just do the next right thing and accept outcomes whatever they may be. Like losing the internet or being unable to watch a favorite show, you will be surprised at what you can peacefully live without. Have Peace and Light!

February 14

Not Good or Bad; Rather Good and Bad

Resentment against people or situations is a major threat to our serenity. Resentment usually starts when we judge a person or a situation as being bad. Our mistake is that there is rarely good or bad; rather all people and situations seem to have good and bad qualities. Everyone has character flaws. Everyone makes mistakes. Every situation, even those that are intended to be fun, has challenges. Difficult situations give us the opportunity to learn and grow. Seeing both sides (the good and the bad) helps us accept situations more easily. We can then understand and forgive (we can even forgive ourselves). Acceptance, understanding and forgiveness lead us toward peace and light.

TO DO: Right now, I will repeat the phrase, "Not good or bad, but good and bad." I will remember that people and situations tend to have both pros and cons. I therefore refuse to be angry or resentful at anybody or anything. I will not judge or measure.

February 15

We Make Mistakes,
But We Are Not a Mistake

Accepting our own humanity is fundamental to serenity and our emotional reconstruction. Cognitive restructuring, or thinking differently, is part of that emotional reconstruction. In other words, we need to keep correcting our stinking thinking. Thinking we are one big mistake because we make mistakes is a form of stinking thinking. There is no reason to self-flagellate just because we make mistakes. All we can do is to try to learn from mistakes (while forgiving ourselves when we don't) and move on. We are human, not a mistake.

TO DO: Today I will repeat the phrase, "I make mistakes, but I am not a mistake." I will accept this part of my Humanity.

February 16

Gratitude: Nothing Is Trite

Gratitude is one of the most spectacular feelings! Gratitude makes everything we have right now, not what we once had or will ever have, enough to make us feel privileged. So that we don't make something that seems trite as trite, because nothing is trite.

Being alive is not commonplace, having our brains working allowing us to be conscious, aware, talking, moving our muscles and limbs is not commonplace. And this perception, this exercise of taking what seems basic, that seems normal, and understanding that this is a great privilege, allows us to give more value to what we have. This doesn't mean we can't dream anymore, that we can't try to improve, but it does mean that thinking that what we already have isn't worthwhile or worthless is a waste of being alive. And in this process of gratitude for valuing what we have, we stimulate our brains and lower our blood pressures. We release more hormones that allow our social interactions to improve. We increase the production of neurotransmitters in our brains which contributes to happiness, decision making and better focus. The more grateful we are, the happier we are with our current situations. We are not shopping with the past, not looking forward to the future. We are in the here and now. And this is the only mental time that exists.

When we get lost in the past or future, we increase the risk of anxiety and depression. Our feeling when we are grateful is of belonging.

TO DO: In this moment I will focus on being grateful. I will take nothing for granted.

February 17

Be Kind to Yourself

"Be kind to yourself, forgive yourself, love yourself and don't push yourself too much. Live one day at a time, as if it were the last. Remember that you are mortal, limited and not Divine, so you cannot solve the world's problems. Stick to becoming a better version of yourself day by day. The simple emerges, for that is where the magnitude of life resides. If you have troubles, admit that you need help. Don't be ashamed. Only then can you get help."

TO DO: Today I will be kind to me. If I am confused or troubled, I will not be ashamed to ask for help.

February 18

Serenity Happens When My Self-Image Changes From a Source of Shame to a Source of Growth

I am learning about how shame affects my desires. I don't submit to harmful desires when I feel unashamed to admit that I have them, that they lead to harmful consequences, and I ask for help. I feel as if I can start to change when I don't feel ashamed about who I am. Shame comes in many forms to me. It may be that I am ashamed of how I look. Or ashamed of my lack of character development. Or ashamed that I can't help more people. Or ashamed that I cannot alone help myself. Or ashamed at what excites me. Or ashamed at my inability to control my eating or drug use or other people.

TO DO: Today, I am going to work on accepting myself as a human being, full of issues, but not ashamed of them. I am not going to judge myself harshly. When I adopt this attitude, I feel so much more relaxed and free from anger. Without shame, I know I can begin real, positive change.

February 19

Happy New Child

I said: "We need to relearn and be again." He said, "What do you mean? How have we been?" I said: "As children, we lived the now to the full. We were happy with the simple, from a walk in the park, playing with pets, with affection and treats at Grandma's house, playing with friends, without charges and complexity. Sometimes we cried, we got angry, sad, but everything went too fast, again we were joking and smiling... And I see that I grew up and this simplicity gave way to comparison: I need this, I need that, I need to have, I need to be this, to be that ... Empty goals imposed by third parties ...Thanks to serenity practice I found myself again with that spiritualized child and I learn to live with joy day by day. If you ask me today what is the purpose of life? I would venture to say Life's purpose is to LIVE FULLY. I wish you to reunite with the spiritualized and vivacious child you once were. That child was very wise!"

TO DO: Today I will reunite with the spiritualized and vivacious child within me. I will focus on simplicity, not comparison. I will accept myself without shame and accept others without jealousy.

February 20

Suit up, Show up, and Sweep My Side of the Street

I need to take care of my business, not everybody else's. Before I made serenity my priority, anger ripped through me when somebody stood me up or cut me off. I felt let down, defeated, due to other people's shortcomings. Today I care less about what they do because I have learned that I ultimately cannot control them. I may be able to influence them, but usually the other person's behavior is beyond my control or not worth the effort of my trying to control them. So, I spend less time pointing out their defects (taking their inventory). Rather, I take my own inventory and work on getting rid of my defects. Knowing I am imperfect and still have much to learn, I try my best to suit up (be at my best), show up (be where I am supposed to be in body, heart and mind), and sweep my side of the street (change my own issues not theirs). It's such a relief trying to do something possible (improving myself) rather than banging my head against the wall trying to do something impossible (changing them). But how does one stop being abused by someone else? Answer: You consult with a counselor about what you can do to change how you handle the relationship, not what the other person can do to change the relationship. Usually what you can do is to stop enabling the other person to abuse you. We enable someone to abuse us when we think we love or need an abusive person - or when we think we can help, save, or fix an abusive person. Interestingly, when we stop enabling, the other person often has a better chance of changing than when we were enabling.

TO DO: Every time I am tempted to judge, criticize, change or control someone else, I am going to use that temptation to ask myself what I can change about myself to be at peace. If I feel I am being abused, I will ask myself and a trusted advisor if I need to admit that I am in a toxic relationship that warrants changing how I participate in the relationship.

February 21

Religion Is for Those Who Don't Want to Go to Hell; Spirituality Is for Those Who Have Already Been There

Hitting bottom is the main impetus for wanting to regain our serenity. Hitting bottom is proof that you need to change your lifestyle. Hitting bottom is Hell. You need a strong spirit to get out of that Hell. Following (without truly believing) someone else's religion is not going to get you out of that Hell. You need a personal relationship with a Higher Power of your own understanding not of someone else's understanding. Although one's Higher Power may be a part of an organized religion, the personal relationship is the key to recovery. The personal relationship is the difference between religion and spirituality*. That personal relationship may be understood through the exercise of spiritual principles like honesty, open-mindedness, love, unselfishness, and compassion. That personal relationship may be with anything that restores you to peace of mind: nature, music, a dog's peaceful eyes, meaningful work, anything that works for you.

TO DO: As you go through your day, keep your spirituality strong on a moment to moment basis by doing spiritually strengthening actions like helpful, forgiving, loving, actions. Maintain a good purpose because living with a GOOD PURPOSE will allow you to turn suffering into joy!

*see appendix, page 437, for a description of spirituality

February 22

As I Miss My Grandmother

As I miss my Grandmother, I remember she had the incredible gift of making me feel magnificent. Even though the world was falling apart, she managed to transmit tranquility and peace. Magnificent not in the sense of feeding the Ego, but of recognizing that I was valuable. Recovery from my loss of peace and light brought this feeling back, made me see the simple, and what was essential became futile. And to my surprise, the simple became my inspiration. In this simple view, today I realize that we are all magnificent and unique. Many, like me, lost their rich and abundant childhood spirituality (no relation to religion) as they aged. I lost my magnificence and started to compare myself and set empty goals, which the more I reached them, the more the emptiness expanded. Goals to show others everything I was not, goals to distance myself from myself, goals assessed only by comparative standards. But such goals are already part of the past. I am grateful for all I went through, after all without this, I would never have found myself.

TO DO: Look at yourself with affection, with respect and consideration. Forgive yourself, be reunited with that wonderful and spiritualized child, who lived one day at a time, focused on joyful events, however small, who fully loved life, even without knowing for sure what this feeling was, even without knowing if he or she would be a doctor, engineer, or farmer. Reunite with that spiritualized child even if you did not become an astronaut or sailor, even if you did not get married, did not have children. No need to be lost in the past or in the imaginary future. No need to rush. The adventure is to simply be better versions of yourself, day by day. Little by little, you will remember how magnificent you are! Start now! I'm cheering for you! Much Peace and Light.

February 23

The Sundial

Have you ever seen a sundial? It is basically a disk with recorded hours and a pin fixed perpendicular to it. When the sun's rays fall on the sundial, a shadow projects on the disk's surface, thus, indicating the hour. Logically, without the Sun, you can't see time on the sundial. There are sundials that bear the following inscription on their disc: "I record only hours when the sun shines."

We can also record only the hours when the sun is shining - and I call this the "way of living according to the principle of the sundial." Dear friend, if you want to make your life, a "sacred" place, do your best to "record only the radiant hours," that is, decide to remember and speak only of joyful and happy moments; use the creative power of the word to express joy. This is one of the secrets of happiness.

If all of humanity starts living according to the "principle of the sundial" registering only good, happy and positive thoughts, and expelling unpleasant recordings, sad thoughts or dark machinations, glad tidings will fill this world!

Why is it that many people remember and express only unhappiness, annoyances, hatred, jealousy, humiliation, etc., all which lead to alienation? It is due to ignorance of the "mental law of happiness" and the "creative power of the Word." These people need to learn they manifest everything they think and say; they need to realize that unhappiness grows when they are fixated on negativity.

Our "mental memory" is like a vehicle, possessed of a variety of passengers: the handsome cowboys, the beautiful ballerinas, the drunks emitting the unbearable odor of alcohol with a body full of sores. But we don't have to obsess on the unpleasant passengers. We can filter the "records" from our "mental archive." We can focus on the positive.

65

What is the use of keeping sadness in your heart? What is the use of remembering how you suffered? The world benefits not from your being discouraged recalling your failures. Sadness, failures - these are all useless baggage. Expel this baggage as you would a thief.

When your mind seems stuck with unpleasant thoughts, or you feel overwhelmed by fear, anger, jealousy or a desire for revenge, your mind is being assaulted by patterns you have created which only rob you of the treasure of happiness.

If a thief comes into your house to steal, even if it is just a pair of shoes, you want to expel him, do you not? So expel from your mind the thieves of hatred, resentment and other negativities which steal from you joy.

TO DO: Let this moment be a mental cleansing. Be like a "sundial", that you record and manifest only the bright hours. Unload the baggage that has accumulated in your mind. Abandon fear and negativity to get rid of melancholy and boredom, and live only the shining moments of the Sun.

February 24

If Your Higher Power Seems Far Away, Who Moved?

Connect to a Higher Power because, at certain times, alone we have no effective mental defense against losing our serenity. Self-reliance cannot provide such a defense. This defense must come from a Higher Power. REMEMBER, A HIGHER POWER IS ANY POWER THAT KEEPS YOU SERENE WITHOUT HURTING YOURSELF OR OTHERS. FOR EXAMPLE, IT CAN BE A SUPPORT GROUP, A RELIGIOUS GOD, A NON RELIGIOUS HIGHER POWER, HIGHER PRINCIPLES, TREATMENT, whatever works in this moment. How do we move away from our Higher Power? We do or think things that disconnect us from it. For example, disconnected thinking involves worry, resentment, fear, compulsivity, hate, anger, etc. Disconnected behaviors involve " immature" acting, misrepresentations, physical abuse, verbal abuse, relapse, etc.

TO DO: Find your GOOD PURPOSE by meditating on how you can serve your GOOD PURPOSE. Begin by doing honest, pure, unselfish, loving acts in each moment. Find people, places, and things that connect you to your Higher Power. Keep reconnecting throughout this day by correcting yourself when you are doing and thinking in a "disconnected" way. Try righting relationships and by making amends.

February 25

The End of Suffering

THE TRUTH OF SUFFERING: There is no way to avoid some suffering here on Earth. There is too much conflict, change, illness, weather calamities, financial disasters, natural disasters, family disasters, etc. to argue that SUFFERING IS UNAVOIDABLE.

HOWEVER, SERENITY IS POSSIBLE IN THE FACE OF SUFFERING. Serenity occurs when we stop lying to ourselves, ACCEPT the truth of suffering, and find a good PURPOSE for tolerating the suffering. THIS RESULTS WHEN WE PRACTICE THE FOUR STEPS.

When we cannot reach serenity in the face of suffering, it is because we are responding to the truth of suffering incorrectly. For example, we think we can escape inescapable suffering by practicing our addictions, to wit: drinking alcohol, using pornography, injecting heroin, gambling, eating obsessively, etc. Or, we think accomplishments and rewards will give us serenity. Or we think we can control the uncontrollable World to avoid unavoidable suffering. We think a geographical cure will help, so we consider moving to an island. We also think we can buy things to avoid suffering. We think buying a pretty car will end it, but then we are faced with stressful payments, and we worry about the car being scratched, and we endlessly clean it until exhausted we realize it will always get dirty again. To avoid suffering, we think we can eat ice cream, hoard money, get married or divorced, etc. BUT ALL OF THIS ONLY LEADS TO MORE SUFFERING. The best way to serenity is through practicing the four steps. This process enables us to ACCEPT the truth of suffering and even find a GOOD PURPOSE in the suffering. What is good purpose? Good purpose (as opposed to bad purpose which leads to more suffering) is often in the practice of compassion either in the sense of not wanting to hurt someone else but also wanting to be helpful. It could also arise through creating something or through service to some just cause. GOOD PURPOSE leads to a stronger, happier you.

TO DO: Try practicing the Four Steps to Serenity. Find a good purpose to deal with suffering.

February 26

The Parable of the Angel and the Imp

A boy saw a man threatening to jump from a bridge. On one side of the man was an angel and on the other side a devilish imp.

The little angel pled with the man not to jump, but the evil imp remained silent, calm, stoic.

Curious, the boy asked the imp why it did not try to persuade the man to jump?

The imp replied with a devilish smile "He's in doubt, he's on the fence, he's already mine."

TO DO: Today I will not be doubtful. I will memorize the Four Steps to Serenity. Whenever I feel as if my serenity is being threatened, I will confidently apply the steps. I refuse to be trapped by the imp.

February 27

The Ocean of Life

I live on an island in the Atlantic Ocean. I swim out into the ocean nearly every day, often in rough seas. The first rule of swimming in the ocean is ONE CANNOT FIGHT THE OCEAN. You can only swim back to shore when the ocean wants to release you. The ocean's waves, currents, tides, riptides, are all too powerful for any human to control. The ocean can also be deceptive for what looks like calm seas may actually have a compression like under current which can suck one under. BUT, in all cases, IF one does not overestimate one's ability and endurance to stay afloat and IF one GOES WITH THE FLOW - one will eventually make it back to shore when the Ocean chooses to create a path.

TO DO: Knowing when to stop trying to control is inherent in the first step to serenity. Today, if you are frustrated, anxious, or downright confused, please meditate on how to make it back to shore. Accept and adapt. Relax, breathe, float, and, as it appears, stroke for the opening which leads you to peace and light.

February 28

The Dark Night of the Soul

The journey to serenity involves a holistic (mind, body, emotional, social, and spiritual) healing process, which many believe begins with a phenomenon called the Dark Night of the Soul. Though at first painful, the Dark Night of the Soul is the initial phase of the process which changes hopelessness into hope, loneliness into connectedness, and a crisis into a blessing.

Eckhart Tolle, Carl Jung, several other psychologists, philosophers and even the Shamans describe the Dark Night of the Soul as a "rite" of passage. Jamie Sams says that Native Americans also consider the Dark Night of the Soul to be a rite of passage, which can strengthen the spirit. It happens when our five natures (emotional, physical, mental, social, and spiritual) go through darkness. We feel helpless and it seems that our world has collapsed. We feel the loss of our connection with the Creator, the Universe, and our true selves. This hard rite of passage forces us to change or die. It makes us courageous, awakens our consciousness, and leads us to our spiritual essence and our holistic healing process. For me, the insanity of everything that I went through, even drunkenly overturning my car with few injuries, shows me that my Higher Power has always been with me even during my Dark Night...and for all of this there is a purpose.

Today, even in the midst of challenges, I am able to appreciate the abundant luxury of simple things. I am able to cheer, to celebrate the happiness of others. Even though I have bills to pay and hard work to do, nothing deters me from living in fullness. When I measure myself with money, blame myself for mistakes, allow others to manipulate me, lose or fail, I can change my attitude.

When feeling imperfect, discouraged, ashamed, lonely, stressed, confused, fearful, resentful, or in any way lost, I am able to see that this darkness results from my closing my eyes, not from the light extinguishing. For me, wealth is being able to share what the darkness has taught me as an expression of hope, not despair.

And your dedication to practicing serenity principles, with its discipline, affection and love for which you give to it, strengthens me and inspires me to dedicate myself more and more to maintain a Rich Life (Peace and Light). I have written this and you are reading this due to our Dark Night of the Soul, and so we unite at this moment in the Peace and Light.

TO DO: Today, I will not despair! I will recognize that any suffering is my rite of passage to a greater consciousness and an abundant life! I will look at suffering not as a burden but as a way to eventually help others and to reconnect to the Creator, the Universe, and my True Nature. I will recognize how my "bottom," my "Spiritual Bankruptcy," my dark night of my soul was necessary to adhere to a new, greater way of life. If I stumble on my recovery path, I will only more vigorously appeal to my Higher Power, knowing that I was once saved by doing so, and therefore faithful that I only need to open my eyes to walk again on the well lit path.

February 29

A Miserable Person Is Someone With Two Feet Planted Firmly in Mid Air

Some of us tend to be grandiose or somewhat imbalanced. We set unrealistic goals and then never do anything to try to earn them. Our imbalanced egos make us either think too highly of ourselves or too lowly of ourselves. Some of us tend to be ego maniacs with inferiority complexes. In any event, it seems to be an impossible challenge for many of us to just live a normal life. So, if things are going well, don't let your brain tell you that you deserve all the credit or else you will turn good things into grandiosity. And if things seem to be constantly going badly, don't beat up on yourself or constantly live in self blame.

TO DO: Devote some energy today to each of your Five Natures: body, mind, emotions, social, and soul. For example, exercise, read, laugh at a situation, and appreciate nature or connect to a good spirited friend. Practice the four steps to serenity by applying them to each challenge you face. If you feel too high or too low, see if you are doing any of the 30 Serenity Killers. Finally, repeat to yourself that your feet need to stay planted on the earth, not mid air.

March 1

When Our Ego Is Out of Whack, We Can Be in the Gutter and Still Look Down on People

Our egos are such dangerous things. Despite suffering self-imposed humiliation after humiliation, our arrogance can still make us think we are better than others. This attitude wreaks havoc on our serenity. This attitude actually can make us feel bad and lonely. We need to be aware as soon as we start comparing ourselves to others. Such comparisons throw our egos out of balance and kill our serenity. We especially need to be on guard for feelings of superiority. When we don't look down on people, we don't isolate and we actually feel more included in society rather than excluded.

TO DO: The serenity poem says, "Not better than, not worse. Comparisons are a curse." Today, I will stop comparing myself with others. I will stop using judgmental language. I will replace egotistical thinking with humble thinking by keeping my self image not to high or not too low, by accepting myself unconditionally, and by gently trying to eliminate character defects like resentment and fear. If I begin to think I am superior to others, I will remember to keep my ego in check.

March 2

An Itch Will Only Go Away
If You Don't Scratch It

If you think you are going to get relief from injuring someone else out of revenge, or by giving in to a harmful temptation, you are mistaken. Seeking relief by misbehavior is like continually scratching an open wound. You will only make the sore grow larger. With regard to resentment, don't nurture it by thinking of reasons to hate. Perhaps try to replace it with understanding and empathy. Another way to get rid of a resentment is to simply detach from the person you resent. You can detach by directing your energy at helping someone else. Redirecting your energy does not mean that you should not create a healthy boundary with the person who has triggered your hatred. Substituting negative thoughts with positive thoughts does not mean that you have to approve, acquiesce or not seek to stop someone else's oppression. But it does mean that you stop carrying around the baggage of hatred which only serves to hurt yourself, "like drinking poison and expecting the other person to die."

TO DO: Obsessing on hurting another does not relieve the craving. Step 4 advises us to fix ourselves, not someone else. Seek counsel on how to create a healthy boundary and seek to spend your day motivated by compassion. When you don't act out of hatred, you will feel happier.

March 3

Beware of Triggers!

What are the events that challenge your serenity? Examples: spending too long caretaking an ailing friend... Procrastinating... Spending too long sitting at a computer. The possibilities are endless and personal to you. A trigger can be a spoon (heroin addicts can especially testify to this). A trigger can be the forest (where I got lost as a child). Yes, a trigger can be anything. It is up to you to discover your triggers. Consulting the 30 Serenity Killers listed in this book may help.

TO DO: Today, list five events that cause you to lose your peace of mind. Begin by thinking about what happened before you last lost your serenity. Typical triggers are being Hungry, Angry, Lonely or Tired (acronym HALT). HALT means you should stop whatever else you are doing and remedy your hunger, anger, loneliness, or tiredness. Similarly, you need to remedy your other triggers (often by applying the four steps). Knowing your triggers is an essential prerequisite to remedying them, so don't give short shrift to becoming familiar with them.

March 4

Out of My Head and Into My Heart

It's not so much what happens to you as what you think about it. Try not to judge a person or situation as good or bad because, with time, good or bad changes. As soon as your brain gets out of control or irritated, tell yourself, "Out of my head and into my heart!" Interrupt bad thoughts by simply repeating to yourself, "Out of my head and into my heart." If you are worried about what others are thinking about you, simply tell yourself, "Out of my head and into my heart" and feel the self-consciousness melt away.

TO DO: Focus on what's in front of you. Say five times slowly to yourself: "I need not feel guilty or ashamed. I am loved" as you simultaneously slow and deepen your breathing. If you think you are not loved, you are mistaken because I love you. Today, stay out of your head and into your heart.

March 5

Don't Let the Bird That Landed on Your Head Build a Nest

You can't help it if someone or something throws you for a loop. Everyone gets overwhelmed and frustrated. No matter how much you think you can control your feelings, no matter how well adjusted you think you are, no matter how well you practice the four steps, every now and then something will happen that will upset you. The key is to not let that bird build a nest in your head. People, places, and things cannot control your emotions. They are just emotional triggers. Remember, you make yourself feel a certain way in response to the trigger. You can also quickly change how you respond.

TO DO: What's a good way to get that bird to fly away? Try to recognize your feeling, and then try to change the bad feeling to a positive feeling. To do so, take a personal inventory and see where your own sensitivity may be contributing to your pain. Then substitute the negative thought with a healing thought plus a healing action. For example, if you feel resentful, substitute resentment with empathy. Hope that the person who caused you the resentment heals. Then try to redirect your attention by helping someone. By getting out of yourself and helping another, you will likely forget about your resentment. The key to getting the bird to fly away rather than building a nest is to find your issue (which you can change), not the issue in the other person (which you can't do anything about).

March 6

The Return of the Dark Night of the Soul

Let us not forget that just as the sun will rise again bringing the light, so the night will fall again bringing the darkness. In life, the darkness occurs whenever I try to control something that I cannot control. For example, this morning I wanted to stand up on a surfboard and ride a wave. However the Ocean had other plans. There were no ridable waves. The more I tried, the darker the situation became. I noticed the waves were breaking nicely near the shoreline, but I knew that those waves would crush me into the hard ocean floor because there was not enough water to cushion my fall. I felt the darkness of an impossible situation. If I overcontrolled to achieve my desire, I would risk severe injury. I screamed at Mother Earth in rage. I raged because I ignored each of the Four Steps of Serenity. I did not know when to stop trying to control. I lacked gratitude even though I was in the midst of enjoying a beautiful day playing on the ocean. I was trying to fix the ocean, rather than maintaining calm, gratitude, and flexibility. And finally, I lost any spiritual connection to the wonder of nature and the glorious power of the sea.

TO DO: It is critically important for us to realize that there will be times when our desire is so strong that we might feel lost again. Don't panic and try to take control. Today, focus on making the adventure the success, not the result. Know that the best way to achieve any result is by engaging fully in the adventure and if the result is to come so be it.

March 7

Don't Fight the Flow

"Don't fight the flow" means don't deny it when you have a problem or even a feeling like anger. This saying directs us to face problems, not argue that they don't exist. So what is this flow? It is, obviously, life. Life is a flow of events which are unpredictable and all too often apparently unwanted, as in the saying, "Shit happens." We are all subject to this flow everyday - most often with little problems. The key is to accept the problem, then respond positively by not turning a little thing into a big thing. Problems tend to resolve in stages, so exercise patience as you take care of problems as best you can. Keep the drama out of it by remembering the big picture that you are OK. This attitude will help you not procrastinate. Of course, there are times when you can't do anything and then you let it be. We always have options so long as we don't deny what is happening. So, not fighting the flow keeps you in a good state of mind because you aren't fighting life, you are dealing positively with it.

TO DO: Exercise acceptance. Do the next right thing according to the four absolutes: Honesty, Purity, Love, and Unselfishness. If you are doing this, know you are acting reasonably so pat yourself on the back.

March 8

First Thought Wrong

When life shocks you, don't react. Never trust your first thought because it usually is wrong. Always test your first thought by thinking of its consequences (good and bad) and always think of possible alternative thoughts before you act. Our first thoughts tend to be harmful to ourselves and others. For example, usually our first thought when feeling stressed, angry, helpless or some other negative emotion is to lash out, withdraw, or escape (fight or flight). This just causes more conflict and stress. We consequently often regret acting upon our first thoughts. Acting upon our first thought is called a reaction. Better to "act upon", not react, because this makes our lives easier.

TO DO: Today, don't react based on your first thought.

March 9

Get Out of the Way

"Getting out of the way" means letting your Higher Power, not your character defects, run your life. It allows you to relax and not live in fear. Your Higher Power can be anything that keeps you serene without harming anyone. Typically, a Higher Power involves a helpful philosophy and community. "Getting out of the way" means that we allow that philosophy and community to lead us to serenity, not our character defects which have failed us. We often choose this Higher Power based upon its history of being effective for others, and we maintain our faith in this Higher Power as we experience its effectiveness in our own lives.

With regard to any problem, getting out of the way reduces stress because we are not shouldering all of the responsibility and doing it all by ourselves without the aid of others who may know better than we do and who can at least give valuable input.

TO DO: Say to yourself: I will get out of the way and try allowing the four steps to guide me today. I will get out of the way because my best attempts at reaching serenity have not been as successful as I would have liked, and I am not ashamed to admit I need help to live a new, better life. Today, I will enjoy letting this new Higher Power run the show for awhile. If I have already been relying on this Higher Power for awhile, I will keep doing so, and not let my character defects return, because I have experienced the Peace my Higher Power gives me.

March 10

Get in the Middle of the Bed

You can avoid slipping if you are in the middle. To get in the middle of the bed, start by memorizing the four steps. Then meditate on them each morning as you make a commitment to practice them each day particularly during serenity threatening moments. Also fully commit to any recovery group to which you belong. Another way to get in the middle of the bed is to REALLY LISTEN when others are sharing their feelings with you. Give a smile to someone. When we start acting a new way, our thoughts and feelings will follow.

TO DO: Today, I refuse to go about my quest for serenity in a lackadaisical way. I will make it my priority. I will get in the middle of reaching toward peace so that I don't slip and therefore regress.

March 11

Give it Away to Keep it

If you help someone else, you will be helped. If you want to lose self- consciousness, be "other" conscious. If you want to feel better, the best way is to try to make someone else feel better. "Give it away to keep it" is a fundamental principle of serenity. "Give it away to keep it" focuses on one person helping another. Recovery from addiction is based on one addict helping another. 12 step programs (like Alcoholics Anonymous and Emotions Anonymous) were started when someone who wanted to stay sober knew he had better try to help another alcoholic or else he would pick up that first, fatal drink. He found another and, together, they stayed sober for each other. I've counseled recovering addicts for twenty one years, and I have been sober for 33 years, and I have noticed that those who stay and reap the rewards of sobriety, are those who encourage and sponsor new recovering addicts (without controlling or expecting results).

TO DO: This concept of helping others to help oneself applies to your journey toward peace and light. To avoid stagnation, a lake must have an inflow and an outflow. Today, ask yourself how you can encourage someone else. Perhaps a smile or a simple act of kindness will suffice? Perhaps volunteering for a few hours is appropriate? Remember to keep your stream clean and flowing to keep your serenity.

March 12

H.O.W. Stands for
Honesty, Open-mindedness, and Willingness

So how do I - someone who has hit bottom (which means someone who has lost all serenity) - change? How? "H" stands for honesty. Honesty to oneself means admitting that you don't know what to do, that your current methods for reaching serenity simply aren't working. For example, drugs, material objects, toxic relationships are not giving you peace and light. Honesty means that you will no longer make excuses to avoid change. "O" stands for open-mindedness. Open-mindedness means you will try a new way to reach serenity uncluttered with doubts and full of faith. "W" stands for willingness. You must be absolutely willing to make your personal serenity the foundation of your life. That is HOW you begin on the path to serenity.

TO DO: Today, I will check the 30 Serenity Killers to guide me as to what I am doing to kill my serenity, then I will apply the four steps and the concepts I am learning by reading these daily messages to regain my serenity. I will not rely on materialism or toxic relationships because I know they will only send me off course.

March 13

H.A.L.T. When You Are
Hungry, Angry, Lonely, or Tired

H.A.L.T. is the acronym for Hungry, Angry, Lonely, or Tired. Common dangers to serenity are hunger, anger, loneliness, and exhaustion because they can threaten our emotional balance. If we don't eat when hungry, we lose our emotional balance. If we don't deal with feelings like anger in a healthy way, we lose our emotional balance. If we don't connect with someone when lonely, we lose our emotional balance. If we don't rest when tired, we lose our emotional balance.

TO DO: Every time you are hungry, angry, lonely, or tired, HALT and address that symptom appropriately. Don't do anything else until that need is taken care of. Think ahead by carrying a bag of peanuts, having your friends' phone numbers in your contacts list, and knowing where to get rest. Deal with these triggers preemptively by creating a good timetable for daily nutrition, exercise, rest, and group support.

March 14

"I try to take one day at a time but sometimes several days attack me at once."
- Jennifer Yane

Losing serenity is often a result of a wandering mind that thinks about worry and regret. Worry involves thinking about the future and regret involves thinking about the past. The bottom line is that we need to live in today. Actually, we need to live in the now. When worries about how you are going to pay your taxes or regrets about why you invested in that stock bother you, you need to refocus on just doing the next reasonable thing according to the four absolutes (honesty, purity, unselfishness, and love). If something needs to be planned, put it in your calendar, do whatever you need to do to prepare today, and then forget about it. If your mind slips into the past, ask yourself what you might have been able to learn from the experience, then let it go. If you are endlessly debating about what decision to make, do a pros and cons list and a cost benefit analysis, tell yourself you never have a "crystal ball" that can magically reveal the perfect outcome, then make the decision and let go of the results.

TO DO: If you feel bad, it may be because your mind is wandering into the future or the past. Live one day at a time by refocusing wandering thoughts back to the moment. A good exercise is to do a few simple physical movements and have your mind trace these movements. For example, untie and retie your shoes while only thinking about untying and retying your shoes.

March 15

If You Do What You Did,
You Will Get What You Got

The person I was will lose his serenity again. Therefore, I must change. The first time I heard this I was offended. I didn't want to be brainwashed, but a good washing was what I needed. I soon learned that changing meant that I was not losing myself; rather, I was just changing the bad parts of myself. Changing meant doing things differently. Examples: helping others without worrying about what I was getting in return and doing my Higher Power's will and not mine. The result was that I did not get the misery I had. Instead, I received a loving family and a blessed lifestyle.

Sometimes, you need to simply change your attitude. For example, if you feel offended by anyone, try changing your attitude by asking yourself if there is something you can change about yourself to deal positively with the offense. Sometimes, it may be that you need to change sadness to acceptance. Sometimes it may be that you need to change hatred to empathy for the other person.

TO DO: Don't fear change. If you do what you did, you will get what you got. Embrace change today. Everything is impermanent so embrace change, don't fight it.

March 16

Look at Your Eyes in the Mirror and Tell Yourself You Love Yourself No Matter What

This may be the toughest one of all. But trust me, it works. You may not even recognize yourself when you do it. When I did it, I was surprised at the nice looking expression that I had never seen. I felt tears of joy. I certainly did not want to punish or criticize myself. Unconditional self-acceptance and love is a key to being serene. When you accept yourself, you will not be jealous or care so much about whether others accept you. You will become less self-conscious and actually more lovable to others.

TO DO: Look at your eyes in the mirror and tell yourself that you love yourself even though you are far from perfect, and even if you feel overwhelmed, hopeless, lonely or sad.

March 17

Magic Magnifying Mind Causes Trouble

Do you feel bad because you feel shocked, worried or confused about making that perfect decision? Do you feel uncertain, even disillusioned? Wondering how you stop saying to yourself, "But what if that happens?... Then I will have to do that... And that will cause them to think that about me... And if they think that, I will never be able to get that job... And if I can't get that job, what was the point of my spending so long in school... Oh, my whole life will be a waste..."

TO DO: Don't catastrophize. Just do the next right thing and concentrate on what you are doing. Exercise mindfulness. Mindfulness means that you are slowly breathing and keeping your mind in the moment. Start by looking at your feet, squeezing your foot muscles, then slowly working your way upward. Take your time, breathing slowly. Once you have reached the top of your head, start noticing your surroundings. Then do your next daily activity, keeping your mind focused on what you are doing. Don't live in the future or the past. Breathe out the stress and in the Serenity.

March 18

Please Let Me Take Life as It Comes and Not as I Would Have It Be

This has become my favorite prayer. My attitude of inflexibility and my desire for things to go exactly as I plan are my two biggest stress inducers. Unless I ask my Higher Power to free me from these defects first thing in the morning, when the snow comes or the smart phone doesn't have enough storage space or the dog barks or the notes get misplaced or whatever other interruption occurs, I feel stressed and even angry.

TO DO: Say a prayer (or simply focus all your energy) early in the day to ask for the strength to accept life's interruptions. As you plan your day, include extra time for things to go awry. Use your sense of humor to laugh at life rather than to be irritated.

March 19

Reach Out. Even When Things Are Good

It is often said that the most dangerous time for losing our serenity is when things are challenging. But it can be just as dangerous when things are good. When things seem to be going smoothly, we may forget to do the four steps, particularly the step which suggests that we connect with supportive people or some other Higher Power. We may neglect meditation or other practices that are keeping us serene. Then when some trigger comes along, we are thrust into despair because we have not been practicing our daily serenity program.

TO DO: Keep connecting with others and practicing your daily serenity program…even when things are good! Each day make a conscious deliberation on the four steps part of your morning routine.

March 20

Serenity Is a Three Legged Stool

"Serenity is a three legged stool: principles, fellowship, and Higher Power. If one of the legs is broken, the stool falls."

This is my Sponsor's favorite saying. He emphasized attention to each "leg" daily because being serene is a daily reprieve. The principles are the four steps, the fellowship is contact with other people who are trying to be serene, the Higher Power is a spiritual force of one's own understanding. The way you stay serene is to keep the table standing by keeping the three legs strong...each day.

TO DO: Make it a daily habit to keep the three legs strong. Try calling a positive person just to say "hello," read a daily message from this book, and take a deep breath while asking your Higher Power to keep you serene today. That's three legs. Good for you!

March 21

Ride It Out

Ride out being overwhelmed. Sometimes you just need to hold your head and cry. Soon the pain and sadness will pass. There will be no explanation for your suffering so don't even try to find one. Crying is absolutely acceptable. Owning your feelings without attaching any intellectual sense to them is sometimes quite healthy. Know that soon your pain will pass. Know that when it passes you will have a greater appreciation for not having that pain. You will also feel incredibly good ("rocketed into the 4th dimension") when you realize that you did not have to act out in some harmful way to cope with the pain!

TO DO: Ride out the pain by supporting your head lovingly in your own hands. It's okay to call someone and share your suffering. Catch yourself if you feel like you want to lash out in anger, withdraw into depression or some other self-defeating behavior. Try applying the four steps to the situation that is causing you distress.

March 22

Sometimes You Win, Sometimes You Lose, but You Can Always Reclaim Serenity

Do you ever get upset because you did not win? Losing is a common trigger for unhappiness. The most effective strategy I have learned to deal with the unhappiness of losing is to redefine winning. Today I define winning as dealing gracefully with the outcome. If I can maintain a peaceful, yet resilient attitude when the outcome goes against my will, then I have truly won. I also allow myself time to appropriately grieve the loss. I am allowed to feel sad or angry for a reasonable period even if I only lost something as replaceable as my car keys or as meaningless as a chess game. I even remind myself that I do not always know whether something I really wanted in the short term is what is really best for me in the long term. For example, when I graduated from law school, I wanted nothing more than to be hired by a prestigious law firm. I spent nights dreaming of the money, benefits and glory of being associated with a renowned firm. But of the seven firms I applied to, not one of them extended an offer. I was forced to go out on my own. I did so not with a sense of dejection but with a sense of adventure. And ultimately, owning my own firm has yielded for me success and pleasure. Failing to get what I first wanted, a big firm job when I graduated from law school, was one of the best things that could have happened to me. When I don't let feelings of loss discourage me, I have courage to keep heading in a successful direction. I take the "dis" out of discourage, and get my courage back. I accept and adapt. True victory is practicing serenity principles regardless of whether we win the trophy, qualify for the loan, see our face on the television, sell the book, or get the applause. It comes from our relationship with our Higher Power and others. It comes from within. As the recovery saying goes, "Happiness is an inside job." True happiness does not come from trying to control the outside World.

TO DO: Today, I will redefine winning. I will make winning giving my all to the journey regardless of the outcome. I will TRUST that my Higher Power has a better plan than what I was planning. If there is a way to try again to achieve something, I might if I am able to make the journey more important than the result. I will accept and adapt according to good values.

March 23

Nothing You Can Own Is Worth Having

Luxury cars, coin collections, gold, people – all cost more than the happiness they were meant to buy. Sooner or later, all things rust, become boring, cause conflict, are eventually sold or stored. There is always the threat of fear that surrounds them: Will they get scratched, stolen, or forgotten? Will they cause family conflict, war? Will the people I seek to own remember me, do what I want them to do? True serenity comes from letting go of ownership, letting go of owning things, spouses, children, ourselves. It is not ego driven. Serenity can't be bought, maintained, hidden, and stored. It comes from unselfishness and love without control.

TO DO: Today, I will not seek to own things or people. I will remember that serenity can't be bought, that it comes from giving up control, appreciating the journey, and being grateful for what I have not from what I desire.

March 24

The 2,500 Ton Phone

Our egos weigh things down. It's not the problem that's heavy; it's our perception that's heavy. One heavy perception that needs to be made much lighter is our fear and embarrassment of picking up the phone and sharing a problem with another person. Had I not heard that I should pick up the phone instead of a drink endlessly during the first 30 days of my sobriety, I would never have picked up the phone and called my Sponsor when tempted to drink on day 31. Picking up the phone helps us share what we are feeling so we can feel better.

TO DO: It is important to have someone with whom you can share your feelings (not just your thoughts). This should be someone who will not necessarily give you advice, but simply someone who you can trust to listen and maintain confidentiality. To find someone, think who might be a possibility, then ask them if they are willing to occasionally receive calls from you for support and friendship. Ask them if they are willing to listen confidentially without giving advice unless you ask them for advice. Tell them you want to express FEELINGS not necessarily thoughts. Obvious possible choices are friends, therapists, children, parents, significant others, etc. If you are feeling any bad feeling (sadness, stress, resentment, etc.) remember a problem shared is a problem halved. Pick up that phone. It ain't heavy.

March 25

Try to remember what bothered you a week ago. Since you can't, should you let what's bothering you today make you miserable?

Is what's bothering you causing you to spiral into depression? You probably will forget what's troubling you, but you probably won't forget if you let it make you spend hours on the internet, ruin your sleep, make you lose interest in things you used to enjoy, and otherwise ruin your day. Most times, it is the initial shock that hurts when we are confronted with an issue. Often, it is a little thing that starts us spiraling downward. It is important to not "sweat the small stuff." It is important to nip bad feelings in the bud.

TO DO: As soon as you feel annoyed, you should use a recovery tool to get over what's bothering you, like sharing the problem with a friend, going to a support meeting, journaling, deep breathing, reading a book, or whatever helps. Writing down something that bothers you and throwing it in the trash might help. Don't sweep your problems under the rug, deal with them one at a time. But there is a time to forget about them. Writing down 5 things you are grateful for (like being able to walk, live in a safe place, have food, a friend, a book, etc.) may change your attitude.

March 26

Five Seconds of Rage
Isn't Worth a Lifetime of Regret

Tennis star Novak Djokovic is well on his way to the $3 million dollar first place finish in the U.S. Open. He has made a few bad shots though, and suddenly he swats at the ball and it hits a referee in the throat. He is disqualified and fined. How many times do we let our reactions cause harm? Is one second of unconscious emotional reaction worth death, insanity, or permanent injury? When you get an urge to react to a situation uncontrollably, follow it through to its horrible end. Any perceived short term emotional release or reward (is it really a reward?) is not worth the long term punishment. That punishment begins with feeling bad about ourselves and may end with our futile attempt to erase that guilt with more harmful actions. By practicing the four steps, we are able to ACT UPON situations rather than REACT to them.

TO DO: The process of eliminating harmful unconscious reactions is to PREPARE yourself for otherwise shocking situations before the shock occurs. Doing a morning meditation, and repeating the four steps throughout the day, preempts unconscious emotional reactions. If we are suddenly triggered, we must think about how that trigger can lead us to disaster.

March 27

We Make Our Own Bologna Sandwiches

"A man may perform astonishing feats and comprehend a vast amount of knowledge, and yet have no understanding of himself. But suffering directs a man to look within. If it succeeds, then there, within him, is the beginning of learning." - Soren Kierkegaard.

Joe was having a casual lunch with a coworker. They both had lunches in bags they had brought from home. As the coworker unwrapped his sandwich, his face turned melancholy. Joe asked what was wrong? The coworker replied, "Oh nothing really… It's just that I am really sick of bologna sandwiches and I see I am having one for lunch again today. Seems like I've had bologna for lunch every day for the past twenty years." Joe asked, "Why don't you just ask your wife to make you something else?" The friend replied "I'm not married. I make the sandwiches myself." The coworker's dilemma sounds ridiculous doesn't it? But think for a moment. How many things do we do out of habit that really only cause us distress, that interfere with our lives? The point is many of us would prefer to experience the same old failures just because we are afraid to change. But the first step is to admit that we have a problem with bologna sandwiches and that we are making them ourselves. Once we admit we are suffering and that the suffering comes from something we are doing (not from something that others are doing to us), we can learn and implement strategies which can lead us to freedom.

TO DO: Today, ask yourself what you may be doing to cause your own suffering. Ask yourself what you need to change about yourself to make you less fearful and stressed. Do you need to realize that holding a resentment against someone is only hurting you? Do you need to make decisions based on humility rather than pride? Don't be afraid to look at what you are doing that may be causing you suffering, then ask someone you trust for help to discover a new way of behaving. You will find that there is a wonderful person within you that you will come to actually love!

March 28

What Other People Think of You
Is None of Your Business

If we are obsessed with trying to figure out what someone else thinks about us, we are obsessed with something we cannot control. Obsessions with things we cannot control kill serenity. Serenity teaches us to go about our business of practicing good principles in all our affairs. Although people usually aren't as concerned about us as we might believe, if they are jealous, hateful, loving, or whatever they may feel about us, that is their business, not ours. What a relief it is to let go of others' opinions about us!

TO DO: You cannot control others and you cannot control what others think of you. Things that you can't control are none of your business. If necessary, create a healthy boundary if someone is bothering you. But don't waste time and energy stressing over what they think about you. Just live according to the four absolutes (honesty, unselfishness, purity, and love) and you will be fine!

March 29

You Are Loved

No matter what you have done, even the worst imaginable, you are forgiven and loved when you are searching for your perception of peace and enlightenment. It is not too late. You don't have to believe in someone else's religion. You simply need to be still and know that you don't have all the answers, that you are not the one in charge, that what you have is not so important, that what you plan need not come true, that you have all that you need, without fear and regret, as you let go of your old ways, and follow the path to peace and enlightenment.

TO DO: Today, do the four steps to peace and enlightenment (serenity). Accept others and yourself, be grateful for needs satisfied, connect to something other than your egotistical, fearful self, and seek to change self defeating behaviors. Perhaps connect to Love.

March 30

You Don't Lose Your Serenity by Making Mistakes - You Lose It by Defending the Mistakes You Made

An imbalanced ego makes us defensive. That ego tells us we are no good if we make mistakes so we try to convince everyone, including ourselves, that we were right. But all that this defensiveness does is cause us stress and insanity because (as we all know) we make mistakes. The four steps teach us to accept our mistakes, not to run from them by acting inappropriately. As we rebalance our egos with humility, we don't need to be defensive.

TO DO: Stop trying to make believe you are perfect. Perfectionism is actually a character defect that only hurts our serenity.

March 31

You Don't Really Need That to Be Happy

Some things you can't have. Since you can't get them, don't worry about them. What is it that you need? Is it really something that is just for ego satisfaction? Is it really necessary to have dessert tonight? Is it really necessary to have that new car, that velvet shirt, that specific answer, that red flower pot? Do you really need that drink or is it going to just let you down later? If it's necessary for sustenance, you will get it. If it's something consistent with love, purity, unselfishness and honesty, just take a small step in that direction. Isn't it nice that you can feel so much better just by simplifying toward goodness?

TO DO: Today, do something healthy for your body like eating something nutritious or taking a walk if you can. Good for you for using this message as one way to maintain a positive attitude! Let go of sadness and desire, and be grateful that you have your needs fulfilled. If your wants are making you miserable, let go of them. You don't really need them to make you happy.

April 1

Make It All Fun

Monopoly takes concentration, calm, resilience, the ability to handle frustration, the ability to handle setbacks; indeed, it can make one extremely angry. In fact, it can be extremely stressful. Yet, people play Monopoly for recreation. The secret of enjoying life is to face problems with a light-hearted attitude. Try to make chores fun. Make believe you are just playing a game. This is not too far-fetched an idea because each chore and problem will either resolve or dissolve, and it will help you to face them with a cheerful attitude.

TO DO: Today I will imagine my problems as just a game. I will be confident that although I may not get what I want, I will get what I need.

April 2

You're OK!

If you're able to read this, your body has enough air right now to function. So you're fundamentally OK. Whatever you think you need, you probably don't. So don't panic because you lack something. Breathe if you can. If you can't, move somewhere that you can. Just keep going in the right direction. This too shall pass.

TO DO: The four steps are particularly helpful when you are in a panic.

1.Accept the situation and be flexible.

2.Be grateful for what you have and focus on the fact that your basic needs are
fulfilled.

3.Connect to that source which makes you feel fundamentally OK. Is that source stillness through relaxed breathing? Is it a vigorous walk? A swim in the sea? A kind act toward others? Cognitive restructuring? A religious God? The act of making amends?

4.Ask yourself what is your character issue that is causing you to panic. Is it impatience? Fear you are not going to get your way? A resentment? Then let goof that character issue.

Finally, repeat to yourself once an hour today: "I'm OK" as you take a slow inhale and even slower exhale.

April 3

You're as Sick as Your Secrets

Keeping things to ourselves because we are ashamed is serenity threatening. So we need to unload secrets about ourselves with someone we can trust. When we do, we usually discover that the secrets are nothing to be ashamed of. We usually discover that we have been carrying a weight that had only caused us to feel bad about ourselves. Even if we are hiding something horrific, it is better for our serenity to unload it by sharing. We should, however, exercise caution. It is our responsibility to find a person who is duty bound for confidentiality. Some options are a wise and trusted sponsor, a clergy person, or a mental health practitioner. But, at the end of the day, secrets are a trigger to emotional relapse and we need to try to dump them.

TO DO: Ask yourself if you are hiding something due to shame. Take some steps toward finding someone you can trust to share your secrets. Share whatever you are holding back. Unloading secrets not only reduces shame, but also allows you to feel more connected to others and less lonely.

April 4

Compare Yours With Something Worse

My friend was constantly complaining because he was in Florida and there were a string of cloudy days in the 60's. I mentioned that it was 2 degrees in Detroit. This brightened up his day. A recovering addict feeling sad she had lost her driving privileges remembered that she was not without food that day. When shocked or confronted with any bad feeling, be grateful for your problems because it could be worse.

TO DO: We can always complain. To feel better, we need to remember that it's acceptable to compare our situation to something worse. Don't feel guilty about that. Perspective is a serenity tool I will repeatedly use today to get me through all the piddling little problems that are thrown at me.

April 5

Sometimes You Can't Fix a Problem, You Can Only Deal With It

I double checked the instructions. While holding down the "program" button, I pressed the "advance time" button, but the time did not change. There was no way I was doing the procedure incorrectly. But the timer would not set. Therefore, I could not program the coffee maker to have my precious coffee ready when I woke up. Another example: a troubled client sends me a threatening email on the first day of my vacation. Another example: a young couple is told that they can never have children. From little issues like my coffee maker not working to challenges like being told you can never have children, there are times when you cannot fix a problem, you can only deal with it so that it does not destroy your serenity or the manageability of your life.

TO DO: Sure it hurts right now, that's unavoidable. However, take gradual steps to get out of the frustration. First, don't allow your frustration to make you do something that will result in bad consequences. Instead, practice acceptance, not judgment. Even if unexpected and unfair, accept that each of us must deal with adversity. Don't feel like you must bear it alone. Ask friends and therapists for guidance and support. Create a plan to deal with adversity. Perhaps, you will have to be a bit more patient to deal with an unexpected problem. Perhaps you will have to be flexible and seek alternative solutions. Perhaps you will have to reprioritize certain life goals to best play the new "hand of cards" you have been dealt. But be patient, the pain will leave. In the meantime, breathe easy and tell yourself you can deal with it. A helpful way to deal with life is to apply the four steps to situations.

April 6

A Problem Shared Is a Problem Halved

So often we are taught to keep everything to ourselves. The following example demonstrates how this self-reliance is a mistake especially when we are upset or impatient. I was standing in line recently at the post office. Each clerk was involved with a customer who clearly had some unusual problem that seemed to require unending attention. There were three other people ahead of me. Each of the three held boxes that no doubt were going to require lengthy attention once the clerks were freed from their current interminable chores. I began to feel the familiar heart pounding that I experience when I am forced to wait in line. I considered my options. I could leave and try again later to mail my overnight envelope, but that would only result in more travel time and would therefore waste more time than waiting for a clerk now. I resolved to wait. I closed my eyes and asked my Higher Power to calm me, but my heart continued to race. I noticed a woman standing behind me. I took a chance and told her, "You know, my biggest weakness is waiting. I can actually feel my heart pounding through my chest." She replied, "I know what you mean, it's especially hard when it looks like the wait will never end." I made eye contact with her and smiled. I already felt a lot calmer. She then smiled mischievously and said, "You know, you can say a prayer I like to say. It goes like this, "Dear God, please give me patience, and give it to me now!" We both laughed. I felt much better. I felt really connected, and my sense of humor was restored. My heart pounding stopped. I was glad to share the wait with her. It was just great to know that I could turn to a complete stranger and honestly share my feelings. Note that I did not complain about the situation, I simply shared how I was feeling. I am sure it probably made her feel better too. I had gotten what I needed: patience (and interestingly) I had in fact gotten it NOW. Honestly asking for help with a negative feeling is often a good risk to take. Your sharing of a feeling may facilitate another to express his or her feelings, and few things make others feel better than honestly sharing feelings.

113

TO DO: Remember that a feeling will not pass until you allow yourself to feel it. Reach out to someone. Make it a point to start with the words, "I am feeling..."

April 7

The Best Way to Be Patient?

Before I made Serenity a priority, I was always halfway there. I was never there. I was always waiting or struggling. I never made it anywhere. I had such big plans. Always looking forward with arrogance and grandiosity, but living with such low self-esteem that I really had no chance to accomplish anything. In living for Serenity rather than ego gratification, I have learned to simply take it one day at a time...to make reasonable plans, but not worry about the results... and best of all to appreciate the beauty of this moment. Even if the moment is challenging, I am able to face it. And soon the challenges pass. I am never struggling to be patient because I am no longer waiting for anything to happen. Rather I am living in this moment. Rather than suffering over not yet getting what I want, I feel grateful I have all that I need right now.

TO DO: Today, I will defeat the agony of impatience and any other stinking thinking by simply living in this moment, by doing whatever I am supposed to do that is right in front of me. What a relief!

April 8

It Would Be Nice, but It's Not Necessary

It's so reassuring to know that most of what we think is so important, really doesn't make that much difference. Too often we think that if someone doesn't do what we want, or if something doesn't turn out how we want it to, or if we don't get this or that, our lives will not be OK. But this is not true. We must learn to reduce our demands to mere preferences. When we do so, we tend to relax. So, a good habit to develop is to say, "It would be nice, but it's not necessary." We can reduce demands to preferences in many everyday situations which tend to stress us out. For example, it would be nice if my son shows up for Christmas, but it's not necessary to my survival...It would be nice if I got a raise, but it's not necessary, and so on. Whenever I'm obsessing over something (or someone) that I wish I could change, I say, "It would be nice if [insert whatever issue is bothering you], but it's not necessary." I even use this tool for most of my selfish desires, i.e. it would be great if I could buy that Mustang convertible, but it's not essential. Of course, this doesn't apply to everything. Sometimes you cannot put up with abuse or you need to change yourself (i.e. stop using drugs). But usually, this simple phrase helps me stop obsessing, gives me gratitude and perspective, lets me let go of things I can't control, and ultimately, be much happier.

TO DO: Right now, I will meditate on the phrase, "It would be nice, but it's not necessary." I will repeat this phrase to myself five times. Then as challenging people, places, and events occur, I will apply this phrase to the occasion.

April 9

Wear the World Like a Loose Garment

Turn something that may be stressful into something humorous. Relax. So what if you got a bad haircut. You don't have to be disappointed or go through the seven stages of death. Nothing is going to put that hair back on your head but time. "Wear the world like a loose garment" is a very relaxing motto. It means that you should try to be comfortable when life throws its little nuisances at you. Don't allow the world to close in on you and choke you. Make a conscious effort to accept life and not resist life because if you resist, problems persist. Don't be jealous because everybody, regardless of wealth and health, has daily problems. Don't turn problems into drama. Don't turn someone else's character defect into a resentment. Don't turn comedy into tragedy. An exercise I do now on an almost daily basis is to become aware when I am getting upset because I am not getting my way. One thing I do is to make believe I am in a movie. I try to imagine how the audience would be responding to my predicament. Nine times out of ten, the audience would be laughing. They would not be laughing sadistically, but they would be laughing because my predicament is truly funny. My predicament is a comedy because most of my predicaments are not permanently harmful to me. Sure they may cost me some time, money or ego gratification, but ultimately most of my dramas are truly funny, and I can only see their humor once I am able to put myself in the audience. Now I frequently end up laughing rather than crying. Seeing the comedy makes me a lighter, happier person. When I became 55 years old, I had an identity crisis. My wife knew I had been working out harder than ever in an effort to resist what I perceived as getting old. She bought me a new pair of exercise pants. I wore them to the gym where I spent hours torturing myself trying to lift weights that were too heavy for me but not "for that 20 year old" linebacker who always showed up in the gym when I did.

One day, two sexy 20 year old female personal trainers were also working out. I thought I looked pretty good in my new exercise pants. I kind of strutted around during my workout, spending a lot of time walking in front of the gals, proud of my new young looking, stylish exercise pants. I may be 55, I thought, but I still can dress in style. After my workout, I went into the locker room and took my pants off to take a shower. I noticed I had forgotten to remove the store tags which were sticking about three inches out of the rear pocket on that plastic string that makes the tags not only clearly noticeable but reminiscent of a huge flag. I immediately felt embarrassed. Then, I mentally shifted into my movie and joined the audience. You can imagine the laugh I had. I later told my wife about it, and we laughed together.

TO DO: Instead of letting little things disappoint you today, use detachment, ego reduction and humor to "wear the world like a loose garment" (and not like tight exercise pants with tags).

April 10

You Know What Takes Down a Big Shot?
A Little Shot

When I start getting cocky, egotistical, and full of myself, I actually become more sensitive to the little ups and downs of life. When I am arrogant, I think that I should not be subjected to what everyone else must endure. This state of mind renders me susceptible to a precipitous fall if I experience a "little shot". A little shot might be a criticism or a small event that I take too seriously. It is anything that happens to pierce my bloated ego.

TO DO: Today I will be careful not to let my ego bloat. I will remember that I am a regular human being who needs to stay humble and "right sized" mentally.

April 11

Surrender to Win!

To conquer our fears and sadness, we need a new way of dealing
with life. We surrender by admitting that our old ways do not work.
We must then be willing to follow new suggestions. The power
of suggestion is very strong. It can cause you to revolt, send you
running way, or it can help you through tough times. It's up to you. It
is better to try to follow good suggestions, many of which you have
been learning in this book. As you begin to see the benefits of a new
life, you will realize that you are surrendering to win.

TO DO: Acceptance and surrender are keys to the kingdom. Today
I give up fighting. I have surrendered and am willing to take
suggestions.

April 12

Do Nice Little Things for Others

To get rid of self-consciousness, anxiety and resentment, make it a habit to start your day by planning to be kind. Then, be courteous and try to do nice little things for others. Even with adversaries, be kind. Try to spend more energy understanding rather than resenting. Don't worry about them understanding you. And don't reserve your "random acts of kindness" for only those so-called very important people you want to impress. Be kind to everyone, including clerks and janitors, those who do the important jobs that most people take for granted. Be the one with a kind demeanor on the elevator; hold the door open. Practice with everyone. The miracle here is that you will find that this habit forces you to be kinder to yourself and consequently happier and more peaceful. In turn, others may be kinder to you.

TO DO: When you are kind to others you are less likely to lose your serenity. So simply do little kind things today.

April 13

If You Don't Think Good, Don't Think Much

Our brains can really cause us problems and make us uncomfortable. A good way to stop feeling overwhelmed is to ask yourself if you really are in trouble or is it just your anxious brain talking? Sometimes we overanalyze. We worry about outcomes. We try to control what we cannot. We tend to think negatively. We tend to ignore good things, and dwell on bad things. Even when things are good, we worry about how long the good things will last.

TO DO: Tell yourself that if you can't think about good things (for example, things for which you are grateful), then you must think mechanically about only what you are doing in the present moment. It's also good to tell yourself to get out of your head and into your heart. You can also think about reaching out to help someone or to do something to serve your Higher Power. Sometimes that service can be not making a problem worse, helping Nature, listening to music, just taking a break for a peaceful walk or some other fun activity.

April 14

If You Stay Humble, You Won't Stumble

Beware of your ego creeping back in. One sign is that you are
taking charge of everyone and everything again. Another sign is
that you are relying on defense mechanisms like resentment and
self-righteousness. Humility is admitting that you're not running
the show - that you really don't know all the answers. Humility is
a difficult thing for many of us to practice because we have spent a
lifetime nurturing our egos. Nurturing our egos means that we have
built up defenses to make it look like we always knew what we were
doing, that made it look like we did not need help. Humility means
that we are strong enough to admit that we cannot control everything
and that our Higher Power can lead us to serenity. Humility puts our
ego back into balance.

TO DO: Today, try to stay humble. A good way is to connect
to HELP (Higher Effective Loving Power). Such power can be
anything that keeps you serene in the moment that does not have
harmful consequences. Enjoying music, exercising, praying to God,
practicing spiritual principles, connecting with a friend, walking
with a dog, helping someone…all can be a Higher Effective Loving
Power. Today, connect to your Higher Power and reconnect when
your ego tries to move in. If you stay humble, you won't stumble
into misery.

April 15

The Three Most Dangerous Words: "I've Been Thinking"

Sometimes obsessively thinking about a situation can be detrimental to your serenity. Your brain can be your worst enemy. Sometimes you can't trust your brain especially if your emotions have been activated. Better to connect with someone you love, or to do the next right thing in the moment. Also, try to stay active. It is dangerous if you are just doing nothing and you are thinking about the past, the future or even just daydreaming.

TO DO: Catch yourself if you find that your mind is wandering or obsessing today. Refocus on positive actions in this moment. Ask yourself what you can do to take care of your Five Natures (body, mind, emotions, social, and spirit), then do an action to take care of one of the Natures. Make it a point to take care of your Five Natures each day.

April 16

Who Wants to Be Held While Isolating?

Sometimes we find ourselves in a state of emotional conflict. We want that which is impossible. We want to be loved, but we don't want anyone to bother us. We want attention, but fear engaging socially. Often, this emotional conflict stems from our desire to have others understand us rather than us understanding them. As we walk on the path to peace and enlightenment, we find that the way we stay serene is to try to be less "self" oriented and more "other" oriented. We spend more time being understanding of others. This actually makes us less fearful and anxious. It is a happier way to live. You deserve happiness!

TO DO: Today I will remember that emotional conflicts can often be resolved if I seek to understand others rather than worrying about whether or not they understand me. I will be confident that this will make me feel less lonely and less self-conscious. Of course sometimes we enjoy being alone, but isolating ends up making us just feel lonely and afraid. We need to gain balance. It is therefore a good idea to socialize.

April 17

I Have This Overwhelming Sense of Wellbeing, It's a Bit Troubling

When is the other shoe going to drop? When things seem to be going well, many tend to fear that it will end with a smack. It's like the old saying, "I see the light at the end of the tunnel, I just hope it's not a train." One key to surviving good times is to stay in the now and not worry about tomorrow. Another key is to make plans knowing that we cannot make results. Yet another is to substitute fear with hope.

TO DO: Today, I will have faith that our Higher Power did not throw us a life float to later let us drown. I will try not to project into the future with all its uncertainty. But if I do look to the future, I will do so with optimism.

April 18

Don't Be a People Pleaser

Worrying about what others think of us hurts our serenity. Even worrying about whether or not they trust us is serenity threatening. Does that person like me? Did I say the right thing? Does my car make me look like I fit in? These are the beginnings of a long list of serenity threatening thoughts. How many can you add to the list right now?

TO DO: Tell yourself right now, that "people pleasing leads to stinkin' thinkin'." Today I will not worry about what others think about me. Rather, I will be true to myself and enjoy freedom from self-consciousness.

April 19

You Really Wouldn't Worry So Much About What Other People Think About You if You Remembered How Seldom They Think About You

Worrying about whether someone likes, understands, admires, fears or trusts you is a waste of energy. First, you can't control what others think. Second, they are probably thinking about their own issues much more than they are thinking about yours. When we realize the World does not revolve around us, we relax.

TO DO: Today I will focus on doing the next reasonable thing. A useful guide is to act or not act in accordance with good spiritual principles after freeing ourselves from our own character defects. I will not worry about what others are thinking about me to maintain my serenity.

April 20

Our EGO Is an Illusion So
Why Let It Bother Us?

How many times do we feel sad, hurt or even worthless because our ego is pierced? EGO pain can be caused by not having as expensive clothes as our friends at a party, or not having our child be as good a student as our neighbor's child, or not having as pretty a garden as our friends have, or not having as long legs as our sister, or blah blah blah blah. Our EGO is built from self-imposed rules that we mistakenly believe we need to survive. It is a phantom which primarily generates fear rather than the intended security. It also causes us to feel guilty or ashamed because it lies to us by telling us that we should be able to control things we cannot.

TO DO: List what hurts your ego and then tear up the list to free yourself. To create the list, ask yourself if what hurts comes from things you use to measure your self-worth or from things that really matter (like having enough food, shelter, or genuinely peaceful times). You are worthwhile just because you are you, and I love you!

April 21

"It's better to put on slippers than to carpet the World." - Kerry Kelly

Are you making things more difficult than they have to be? Is all of this trying to control the World just causing you stress? Is all of this manipulation getting you what you want or is it just causing others to resist you? Are any rewards worth the aggravation? When I was drinking, I can remember wasting long hours at the barstool insanely pointing out to everyone exactly what was wrong with the World. In recovery, we learn that serenity is the priority, and that this treasure occurs when we change ourselves, not others. If someone asks for help, we try to do so. If others can't seem to respond to our help, we find solace in thinking that others have the right to find their own loving Higher Power. When we stop controlling others and start changing ourselves by practicing the four steps, we come to realize that the World is not so bad. We realize that others don't have the power they used to have over us. By changing ourselves, our perception of situations change, and this change has the wonderful effect of improving situations which used to baffle us. I no longer am stressed or depressed, and all I had to do was change my attitude, not carpet the World.

TO DO: Today I will take comfort in knowing that my daily serenity practice is like putting on a pair of slippers that will keep my feet comfortable. I will start my day by connecting to my Higher Power (God through prayer, the universe through meditation, a friend through an email, my support group through service, nature through a walk, the ocean through a swim, music through listening, yoga through motion…whatever my Higher Power is in this moment). I will connect to that force which leads me on the path to peace and enlightenment. I will then reconnect to my Higher Power as the day progresses.

April 22

Give Time Time

Eventually it will all work out. I need to be less impatient. Problems either resolve, dissolve or are solved. Letting problems destroy our serenity is letting something temporary beat us. It is so important for us to quickly accept life on life's terms and find out what we can change about ourselves before we try to change problems. I used to think I was the only person on Earth who had problems. In recovery, I have learned that everyone has them and that they are often good because they create growth opportunities. I do not fear problems when I am working a good serenity program. If I am letting a character defect like anger or impatience motivate me to fix a problem, I need to get rid of the character defect before I address the problem. To rid myself of character defects, I have many tools such as sharing my feelings with someone else, making a gratitude list, keeping perspective, taking a ride in my car, walking my dog, or sometimes just giving time time. Sometimes I need to remember not to DWELL on the problem and just move on and take care of a different problem. One thing is for sure, there will always be a new problem even if my current problems end. I must accept that such is the nature of life. Ultimately, with time and a serene attitude, sometimes a problem that I have judged as being bad actually turns out to be of some benefit.

TO DO: Right now I am going to change my attitude before I change the World knowing that problems that seem so overwhelming now will dissipate and that I can best deal with them if I don't let a character defect influence my actions. When my impatience arises, I will ask myself if the problem needs to be resolved right now or can it wait. Too often I make emergencies out of non- emergencies. A reasonable exploration of alternative ways to solve problems may be beneficial. I will give time time.

April 23

Forget About Walking a Mile in My Shoes. Try Living an Hour in My Brain.

Some of us have overactive brains. We argue with ourselves. We get worried. We overanalyze. We have adversarial mental committee meetings. All of this just makes us anxious, stressed, and depressed. At least we are not alone in having tormented minds. But there is a solution.

TO DO: Don't think. Breathe. Do the next reasonable thing. Have faith that HELP (Higher Effective Loving Power), be it a support group, living according to good moral principles, love, whatever gives you spirituality) will keep you serene.

April 24

"The Only Difference Between a Flower and a Weed Is Judgment"
-Wayne Dyer

It's not what's happening, it's what we think about it. A rainy day may be depressing to one person and peaceful to another. With time, my alcoholism changed from something horrific to something positive because it led me to practice serenity principles and to become a therapist, both of which have immeasurably improved my life. Judgment can be based on preconceptions, other people, our own moods, and many other factors that are not even related to what is really there. Judgment can make us feel depressed, anxious, ashamed, and even resentful. Judgment seems to be so heavily influenced by our own attitudes that we may be better served simply not to judge. It may be wiser to accept and try to be positive. Especially when something is frustrating me, I try to remember not to judge the situation as good or bad because time often changes my judgment.

TO DO: Today, try not to judge and if possible try to see something positive in a person, place or thing that you find negative.

April 25

At the End of Each Day, List What You Are Grateful For

We sometimes can feel hopeless, resentful, fearful, overwhelmed, and many combinations of these painful feelings. A great exercise to turn around our attitude is to take a few minutes at the end of each day (or immediately when shocked or upset) to remember the things we are grateful for. Don't think about things that happened in previous days. Just focus on the good things that happened that day. This exercise will make you feel like life is good. It will give you joy. Sometimes it takes a little more effort than thinking about the bad things or being irritated. In fact, it is especially important to make a mental gratitude list on days you think were bad. After a few weeks of practice, you will find your mind defaulting more naturally to the good things than the bad things.

TO DO: Immediately after something nice happens, be conscious of it and say to yourself, "Thank you." At the end of the day, make a mental list of five good things that happened to you that day. It can be that someone smiled at you. It can be that you had something tasty to eat. It could be that you could look yourself in the eye in the mirror.

April 26

Don't Feel Bad About Feeling Bad

Don't feel guilty or ashamed just because you feel a certain way. If you beat up on yourself for letting something bother you, you are being a perfectionist and you are denying that you are a human being. We all make mistakes. We all let others (especially people we are attached to like "significant others") drive us crazy sometimes. The solution is to acknowledge that you are making progress but that you are not perfect. Giving yourself a break will keep you from turning a temporary bad feeling into depression or misery. Giving yourself a break relieves stress and is a positive personality change. It also helps you make decisions because you won't worry about beating yourself up if the results don't turn out as planned.

TO DO: It is normal to feel annoyed at times. But as soon as possible (especially before going to sleep), give yourself a break and relax. Exercise acceptance. Ask yourself if you have done everything reasonably necessary to deal with a problem, then forget about the problem and breathe. Finally, use gratitude, perspective and loving thoughts to turn your attitude around.

April 27

Don't Jump Over Mouse Turds
With a Pole Vault

Do you create complicated solutions to simple problems? Do you waste time and energy over little things that are relatively unimportant? Then you are using a pole vault to jump over mouse turds. You will lose your serenity if you don't start putting things in perspective. Don't sweat the small stuff. Keep remembering in the Big Picture, you are OK. Keep separating wants from needs. Don't mentally make little problems become big problems. When confronted with daily issues, first ask yourself, "How important is it ...really?" Is it worth your serenity? Never.

TO DO: Keep your sense of humor especially if something little is irritating you. Exercise mindfulness (breathe and think about what you are doing). Read the Serenity Poem and remind yourself to be grateful that what you're worried about is not really worth the worry.

April 28

We Need to Focus Less on the World Outside Us and More on the World Within Us

That person seems stupid. I would sure like to have that car. Why did that person treat me that way? I have too little money. I have too much money and I don't know what to do with it. Why won't she see my point of view and agree with my political opinion? The weather is awful. My husband is late again. The list of things I could focus on in the outside world is endless. Most of the time focusing on them causes me misery.

TO DO: Today, I may need to change something I can change such as the World within me. I need to do this before I attempt to impact the outside World if I decide to even try to impact the outside World. So, today I am going to focus less on the outside world and more on my inside world. Am I expecting more out of life than is reasonably possible? Am I being selfish, greedy, indignant, resentful, humorless, dishonest? If any of these character defects are operating within my world, I am simply going to try to do the opposite. If I feel hate, I am going to find a reason to love. I have faith that changing my inside world can give me the peace that I used to think only came from controlling the outside world. Today, I know that trying to control the outside usually frustrates me and serenity is my priority today.

April 29

That Train Is Runnin' Around in My Brain

"That Train is runnin' around in my brain. And I don't know what to do with it. And I just wish it would slow down. That train is runnin' around in my brain, and it's drivin' me insane, just like the poundin' rain, and I wish it would just shut up, it's causin' me pain. Like a clangin' chain, that train is runnin' around in my brain."

I'm fairly confident that peace of mind has very little to do with material success or arranging the world the way I want. Rather, it depends on what I am thinking about. My brain can sometimes be like a Manhattan subway train, rattling and crowded, full of multitudinous, debilitating conversations. I'm convinced that the only way I am going to find peace of mind is by emptying the subway car. By doing meditation and emptying my mind, I seem to get the serenity that I thought only material success and world arrangement would bring. For me, this form of meditation reduces anxiety. Meditation seems to lead to the spirituality that keeps me serene.

TO DO: Try taking a few deep breaths while repeating to yourself, "Be at peace." See what the effects are. Try to lengthen these meditations day by day.

April 30

Don't Ignore Your Physical Self

If you are feeling bad, the cause may be that you are physically out of balance. There are many ways to make yourself feel better emotionally: acceptance, lowering expectations, reliance on HELP, etc. However, there is more to feeling better than emotional wellness. One can't ignore the importance of a healthy physical self. Numerous studies show that regular exercise decreases depression, anger, and stress.

TO DO: Make time to get off that couch and work out. Eat correctly because if you fuel yourself with better fuel, you'll operate better. Start small by doing a little exercise for a short time and build up. You know you will feel better if you treat yourself better. And don't be too hard on yourself. If you are carrying a few extra pounds, don't make a big deal out of it. This is critical in not carrying this health thing too far.

May 1

Fear Is the Feeling That I Am Not Going to Get My Way in the Future

Don't think about whether you are going to get the outcome you want. Substitute serving your will with serving the will of your Higher Power. Your Higher Power wants you to do the next reasonable thing in this moment free from the impediments of your character defects. This is the best you can do to maintain your serenity. Don't worry about whether things will work out exactly the way you envision. You cannot control results. This attitude will help eliminate fear.

TO DO: Today I will keep bringing my mind back to the present if I start worrying about whether or not I will get my way in the future.

May 2

Fear, Anger, and Resentment
Are Your Will Overcontrolling Your
Future, Present, and Past

Fear, anger, and resentment are your will operating in three different time zones. Fear is the feeling that you will not get your way in the future. Anger is the feeling that you are not getting your way now. Resentment is the feeling that you did not get your way in the past. These feelings are therefore based on selfishness (the desire to get your wants fulfilled). Selfishness is the root of despair. Fear, anger, and resentment (resulting from selfishness) are perhaps the three greatest threats to serenity.

TO DO: Make a decision to turn your will and life over to the care of your Higher Power as you understand your Higher Power. Your Higher Power can be any kind of positive help, i.e. a mentor, recovery principles, a good purpose, a therapy modality that works, music, nature, or a spiritual feeling that you can't explain that gives you a sense of peace, etc. Your old Higher Power was your imbalanced ego which ultimately caused you and others suffering. It wanted you to only look out for yourself. It wanted you to be dishonest, selfish, impure, and hating. Your loving Higher Power wants you to practice the four absolutes which are honesty, purity, unselfishness, and love. Do your loving Higher Power's will in this moment and you will no longer be fearful, angry, or resentful.

May 3

Fight or Flight; That's Not Right

Our bodies still think we live in the jungle. The snakes are bills, bosses, complicated financial news, health insurance issues, etc. Our bodies' initial responses are to fight or flight. Both of these responses only escalate the problem, escalate the stress. When given stressful news that appears threatening, the first step to serenity is just absorbing the blow and not reacting. No need to immediately intellectualize a response; just absorb it until the instinct to fight or flight passes. If these instincts don't pass, call someone safe like a friend to discuss the problem. This strategy will keep the problem from becoming trouble. Fight or flight does not work as well as compromise.

TO DO: Imagine that stress is a snake. Most snakes are harmless. In any event, you don't need to run away or lash out at it. Just gently support your head and breathe slowly and the snake will be hypnotized. We can't do anything productive when we are stressed out. We must let it pass. Only when the instinct to fight or flee passes can we think of a rational, serene solution to a problem. Perhaps read the Serenity Poem, take a walk, breathe slowly and chant to yourself, "Fight or flight, that's not right."

May 4

God Is a Comedian Playing to an Audience Afraid to Laugh

Are you too serious? Are some of the tragedies you perceive in your life really comedies? Taking ourselves too seriously can lead us to relapse. It is far better to shake our heads and chuckle over something that doesn't go our way than it is to lose our peace of mind. It is better to remember that we don't have to live up to our own or others' high expectations. It is better to remember that we are far from perfect and don't always have to implement a perfect solution to everything. How do we lighten up? It actually takes some serious faith that our HELP (Higher Effective Loving Program) will protect us no matter what happens…that we will be OK if we keep serenity as our priority and try to do what it takes to keep serenity… that Life and Ourselves may be throwing us some loops but that the steps to serenity is a safety net. It takes an attitude that we will not let the ordinary ups and downs of life drive us crazy…that it's OK to laugh over them because we have been given the gift of serenity.

TO DO: Look for the humor by accepting life on life's terms with all of its unpredictable twists and turns. Don't take things too seriously.

May 5

Humility Is Willingness to Learn

If you know that you don't know, you are in a powerful position. Learning is easier than faking knowing. One factor which may be tied to our lack of serenity is the need to look like we have all the answers all the time. We tend to put on facades, fake fronts to try to impress others. But inside we know differently so we feel stress. Others often see through our facades and we become humiliated. As we do the steps to peace and enlightenment, we turn this humiliation into humility. We recognize that we can accept ourselves even though we are not as important as we thought we had to be. We learn to appreciate ourselves for who we are, not some egomaniacal version of who we would like to be and who we would like others to think we are. We become open minded to learning, and this actually makes us feel better.

TO DO: Today, I will keep an open mind and be willing to learn. Exercising humility will bring me closer to my personal Higher Power which will keep me serene.

May 6

I Am My Own Best Friend

Life tends to expose us to many negative people and influences. We all know people who act like they have the weight of the world constantly upon them every day. We find them at work, at school, in grocery store lines, even while we are stopped at a red light. We also are continually exposed to overwhelming negative stimuli like newspapers, television, the internet, all of which bombard us daily with all the new ways the world seems to be struggling. Clients, customers, parents and children complain to us. They grumble and use negative words to express their plights. If we let them drive our bus, we can become fearful, anxious, and depressed. Sometimes that negative person can be ourself. We use negative self talk and beat ourselves up for making a mistake. We can be our own worst enemy by isolating and slipping into loneliness. In the face of all of this negativity, an excellent way to keep a positive attitude is to say short positive messages to yourself, to be your own best friend. Dr. Emile Coue' was a noted physician in the 1920's. He described how he helped his patients heal themselves from such diseases as rheumatism, tubercular sores, paralysis, fibrous tumors and ulcers by autosuggestion. He is credited with the phrase, "Day by day, in every way, I am getting better and better."

TO DO: I've found that I can turn around a negative or nervous thought by repeating the phrase, "I feel physically good." See if this phrase works for you, or perhaps you can create your own. Just the act of physically smiling can help you feel better. Smiling also attracts other happy people to you. You can draw on autosuggestion quickly, and it can change your attitude so that you can feel more relaxed no matter what bad feeling you are experiencing.

May 7

Count the Angels Not the Devils

I used to dwell on how people had hurt me. I carried the weight of resentment even on vacation. I imagined that people hated me even when they were not even concerned with me. Today, I count the angels instead of the devils. Teachers, doctors, the list is great. I can appreciate all of the people it took to create the technology that allows me to correspond with you right now. I can even see where many of the people I used to resent have helped me to grow.

TO DO: Today I will count my angels to counteract any ingratitude. I will also seek to understand rather than hate, empathize rather than resent. I will make it a point to get rid of my resentment because resentment only hurts me.

May 8

You Look Good in Orange,
Just Not All the Time

The following story shows how important it is to practice step 3:
"Connect to HELP (Higher Effective Loving Power)."

"It's late 2020 during the resurgence of the pandemic and I have
been quarantined with my wife for too long now. She scrapes the
bottom of her cereal bowl with a spoon - interminably – trying
to get that last drop of ice cream. The sound is like fingernails
on a chalkboard. I am about to explode, but thankfully I am well
practiced at the steps to peace and light. I close my eyes and accept
the situation; I adapt rather than try to change her (there is no escape
from her eating); I go directly to step 3 by leaving the kitchen and
calling a close friend. I am not embarrassed about sharing. In fact, as
I explain to him the situation, I can see the humor in it. I say, "I am
glad there are laws against murder. Otherwise, I would be in jail for
murdering my wife." He replies, " Yep, you are lucky. You look good
in orange, just not all the time." We both laugh together.

TO DO: Today I am going to apply some or all of the Four Steps
to Serenity. In situations where others are scraping their fingernails
across the chalkboard, I am going to accept and adapt, be grateful
and flexible, connect to HELP, and fix myself not them.

May 9

I Want What I Want When I Want It

Nothing is as surefire a recipe for frustration than demanding what you want. "Self will run riot" is a fundamental characteristic of misery. Serenity results from aligning your will with your Higher Power's will. Your Higher Power does not have to be religious or have intermediaries. Your Higher Power can be anything that restores you to serenity like doing actions that are guided by the four absolutes (1. Honesty, 2. Purity, 3. Love, 4. Unselfishness).

TO DO: Ask yourself if you really need what you want right now. Ask that your Higher Power's will be done not yours.

May 10

It's Your Turn

If you feel overwhelmed because you are getting LOTS of life thrown at you, one helpful message may be to say, "It's just my turn." Everyone - regardless of health, race, wealth, or anything else - gets lots of seemingly unending problems thrust upon them at once. It's critical to realize that you cannot always control problems like parents getting older, children losing their homework, cars breaking down, identity theft, and on and on and on. Despite trying to take great precautions against certain problems, sometimes all you can do is the footwork necessary to not lose your peace of mind when things go wrong. That said, if life is continually overwhelming due to, for example, some abuse you are experiencing, you need to ask yourself whether enough is enough. If you are experiencing emotional or physical abuse, ask yourself when are you going to be sick and tired of being sick and tired such that you take steps necessary to create a healthy boundary.

TO DO: Remember that everyone gets lots of problems thrust upon them at different times. Don't expect everything to get done today. Acceptance and doing the next reasonable thing will get you through problems. There will always be new problems. Such is the nature of life. So if you are counting on the resolution of problems to give you lasting serenity, you are misleading yourself. Try being grateful for what you have rather than longing for something to happen to satisfy your desires. Relax and breathe easy.

May 11

Joy Comes From Gratitude

The key to becoming happy, joyous, and free is to NOT MAKE A BIG DEAL OUT OF GETTING THERE. You are happy if you're not unhappy. You don't always have to be whooping it up. Sometimes you may be sad or anxious because of a difficulty, but you still qualify as a happy person if you don't turn temporary sadness or anxiety into misery. "Free" means you are not bound by self-defeating behaviors. A friend was doing well with "happy" and "free" but struggling with "joy" until a wise person asked him, "What is the first thing that comes to your mind that you are grateful for?" My friend replied, "Well I woke up today" and spontaneously laughed with joy! It's the simple stuff that we are grateful for that gives us true joy.

TO DO: Keep a grateful heart to feel the joy that ameliorates nervousness, sadness, and fear. One way to feel grateful is to make a list of all of the angels (people) who have helped you over the course of your life.

May 12

Let Me Take Life as It Comes,
Not as I Would Have It Be

The computer won't work. I don't know why. There really is no reason for it to be behaving this way. It is wasting my time. Now I am going to have to call the I.T. people, and I just don't have time for this because I need to get out the door. Oh No! How many situations parallel the above scenario in your life?

These unexpected little shocks and tragedies can ruin our whole day. Better to accept life on life's terms, not our own. Even when we can't figure out why something comes along which interferes with our day, we must accept the unexpected and remember that we do have time to do what we must, even with all the curve balls.

TO DO: When overwhelmed, repeat, the phrase, "Please let me take life as it comes, not as I would have it be." Try adding this phrase to your morning meditation to preempt the inevitable surprising challenges that come with the day.

May 13

Life Is Not an Emergency

For me, ordinary duties become emergencies when I (1) feel I have to get everything done that I write in my calendar, (2) fear that if I put even small things off they'll just build up so that I'll never get to them, and (3) don't schedule enough time between appointments. I consequently tend to stuff too much into one day. I tend to create artificial deadlines. I fear that if I don't get everything done today, it'll pile up and then I'll be "under the gun." So, I make the mistake of creating an emergency due to my fear of putting myself under the gun later. This occurs because I am overly conscious of the negative consequences of procrastination. Ironically, I have many clients who always procrastinate because they feel like there are so many things that must get done that they become afraid to start doing any of them. They feel like there are so many overwhelming emergencies, they just don't know where to start. So they become paralyzed and procrastinate.

TO DO: Solution to problem 1: Feeling I have to get everything done that I have listed on my calendar just plain isn't true. When I have this attitude, I am falling victim to the impossible desire for my life to be complete with nothing left to do. The truth is that my life is a constantly evolving journey that is certainly never wound up in a neat little ball and complete. So, I just have to try to better prioritize and do less. If I can't get something done, I go to the next day in the calendar and mark it "Do what's left from yesterday." Solution to problem 2: Regarding my fear that if I don't do it now, it will never get done is also a bunch of hooey! If it doesn't get done today, tomorrow or the next day, then it's because I either had something more important to be done or I'm dead in which case it won't matter. I must also note that I used the word "FEAR" in stating my problem. Anytime I use that word, I've got to wonder if this is a "boogie man" I'm creating or whether I really have anything to fear.

The acronym for fear is False Evidence Appearing Real. Fear is illusory. I must therefore ask myself, "What am I afraid of?" Again, prioritizing is the key to dealing with my fear of not getting everything done. Solution to problem 3: To schedule more time between meetings, I need to take into account human functions like driving time, running into somebody who may need a kind word, or even helping someone who may have a real emergency. I've got to remember that red lights happen too. They weren't just put there to make me angry and impede my way. Everybody has to stop for them. The bigger picture, of course, is we all have a right to move along with our lives and sometimes that means it is my turn to wait. Scheduling "in between time" gives me more time to make others feel better. I've found that if I take a few minutes to "stop and smell" the roses, my mind relaxes. By living in the above simple solutions, I have eased a lot of the emergencies out of my life, and I have continued to be more productive too. I'm easier on myself, and I achieve my goals more often.

May 14

Are You Analyzing It or Doing It?

I spend too much time analyzing whether or not I am having fun, rather than having fun. I spend too much time analyzing why I should pray, rather than praying. I spend too much time analyzing whether or not I should call a friend when I am losing my serenity, rather than simply calling him. I spend too much time analyzing whether or not I am a good person, rather than just being a good person. One key to serenity is to DO rather than to ANALYZE.

TO DO: Today I am going to apply the four steps to my life. I will empty my mind about measuring and judging and appearing a certain way. I am just going to do good acts. For example, if I feel upset, I am not going to analyze whether or not I should share with someone else, I am just going to share my feeling and see if that helps. I am going to tell my friend that I am practicing the four steps and that I am calling because I am connecting to HELP (Higher Effective Loving Power) by calling.

May 15

Love – No Matter What

Not only an unconditional, loving attitude toward others, but an unconditional loving attitude toward yourself helps keep you serene. If you are feeling bad, trying to escape by turning to a bad habit or acting out with a negative emotion, is an act of self-loathing. You deserve to care about yourself just because you are - not because of your inflated ego, what you accomplish, or what you do or do not have. Conditional love focuses more on the conditions than the love. It creates stress, fear and negativity. If someone wrongs you, deal with the wrong by creating a healthy boundary or by focusing on how to obtain justice. Don't let the wrong cause you to take on the heavy baggage of resentment against the person. Try to exercise understanding by thinking about the harmful influences the person may have experienced. Better to feel pity or just ignore the offending person rather than to allow resentment to weigh you down.

TO DO: Don't imprison your loving attitude with conditions or else you will fail to experience the love which is so useful to your own serenity. Avoid anger and resentment by trying to find a reason to love rather than hate.

May 16

Lower Expectations Equal Higher Serenity

One way to ruin our serenity is to have too high expectations of ourselves and others. Inflated expectations cause stress. Such stress may actually cause us to perform worse. It is far better to have reasonable expectations to minimize stress and disappointment. We can then be pleasantly surprised should we outperform. Lowering one's expectations does not require lowering one's optimism. We should always be encouraging and hopeful that we and others will try reasonably; we should always approach challenges with confidence. However, we must also bear in mind that none of us are perfect, and that intended results are never guaranteed. By lowering our expectations, we become less dependent on others (and external circumstances beyond our control) controlling our serenity. A perfect example is my use of the telephone. Let's say I'm calling a client, and I have high expectations that the call will go smoothly such that I'll accomplish exactly what I set out to do. First, I expect to find the telephone number easily in my smart phone contact list. I scroll through it and can't find it. I am shocked, disappointed. "How on earth (actually I'd probably say something much worse) can that guy's number not be in my doggone (trust me, I'd say something far worse) smart phone." I'd worry that my entire office system was askew if I couldn't keep organized enough to find a simple, stupid telephone number. I'd then do what I usually do in such instances - flip through my paper file where I probably scribbled the client's number. As I flip through each page, I would feel more and more irritated and even hostile. "What an idiot I am. What a waste of time. If I had only done what any simple minded idiot could have done and taken a second ... and..." the negative messages (self-flagellation) might go on until I was actually questioning whether I was so stupid that I shouldn't even be a counselor, that I probably should just close down my office and "What is the meaning of life anyway if God himself should so punish me that I can't find this stupid phone number?" By the time I find the phone number, I would be so angry I'd probably be unable to deal well with the client anyway.

Now, let's take the same scenario with lower expectations. Once again, the phone number isn't in the contact list. But this time, I didn't expect it to be in the first place. Rather, I started looking for the number knowing that I had been in a hurry on Friday afternoon to go see my son play baseball and that I had scribbled it somewhere close by and that if I took a minute and patiently looked for it now everything would be just fine and dandy. With lower expectations, I would tell myself that I am as imperfect as anyone else so why not give myself a break. By the time I find the number, I would still be serene (or as serene as can be expected on a Monday morning) and I would call the client with a positive attitude. In this case, I lowered my expectations to make myself feel better so that I could be in a good frame of mind when trying to counsel a client.

Another way to have lower expectations (and therefore higher serenity) is to make plans, not results. If we make plans and don't expect results, we have a better chance to avoid frustration because whenever we try to do something, we can't be sure it will turn out exactly the way we envisioned it. More often than not, some strange twist occurs which "lays to rest our best laid plans." Accordingly, we should never set out to do anything hell bent on getting certain, exact results or else we will likely be frustrated. It is wiser and infinitely more comforting to be flexible and content if our plans seem to be headed in the right direction. Furthermore, with a little faith, we will usually get results which are better than anything we had envisioned if our plans are guided by love, honesty, unselfishness and a pure, not jealous heart.

TO DO: Today I will remember not to have overinflated expectations of myself and others. I will remember that an expectation can be a premeditated resentment. I will practice the four steps to peace and light and particularly focus on keeping a reasonable attitude and doing the next reasonable thing.

May 17

Stay in the Moment

"Look to this day, For it is life, the very life of life. In its brief course lie all the realities and verities of existence, The bliss of growth, The splendor of action, The glory of power - For yesterday is but a dream, And tomorrow is only a vision, But today, well lived makes every yesterday a dream of happiness, And every tomorrow a vision of hope. Look well, therefore, to this day." Sanskrit Proverb. "One Day at a Time" is a fundamental serenity suggestion. It reminds us to stay in the now - to focus on what we are doing, rather than regretting the past or fearing the future. Living "One Day at a Time" or in the "now" is important because we must be focused on what we are doing to stay serene. We cannot afford to let our minds wander into regrets or fears.

TO DO: A useful phrase to repeat in order to keep you in the now is: " No There, Just Here, No Then, Just Now!" This will reduce stress and other bad feelings (especially fear, anxiety, and restless mind syndrome).

May 18

Stop Asking "Why?"

If you find yourself trying to figure out what the meaning of life is or why random tragedies occur, you may be asking "why" too often. You may be causing yourself to be overwhelmed by thinking about issues which no human is fully capable of resolving. These mental committee meetings may be causing you to become indecisive, confused and "restless, irritable and discontent." This state of mind is one step away from an emotional relapse.

TO DO: Relax, remember that often only God (or some force beyond our intellectual understanding) knows why. We are not capable of knowing all the reasons. Repeat the chant, "I just don't get it, cried I, throwing my arms up against the sky, You're not supposed to, was the reply, You're not supposed to, was the reply." Let go!

May 19

Just Because They Aren't Paying Attention to You, Does Not Mean They Don't Love You

Before I started practicing the four steps, I thought that the path to serenity included fame and getting lots of attention. Sometimes even today, I can be like a needy baby. I think if people aren't paying attention to my worries, my problems, my actions, they don't care about me. Well that's another thinking distortion I need to vanquish in order to stay truly serene. People have issues of their own. They can still care about me, even if they are not paying attention to me.

TO DO: Today, I will take comfort in knowing that I am still loved even if others aren't calling me or paying any attention to me. I will live my life and let others live theirs. Live and let live!

May 20

When You Open up, They Open Up

Serenity involves practicing the 3rd step which includes not only connecting FOR help but also TO help others. Often if I open up to someone else about an issue I have, they are more likely to open up and share with me. Perhaps this is because the other person no longer feels ALONE. This connection helps the other person and me. For example, I took a chance and recently opened up about being a victim of a scam, and I was surprised when two other people reported that they had been similarly victimized. This took a lot of courage for me to bring up. I was also careful to open up about it in a SAFE place (in an online forum where I was completely anonymous). Opening up with others who have experienced similar challenges and interests is a great way to give and get help. Hence finding recovery groups with people who have experienced similar challenges or interests, like AA, or parents of disabled children, or a stamp club, or a Church is an effective way to practice the 3rd step. Whenever I share about my issues in such a group, it makes it easier for someone else to talk about their problem and thus solutions emerge.

TO DO: Today I'm going to take a chance and share something personal about me. This will get it off of my chest and also perhaps help someone else. I will take care to do so in a safe place and with safe people, but I won't let shame or fear stop me from sharing.

May 21

"The only pressure I'm under
is the pressure I put on myself"
- Mark Messier

I only have to live up to my own standards, not anyone else's. Another person may be a trigger for stress, but I am responsible for the stress. No one else can drive my bus. I don't need to worry about someone else's measurement of me or living up to their expectations. I am grateful I have made the practice of serenity principles my priority because I am no longer controlled by others; I only have the issues and challenges that I set for myself.

TO DO: Today I am going to take it easy and try to do reasonably well in taking care of my responsibilities. It is ok for me to relax and have fun too. Staying loose keeps me from thinking I need to please everyone.

May 22

The Trick to Serenity Is
Learning to Live With Uncertainty

Don't turn uncertainty into fear. Remember that you can't know everything. You can't predict anything (outcomes especially). For example, you can't know if a law will change, how an investment will perform, whether you will get that job, or whether you will get sick. No amount of money can resolve uncertainty so don't isolate and worry about it. Uncertainty is a natural way of life for all of us.

TO DO: Have a busload of faith that your Higher Power will give you no more than you can handle. Your Higher Power can be whatever keeps you serene without bad consequences (group support, faith, the act of helping others, spiritual principles, the loving universe, a religious God, or a non-religious Higher Power, creativity, a Good Purpose, the four steps, etc.).

May 23

There Really Is a Step for That

Take any problem in your life. Think about how you used to handle it before you started on this path to serenity. Were you able to keep your serenity? Most of us will probably answer, "No."

Now, ask yourself what step (of the four steps) can you apply to your current problem. Sometimes it's actually best to start with step 4 to determine what character defect you need to fix. Then you can get rid of that defect by doing step 3: connecting to HELP.

Sometimes you might decide that overcontrolling is a problem. Then, step 1 applies because step 1 reminds us that we can't control people, places, and things.

Perhaps you are caught up in too many wants. Then step 2 will remind you that you can relax because even though all of your wants will never be fulfilled, all of your needs will! Applying the four steps to issues will reduce stress and worry and help you make better decisions. It will also keep little things from building up, overwhelming you, frustrating you, and confusing you.

TO DO: Today, I will try to live according to the four steps. I will also try to see if a particular step or combination of steps will relieve a problem and help me make better decisions.

May 24

Loyal or Co-Dependent?

Do you know whether you are being loyal or codependent? Loyalty is a healthy allegiance and collegiality with another for mutual benefit. Codependence is an unhealthy addiction to someone. Codependence is an imbalanced, debilitating relationship born from a misperceived need rather than love. Usually one party gets hurt more than another in a codependent relationship. Often, the codependent person thinks that he/she is actually helping the other whereas the truth is that the codependent person is hurting the other person by making excuses for the other person and doing what the other person should be doing for himself/herself. You can determine if you are codependent by assessing whether or not you are getting hurt, True serenity involves eliminating codependence. Realizing that we are not responsible for another's happiness is very important to peace of mind.

TO DO: Today I will be on guard for allowing someone else to take advantage of me. I will stop myself if I can see that the results of my trying to help another person is actually weakening that person. Most of all, I will not allow myself to be victimized. I will love and seek to help, but not to the point where I am getting abused and mistakenly hurting rather than helping.

May 25

What Has No Solution Is Solved

There is no solution to my parents getting older. There is no solution to the various ways I can try to sell my car. There's no solution to the confusion created by common everyday problems, and no surefire way to control a situation. There's also no solution to alter or redo things that have happened in the past. So we deal with the past by looking at it with love and self- forgiveness rather than shame and guilt, then give value for learning from it and make amends whenever possible except when to do so will injure ourselves or others. Then we let the past go. We stay in the present moment. Often people, places, and things cannot be fixed, changed or controlled. The thing we can change is our attitude. Do we try the solutions that did not work in the past, like switching drinks, geographical cures, switching jobs? Or do we relax and practice the four steps.

TO DO: Today I will not wrack my brain trying to solve an unsolvable problem. I will ACCEPT and ADAPT. I will accept confusion, uncertainty and incompleteness. I will practice the four steps by accepting, being grateful, realizing I am not alone, and changing my attitude from wanting everything to be clear-cut and simple to enjoying the adventure and being flexible.

May 26

Let Them Be

They are who they are, not who I want them to be, and it's not my responsibility to change them to meet my desires. It helps me to let go of trying to control them if I remember that if they were who I want them to be, they might end up getting into more trouble than they are in now. In other words, I must accept that I don't know what's best for everyone else. I must let people be themselves. I must learn that everyone is human, so everyone has their own issues. This should not be a cause of resentment for me, but cause for appreciation, sometimes gratitude and sometimes empathy. Just because someone is different, and has different goals, does not mean that I need to fix or change them. Unless it is a clear cut crisis where, for example, the person is in denial and needs an intervention due to an addiction or some serious problem or other illness, I need to let go. Letting go of others is a way to reduce my own stress and actually makes me happier. Just because they are different, does not mean that they are wrong.

TO DO: Letting go of control of others makes you less resentful and more serene. So, today, enjoy the differences. If someone is making you miserable, you may need to remove yourself from the situation and create healthy boundaries. If someone is in denial about a serious problem which is clearly hurting the person, you can consider intervening. However, more often than not, you don't really need to do anything but let the person be.

May 27

Those Who Laugh – Last

This saying reminds us to take it easy and not be afraid to see the lighter side of things. It also reminds us that we are saved from misery when we can look back at honest mistakes we and others have made without shame or anger but with a sense of humor. Sometimes it is healthy to laugh at the mistakes we and others have made rather than cry over them. We are truly laughing "with" and not "at" ourselves and others. We need not be a glum lot just because we are imperfect or certain things didn't work out as we wanted them to. Those who laugh have lasting serenity.

TO DO: Today I will try not to take life too seriously. It's OK to laugh. It is great medicine to reduce stress and other bad feelings.

May 28

Happiness Is Not Getting What You Want, It's Wanting What You Have

"Wants" create stress. Sometimes when we get what we want, we discover that we don't really enjoy having it. We find out that things we wanted really are not fulfilling and are actually "a drain to maintain." We also discover that getting what we want was not worth our selfish attitude. We see that wants took our focus off of serenity and on selfishness. The 12 step recovery text affectionately called The Big Book says, "Selfishness is the root of our problem." Another pitfall of wants is that negative "feel bad" messages usually result from our perception that we have not, will not, or did not get what we want. We all instinctively want things to go our way. But our wants often conflict with others' wants such that things often don't go our way. And when they do go our way, we find out that what we wanted was not what we wanted when we got them. From material wants (the biggest boat) to simple daily wants (avoiding a stop light), wants frustrate us. Far better to appreciate what we have and distinguish wants from needs.

TO DO: Today, I will say a mental "thank you' for three things and situations I have that I need.

May 29

"You Complete Me"

If you have ever sincerely quoted the Tom Cruise character in the popular film Jerry McGuire by telling someone, "You complete me," you may have felt good for the moment, but in the long run you were asking for trouble. Codependence causes stress. You are an individual, complete in and of yourself. Although you need fellowship and support to stay serene, you do not need anyone else to validate your completeness or to make you feel worthwhile. When you depend on someone else to complete you, you are using the other person like a drug. It is a blessing to love another, but trying to control another or depending on another for fulfillment can cause misery.

TO DO: Today, tell yourself you do not need others to love yourself.

May 30

Consciously Breathe Away The Stress

Conscious breathing is far different from the unconscious, unthinking, automatic breathing we usually do. Conscious breathing takes concentration and it may be the most effective antidote to stress. At least, it should be the first line of defense. Remember to do conscious slow breathing coupled with visualization of a peaceful place and the mental repetition of a relaxing phrase. My visualization is my little white dog, and my phrase is "I unconditionally love and accept myself." This is a great way to practice Step 3: Connect to HELP.

TO DO: Today become aware of the rate you are breathing and slow it down until it takes at least three seconds to inhale and five seconds to exhale. Repeat four times while adding a visualization and relaxing phrase. Consider setting your alarm to remind you to do this 10 second exercise every three hours.

May 31

Anger Is Only One Letter
Away From Danger

Don't let your anger or rage go unchecked. When feeling hostile or enraged, deal with it as early as possible. If you don't, it can be so painful that you may do something extremely harmful just to put out the fire. Anger is sometimes unavoidable. What you do with it and when you do it are under your control. If you know it's a common problem, focus on preventing anger even if you are not yet angry. First thing in the morning, make an action plan on how to avoid emotional upset as you go through the day. The action plan should focus on how you can fix yourself rather than fix other people, places and things. Take breaks throughout the day to breathe slowly. If something triggers your anger, and you feel offended or insulted, tell yourself to relax because if you act out in anger you will suffer the consequences you have suffered before (like alienating friends, spouses, children, dogs, etc.) Follow the rage through to its bitter end by remembering how hung over and exhausted you became after a hateful attack.

TO DO: Today, before doing that angry email or hurtful attack, take a break, do something else, then reply when not irritated. If you feel compelled to do something, don't. Commit to a daily action plan to deal with potential conflict which might cause anger.

June 1

Don't Blame God

My friend hated God because his Father committed suicide. "How would God let this happen?" thought my friend. In recovery, I have learned two main things about God. First, God is defined as a power greater than yourself that can restore you to sanity. For example, if I am a drug addict about to relapse, my Higher Power may be a friend who I can call for help. For that moment, my friend is a power greater than myself , and if by speaking with him I am saved from relapsing, the friend was able to restore me to sanity. Step 3 of the Serenity Steps would designate my friend as H.E.L.P. (Higher Effective Loving Power).

The second thing I have learned about God is that there is a difference between Life and God. Life includes toxic people, challenging places, human choices, other's mistakes, my mistakes, my disease, geological vicissitudes, etc. God or HELP (that loving, powerful effective force) is there to help us deal with Life, and God will if I don't let my ego tell me I need to control the situation alone, without turning to HELP. God or Help or Good Orderly Direction will let me be at peace and not have to turn Life's issues into terrible consequences. Remember, God is an all-encompassing term in our four step program that we call HELP which stands for Higher Effective Loving Power. It can be any HELP that will restore us to serenity in that moment. So don't get hung up on the word God. No one can foist his or her own definition of God on you!

TO DO: Instead of blaming God today, I will ask God for strength to stay serene to deal with Life and to be grateful. I will not fight the spiritual sense of peace that I feel by turning my life and will over to the care of HELP in this moment.

June 2

Hating Only Hurts the Hater;
It Does Nothing to the Person Being Hated

We need to get rid of hate for our own good. But how do we eliminate hostile and hateful thoughts? The best way is to forgive, and the best way to forgive is to hope for the health and welfare of the person we resent. One way to hope for some people is to pray for those they resent. "If you have a resentment you want to be free of, if you will pray for the person or the thing that you resent, you will be free. If you will ask in prayer for everything you want for yourself to be given to them, you will be free. Ask for their health, prosperity, their happiness, and you will be free. Even when you don't really want it for them, and your prayers are only words and you don't mean it, go ahead and do it anyway. Do it every day for two weeks and you will find you have come to mean it and to want it for them, and you will realize that where you used to feel bitterness and resentment and hatred, you now feel compassion, understanding and love." P.552 of the Big Book (Alcoholics Anonymous text). If this prayer can work for addicts, it can work for you. Nevertheless, at first, any normal, rational person will think that hoping for the welfare of someone who has wronged, offended, insulted or irritated us is insane. I know I did. Nevertheless, this theory is at the centerpiece of many recovery strategies. For example, exercising forgiveness may be a part of your cognitive behavioral therapy. Another example: the Bible is but one resource that repeatedly states that we are all sinners, but the difference between those in Heaven and those in Hell is that those in Hell never asked for forgiveness or forgave those who sinned against them. Don't create a living Hell; try to forgive.

TO DO: Today I will remember that anyone I hate is probably not thinking about me so I won't give that person free rent in my brain. I will hope for their recovery.

June 3

"The most heated bit of letter-writing can be a wonderful safety valve – providing the wastebasket is somewhere nearby."
-Bill Wilson

It's good to get anger out in a healthy harmless way. Journaling is one such way to vent. Anger let out against people causes retaliation. Retaliation causes you to increase your anger. Dealing with retaliation complicates our lives when our goal in serenity is to simplify our lives. Foisting anger on others creates a bad spiritual balance (bad karma). Bad spiritual balance is also bad for our serenity. Remember today that it is our goal to do what's good for our serenity, not what is necessarily good for our ego defenses or selfishness.

TO DO: Today, I will try getting my anger out by journaling. But I won't let the anger interfere with my life by sending that journal to the subject of my anger. I will also wait until anger passes before I communicate with others.

June 4

Change Is an Action, Not a Thought

You become serene by following through on your commitment
to change. For example, you do the four steps. You make positive
changes by doing things differently. Once you do the new actions,
you will think differently. This is how you become serene. "You just
bring the body and your heart and mind will follow." New actions
include connecting with others and revealing your true self, having
a mentor, picking up the phone when you need help, etc. It's really
that simple. These new actions are not threatening to anyone's
philosophical or religious beliefs. However, your voice that still
wants you to be depressed may tell you they are a threat. Listen only
to the voice that wants you to be serene.

TO DO: Today, I will not listen to the voice in my head that wants to
keep me depressed. I will do serenity footwork!

June 5

Tomorrow's Resentments Are Fed by Today's Expectations

Keep reasonable expectations of people, places, and things. People (including others and ourselves) are imperfect and cannot live up to ideals. Places have challenging weather patterns and difficult terrains. Things break. If we EXPECT things to be perfect, we are bound to be resentful. Left unchecked, resentment is a trigger for misery.

TO DO: Today, stay positive but keep expectations within reason.

June 6

An Attitude of Gratitude Is the Best Defense

The best defense against frustration and sadness is an attitude of gratitude. I just make a list of five things I am grateful for whenever I am starting to feel angry, offended or as if life isn't fair or things never go my way, or whatever it is that is making me feel bad. Items that have been on my list are being free from pain, having enough food, having shelter, being able to walk out my front door without fear of being shot, having my sight, my limbs, and not having hurt anyone out of anger.

TO DO: Especially on a day like today when my baseball game got rained out, I am going to write down five things I am grateful for and put the list in my wallet and look at it later if I start to feel frustrated or dissatisfied again. Maybe I can't play baseball, but I am thankful for you who are reading this, for my dog, for waking up without a hangover, for others who provide me with HELP, I am grateful for freedom from pain and shelter from the rain. What are you grateful for?

June 7

Get Comfortable Being Uncomfortable

If you are angry, frustrated, or otherwise uncomfortable psychologically or physically, this is not unusual particularly if you have just started to dedicate your life to Serenity. Discomfort is to be expected because you are going through emotional change. But you do not have to make these unpleasant feelings cause you to relapse back into bad habits or your old way of thinking. Just go about your life anyway. In time, the discomfort will pass and you will get the peace you were always trying to get but going about getting it in the wrong way. Even if you have been practicing Serenity principles for a long time, Life may challenge you and you may have to go through discomfort again while you adjust to the new challenge.

TO DO: Today, don't run from bad feelings. Keep practicing the four steps to get through it. You can live with the discomfort because it is born from positive change. Soon you will feel FANTASTIC!

June 8

The Black Snow

One winter, I woke up, looked out the window and saw snow. Be assured this was not the fresh, new fallen snow, described in fairy books; rather it was the black snow typically found on the streets of Northeast Ohio after being subjected to day after day of automobile exhaust systems and snow plows. I tried not to feel negative about the black snow. I repeated (almost chanting) to myself that the snow did not bother me, that in fact the black snow was beautiful because here on God's earth, everything has beauty. Guess what? I just became more miserable because I was in denial about how I really felt about the snow. I tried changing my messages. I told myself that the black snow was ugly. I admitted that I didn't like it, but that it was okay the way it was even though it annoyed me and I preferred it to be different. I therefore changed my attitude from denial to acceptance. I immediately felt much better. Notice that I didn't spend a long time debating why I lived in Northeast Ohio. I didn't compare myself to people who live in Florida. I didn't wish that the snow would magically disappear. I kept it simple. I changed myself. I did not change the situation. Funny thing: as I realized that my needs were being taken care of because I was in a warm, cozy house, I became grateful and I started to chuckle with a bit of joy. Not only was I able to accept the black snow, but I was able to have a sense of humor about it. Even funnier? As I continued to gaze at the black snow, I saw a shadow that struck me as kind of, well yes, beautiful.

The lesson I therefore learned was that I could feel better even while looking at black snow. However, I first had to be honest enough to admit that I thought the snow was ugly. "Acceptance is the answer to all my problems today. When I am disturbed, it is because I find some person, place, thing, or situation - some fact of my life - unacceptable to me, and I can find no serenity until I accept that person, place, thing, or situation as being exactly the way it is supposed to be at this moment. I accept that person, place, thing, or situation as being exactly the way it is supposed to be at this moment. I accept that person, place, thing, or situation as being exactly the way it is supposed to be at this moment. Nothing, absolutely nothing happens in God's world by mistake. Until I could accept my alcoholism, I could not stay sober; unless I accept life completely on life's terms, I cannot be happy. I need to concentrate not so much on what needs to be changed in the world as on what needs to be changed in me and my attitudes." page 417 of the Big Book. Acceptance is the foundation for how you can deal successfully and serenely with anyone and anything. For example, unless you accept your boss, spouse, child, neighbor, bad habit, house, car, or black snow exactly the way he, she, or it is supposed to be at that moment, you will be disturbed and unable to deal with that situation in a healthy, serene way.

TO DO: Today, I will apply the four steps to the black snow in my life.

1. I will accept my feelings.

2. I will then determine if the trigger of those feelings involves something that truly affects my wants or my needs.

3. Then, I will connect to my Higher Effective Loving Power (a call to a friend to share my feelings? a pause and meditative reflection? A listen to a favorite song?) which will open my mind and expand my consciousness so that I can

4. fix myself by changing my attitude from self pity to gratitude.

The result? Serenity! As soon as we accept our true feelings, and allow ourselves to feel them, we feel better and are in a better state of mind to make a reasonable decision.

June 9

I May Not be Much,
but I'm All I Think About

Do you find that you spend a lot of time thinking about how you are going to get your way? Do you spend a lot of time thinking about how people have done you wrong? When you walk into a room, do you feel as if everyone is watching you? Do you start a lot of phrases with "I want?" Serenity involves becoming less concerned with getting our wants fulfilled and appreciating that our needs are fulfilled. Serenity also arises when we are less self oriented and more empathetic and compassionate toward others.

TO DO: Today, try doing something nice for someone else and perhaps do it anonymously or without them expecting it.

June 10

If You Think You Know, You Got a Lot to Learn

If you are confused, that's OK. Don't let that confusion make you upset. Remember, no one has all the answers. And anyone, who thinks he does, is misleading himself. If you are unsure of whether or not you need HELP (Higher Effective Loving Power), don't automatically conclude that you don't. Rather, give HELP a chance and see if your life is easier (with less bad consequences). If you are confused about whether or not you can have a Higher Effective Loving Power, remember that you don't have to have a perfect idea of one. Ask yourself if your current way of searching for Serenity is working and whether or not it's time to pick a healing Higher Power. If you think you know how to stay serene without HELP, you may have a lot to learn. But you can learn if you are willing to take a chance and get HELP.

TO DO: It's time to let go of knowing everything. Try reducing your ego. Do so by becoming humble and teachable today. When you do, you will lose the confusion or at least be more comfortable not knowing everything. Your HELP can begin by your simply sharing what is troubling you with a friend and perhaps asking for some advice.

June 11

If You Want to Make God Laugh,
Tell Him Your Plans

Things don't always work out as planned. In fact, things NEVER work out exactly as planned. So, if you are thinking life is not fair or life doesn't make sense and that this is a good reason to stay in your room and eat doughnuts all day, then you are not being entirely realistic. You are asking for more than what life can give you. It's OK to make plans, but you can't be God so you can't control the results. Trying to control results and people cause depression.

TO DO: Today, let go. Have faith that your loving Higher Power has a better plan for you; it's just that you may not be able to see it yet. Remember your concept of God does not have to be a traditional, religious concept (although it can be); God can be any positive, healthy force you want that helps return you to sanity.

June 12

"It takes a busload of faith to get by."
- Lou Reed

Sometimes we feel completely lost. We feel like there is no Higher Power, no friend, nothing that can help us. We just can't figure it out. You don't even know when the suffering will end. As Lou Reed's song says: "You can't depend on your family, You can't depend on your friends, You can't depend on a beginning, You can't depend on an end..." At that time, we need to just have blind faith...even if you don't know what you have faith in.

TO DO: When you feel lost, hopeless or totally overwhelmed, faithfully search for HELP. Hope will be restored because FAITH works. Repeat: "I have a busload of faith and I will get by."

June 13

Me, Me, Me, Like an Opera Singer

Before I started practicing the Four Steps to Serenity, every time I walked into a room, I thought everyone was staring at me. Come to think of it, wherever I went, it was all about me. Someone else could be dying in the hospital and I was worried about how that affected me. Serenity requires us to focus less on ourselves and more on others. Serenity asks us to deal positively with challenging experiences. When we simply live the experience without making it all about ourselves, we avoid "pity parties" or "egocentric grandiosity" which can lead us down the rabbit hole of depression. Once we rebalance our ego, we will vanquish fear because we won't be so obsessed with what happened, what is happening, or what will be happening to the almighty ME. We will change into a more relaxed person as we gain humility.

TO DO: Live each experience today without making yourself and your desires the focus. If you feel down because you are not getting your way, remember that life is not all about you. Perhaps expand your consciousness by corresponding with someone else to brighten their day.

June 14

Humility Is Like Underwear,
It's Necessary but It's Indecent if It Shows

Humility is the opposite of humiliation - although humiliation becomes humility if it is dealt with well. When we hit bottom, we experienced humiliation. As we progress in serenity practice, we experience humility. Humility empowers. When present, humility eases stress and self- consciousness because our ego defenses don't have to work overtime to justify misbehavior. However, if we try to help others for praise and accolades, we are back to letting our egos control again and the stress and self-consciousness will return - as if someone is seeing our underwear.

TO DO: Today, simply do the next reasonable thing. Don't worry about whether someone sees you do it or not. This will free you from needing others' approval and heighten your peace of mind!

June 15

To Change How You Feel,
You Must Change How You Think and Act

This is one point of this book. By reading a message, you are choosing to change how you think and act. This in turn will change how you feel. If I am resentful, I must think about resentment in a different way. Instead of bathing in it and feeling worse and worse, I must think about getting out of that bath and substituting resentment with empathy and forgiveness. But this change of thinking is only the beginning. I must combine my change of thinking with a new action whenever I begin to feel resentment. That new action may be doing something kind for the person I resent. It may also be something that has nothing to do with the person I resented. Perhaps something fun. I like playing the guitar even though I'm lousy at it. I am blessed to be able to take care of and play with a puppy.

TO DO: Today I will turn a negative emotion into a positive emotion by changing how I think about what is triggering the emotion and then doing a positive action.

June 16

I Can Be Complete
Even When Life Is Incomplete

My biggest trigger for misery is thinking that I can only be happy when problems resolve. What I have learned in my pursuit of Serenity is that even if one problem seems to end, there will always be another problem. I have learned that this is the nature of life and that I can view problems as being good. I can perceive problems as a natural consequence of living. I can be grateful for problems because their existence means that I am alive. I can also feel complete as a human being even though problems persist, even though results seem incomplete and pending. Completeness comes from my sense of connection with my serenity process...with my doing the four steps in the moment.

TO DO: Today I will repeat to myself that I am complete even though life is incomplete. I will not allow problems that seem to last forever to tangle my mind and make me feel as if I cannot be happy and serene.

June 17

Don't React, Act Upon

You have just received an email which is insulting, inaccurate, and has caused your blood pressure to elevate such that you actually feel your chest twitching. You are in shock. You click reply. Although you think you are citing facts and being rational, you don't proofread your reply because you want to get it out of your mind and off to the offender immediately. What is the result? A day or two (after you have completely alienated the other person), you shake your head and say "I did it again…I wish I had never sent that email." It is ALWAYS advisable to wait until anger subsides before you respond to anything. When you are angry, you cannot fashion a response that fully accounts for all of the relevant factors. When you feel insulted, you cannot account for who you are responding to (is it a boss, friend, colleague, spouse). You can't exercise empathy and understanding. You can't even look at the facts objectively. Even if someone says something that provokes you, you can say "I'll respond to that later."

TO DO: Today, act upon, don't react. Wait until the anger and shock passes. When compelled to do something, don't. Be patient and follow a knee jerk reaction through to its bitter end. Before responding, consider the status of who you are responding to. Apply the Four Steps of Serenity: accept, realize that your needs are fulfilled, connect to HELP, and deal with your emotion in a healthy way taking care to give yourself time to calm yourself. You will return to serenity soon enough and will be thankful you didn't react.

June 18

Patience First

When impatient or confronted with a shocking problem, the first thing you want to do is nothing. Just wait until the emotions calm. Slowly accept. You might want to repeat the four steps over and over again. But whatever you do, do not respond when you are emotionally out of whack or you will give an unintended response. The next step is to determine if there is a way to change the situation. Before acting upon your idea, you may want to get a second opinion from a trusted advisor. Remember in 99.9% of the shocks you are confronted with, the worst case scenario is a rarity and is survivable. Usually you can be patient because what you think you needed now, can wait.

TO DO: Today I will think of the consequences before I act. If I feel as if I am out of patience, I will pause until I can make a calm decision. Today I will keep reconnecting to my Higher Effective Loving Power, whatever it is in this moment, and breathe consciously and calmly.

June 19

If You Can't See God,
First Remember He's Not in Your Mirror

This proverb reminds us that we are not in charge of everybody and everything. Our serenity is better served if we turn our life and will over to the care of a Higher Effective Loving Power (H.E.L.P.). This "turning over" simply means that we are going to follow suggestions which work to keep us serene. We cannot continue to run the show because by running the show, we ended up frustrated. My ego is the problem if I start playing God. Part of being serene is reducing that ego and becoming humble.

TO DO: Today I will remember to stop playing God. I will remember that I am not in charge. I will enjoy the relief in recognizing that I do not have to be responsible for everyone and everything. I will humbly follow Good Orderly Direction.

June 20

Be Gentle With Yourself

Would you treat other people as badly as you treat yourself? Would you use the mean words with others that you direct at yourself? Would you be as hard and demanding on others as you are with yourself? Would you hold others up to the standards that you set for yourself? Do you ever call yourself a loser, worthless, a failure? Do you often feel guilty or ashamed? Serenity teaches us that we should not be ashamed of making mistakes. Serenity teaches us that we are not losers; we are not evil; we are not weak willed. It is wrong and harmful for us to beat up on ourselves because we are human and therefore imperfect. It is wrong and harmful for us to continually blame ourselves for the harm we have done others. We must forgive ourselves to be serene. We must learn to use gentle encouraging words when we talk to ourselves. We must learn to be on our own side.

TO DO: Today tell yourself that you are a good person. Tell yourself you are not weak. Cut out mean language when you think about yourself. Forgive yourself as a means to breathe easy, relax, and enjoy your serenity.

June 21

Don't Accept Invitations to Pity Parties

Be aware of what gives you self-pity. For example, many feel sad
just because they are around sad people. Yet this does not have to
be the case. Don't let others bring you down. Instead, make it your
job to be the one they turn to in order to feel better. "Be the light of
the world." Another invitation to sadness is to decide, "I'll be happy
when something happens." Allowing yourself to be happy when you
make a million dollars or sell your screenplay or move to Wyoming
is possibly the worst attitude you can have. It is a prescription for
misery for you and everyone around you. Instead make a decision
to change your attitude now so that you can be happy now. This
doesn't mean that you should ignore sad feelings. In fact, if you
just gloss over, deny or ignore your sad moments, they will affect
you sometime in some way. It is better to admit you are sad and
immediately take steps to deal with the sadness in a healthy way. So,
it's okay to be sad. But don't wallow in it until it matures into self-
pity or misery. Do something (examples are prayer and sharing) to
leave that pity party.

TO DO: Today I will remember that sadness is inevitable but misery
is optional. Examples of healthy ways to deal with sadness are: (1)
call a trusted friend and, after asking for a few minutes of his or her
time, tell the friend that you are feeling sad and why you are feeling
sad. It is often said in therapy sessions that "a problem shared is a
problem halved." Note that talking to another in such a way makes
the other person feel important. (2) say a prayer to your Higher
Power. Try something like "Dear God, I feel sad because...
Please take this sadness from me." This faith can lead you in the
right direction. (3) Try doing something creative like painting a
picture or playing an instrument or just sing along with a favorite
song or try to find a new one. (4) "Scrub the floor" and straighten up
that apartment. (5) Email someone who is lonely; (6) What else can
you think of that is positive?

June 22

Change Anger to Gratitude

My friend left his car in my driveway where no one ever parks, and I backed into it. I was immediately angry at him. Instead of letting that anger build and ruin my day, I thought of reasons to be grateful for him. I remembered the great idea he came up with to save me money. I remembered how supportive he had been over the years. As I consciously told myself reasons to be grateful for him, my anger dissipated and I actually relaxed and felt happy. If you can't think of a reason to be grateful for something that the offending person did for you, focus on the fact that the person's mistake has given you the opportunity to practice good character attributes like patience, forgiveness, and understanding. Remember that we develop character from tough times, not easy times. This practice will help improve your personality and make it easier the next time someone interferes with your rights.

TO DO: Has anyone caused you to feel resentful? Think of something you are grateful for about that person, even if it's just that he or she has given you an opportunity to grow. You are doing great by switching your attitude. Good for you!

June 23

Do You Need Permission to Feel Good?

"I 'shoulda' done that… If only I 'woulda' done that…That 'coulda' happened, but didn't…My mother in law, wife, children are a mess…I'm not as rich, good looking, fast enough as I expected…My license is suspended. I'm too fat, thin, and strange." Even if you have failed at everything and life is not what you want it to be, you still do not have to be miserable or hopeless. The end of misery begins when you realize that you do not have to give yourself permission to feel good. In other words, you do not have to reach a certain standard to allow yourself to feel OK.

TO DO: Say, "I'm not guilty, not ashamed today." Forgive yourself and celebrate. Repeat the following five times: "Even if I totally fail in life, I unconditionally love and accept myself." Then just do the next honest, pure, unselfish, and loving thing. Nevertheless, of course, if you feel bad because of a bad habit, heed that signal and seek help to change. Similarly, if you feel bad because you hurt someone else, it may be time to make an amend to that person. But don't let failures and mistakes get you down today because you are human and live in a challenging World.

June 24

You Can't Save Your Ass and Your Face

Sometimes you have to let all those ego defenses down. You have to stop being afraid of what other people think about you. You may also have to stop blaming others and finally take an honest look at yourself - without beating yourself up but with the goal of trying to help yourself. If you want to be serene, you may have to admit that your bad habits are out of control. You also may have to accept that you need to change your lifestyle, improve your practice of the four steps, and make balance the goal rather than material gain.

if you want to feel better today, you may have to admit that people, places, and things are not the problem, but rather how you respond to them is the problem.

TO DO: Today, I refuse to make lame excuses to protect my sensitive ego. No more saying it is someone else's fault. Today I will honestly look at myself. The goal of serenity is to be "happy joyous and free." The only way I can get there is to change me, not them. Today I will not worry about saving face, rather I will save my ass!

June 25

Ask What's Wrong

One of the best ways to improve your serenity is to try to improve relationships without controlling others or trying to get them to do what you want. It may help to let others explain what may be bothering them. The best way to discover how is to humbly ask "What's wrong?" or "What can I do to improve us?" or any heartfelt phrase to lovingly prompt the other person to open up. When you begin discussing what's wrong, if you are fortunate enough to get an honest answer, don't argue especially if the other person says what is bothering them is something about you. Another's feelings of being wronged do not need to make sense. Feelings rarely make sense. Don't expect to understand or agree with the other person. Don't try to explain why you felt you were right at the time the other person felt wronged by you. Simply say "Thank you for telling me." Remember the goal is to mend the relationship, (and the first step is to get the other person to express his or her feelings) not for you to prove how you were right or justified. For example, perhaps you have a problem with your significant other. After he or she tells you what you have done and you have thanked him or her for opening up, tell the person that you are going to think carefully about what he or she said and see what you can do to change. Since most things that happened in the past cannot be changed, you may have to explain that you are now going to amend your behavior as best as you can so that it never happens again. You may think that what the other person perceives as wrong is something you both need a counselor to assist you in resolving. At the very least, you now have something you can deal with because you have enabled the other person to let you know what you need to deal with to change the relationship. Without such knowledge, no progress can be made.

Before you ask what's wrong, you will have to likely overcome fear of the pain of having your feelings hurt. To do this, expect that you will feel some pain when you ask what's wrong, but also know that asking could be the only way in the long run to regain peace in the relationship. Accept that you have faults and decide that you will not beat yourself up. You'll find that a reduction of your ego with a commensurate increase in your humility will help you overcome your fear of getting your feelings hurt. Focus more on compassion for the other person than self-consciousness.

TO DO: To renew trust and understanding, sweep your side of the street by making amends without blaming the other person or allowing your own shame to stop your positive change. Get rid of your fear of asking "What's wrong" by asking your Higher Power to focus on unselfish love rather than self-conscious fear. Before you make amends, ask a trusted advisor about how to proceed. Asking what is wrong is usually a great beginning to making amends and healing relationships.

June 26

Worry Doesn't Change the Outcome, It Just Makes You Feel Bad in the Meantime

Worry is a waste of energy. It makes us suffer before we even know if there is any reason to suffer. It doubles the pain if something happens we don't like. It causes us to over prepare for bad outcomes when we don't need to. It just plain feels bad. It can make you want to escape by using a bad habit. Worry or anxiety are fancy words for fear that something you want won't work out. The negatives of worry far outweigh any positives. Even if something bad is likely to happen, there is NO POINT in suffering before it happens.

TO DO: Catastrophizing is thinking the absolute worst will happen. It is the foundation of worry. Ask yourself if what you are catastrophizing about is even a possibility. The answer is probably not. Then write down more realistic outcomes. Look at worry and catastrophizing as a waste of time and energy, then focus on doing the next reasonable thing in front of you. If possible, help someone else to take the focus off of you.

June 27

A Good Purpose Beats Negativity

Your Higher Power's will is for you to be happy, joyous, and free. You accomplish this state of mind sometimes quickly, sometimes slowly, by living for a good purpose. Don't worry about the results because you can't control them. Don't measure your self-worth by results. You are not a failure even if you don't get that job, leave a large inheritance, can't pay your bill, or can't save your friend, etc. Simply try to live for a good purpose.

TO DO: Today, I will try to live for a good purpose by turning my life and will over to the care of my Higher Power (which may be higher values). I will not worry about the results because they may be something different and better than I can envision.

June 28

The Problem Is Not the Problem

Written by a friend during the Pandemic of 2020, the following is applicable to dealing with any challenge:

"There is a maxim that says 'The Problem is not the problem, the Problem is the way you react to the Problem.' Although I share in grieving the losses caused by the Pandemic, I also see this Pandemic as an opportunity to review our values and to seek a profound, transformative, serenity enhancing WISDOM. For example, it is forcing me to remove my illusion of permanence, appreciate evolution, understand what is truly important, dissolve harmful attachments, enlarge my vision of humanity, gain humility, open my heart, reassess my priorities, explore new opportunities and technologies, give more importance to life, appreciate family and friends, get me out of my doldrums, appreciate simplicity, be more creative, appreciate art and music, live less wastefully, vent emotions without drugging, reach a new paradigm, use the Light for peace, be more faithful to overcome fear, use household items more efficiently, take more time to interact with others, not take sporting events for granted, be more grateful for fundamental necessities, celebrate the healing of our environment from harmful emissions, heighten my sense of perspective, live with more flexibility, give less importance to materialism, accept my powerlessness over people and nature more deeply, enjoy the adventure of living, and heighten my love for humanity.

In my opinion, The great opportunity that the Highest Power is giving us at this moment is to relearn LOVE.

A lot of soul in this hour.

Peace and Light.

TO DO: THIS TOO WILL PASS! It's just a matter of time. In the meantime, don't let any pandemic or difficulty drive you into FEAR. Instead react with positive, faithful wisdom. Without denying any heartfelt grief, take a moment and focus entirely on some positivity the pandemic or other challenge is revealing in your life. Find your GOOD PURPOSE by meditating and asking your Higher Power or your Higher Self or your Rational Self how you can serve your GOOD PURPOSE. Begin by doing honest, pure, unselfish, loving acts in each moment. Can you add to the list of positive things you can do?

June 29

There Is a Little Pain in the Ass
Related to Everything

It's a sunny day and I am supposed to be enjoying my day off from work by fishing. But my line gets tangled, and the sunscreen burns my eye, and it seems the only thing my fishing hook will catch is my now bleeding finger. I scream, "How can this be? This is supposed to be fun! What a pain in the ass!" My most profound disappointments occur when I think that if I do something it will not have a measure of suffering. For example, I think going to the baseball game will be fun. But I am in denial about the fact that I have to park, pay for the ticket, put up with potential vulgar comments of people around me, and negotiate the weather. Another example: I think having a dog will give me love. But I forget about the related suffering of having to take care of the dog when he's sick, the expense of buying dog food, etc. Sometimes it is hard to stay faithful to my spouse. So I want to cheat. But there is suffering for adultery: AIDS potential, the immorality, the potential for hurting her, the loss of trust, etc. I think having a lot of money is a great thing. However, I forget about the suffering of having to manage the money, actually paying the bills, and buying and managing the things I can get with the money.

TO DO: Today I will figure out what suffering I am willing to put up with. I will remember that there is a "pain in the ass" related to everything so I will not let these pains surprise me and shock me. I will not let the fact that there are problems with everything depress me or make me become hopeless. I will also try to remember that most difficulties have another side to them which I may find enjoyable or meaningful. Most importantly, today I will not let life's inevitable pains spoil my grateful and joyous attitude!

June 30

"Happy, Joyous, and Free!"

In one of the most widely read, frequently used, and dearly loved books on recovery from addiction, the affectionately called "Big Book", it is written that the goal of life is simply for you to be "happy, joyous, and free." The key to reaching this goal is not to make a big deal out of it. Often, you are happy if you're not unhappy. You don't always have to be ecstatic. Sometimes you may be sad because of a difficulty, but you still qualify as a happy person if you don't turn temporary sadness into misery. "Free" means you can wake up in peace. After one year clean and sober, I knew I was happy and free but wondering if I was experiencing joy. I mentioned this to my Sponsor who asked me, "What is the first thing that comes to your mind that you are grateful for?" I replied, "Well I woke up today, I didn't come to from a hangover." I laughed with joy, and the following words flowed out from my heart, "My life is full of so much joy! I can even be content when things don't seem to be going my way. I am able to find peace in the midst of struggles. I have learned what I can and cannot control. I can now see that I have a joy that did not exist before I made serenity the central theme of my life rather than materialism, selfishness, and egotism.

TO DO: Today I will appreciate how happiness, freedom, and joy have returned to my life. I will remember how rare these states of mind were before I began practicing serenity principles. So, today I will do a gratitude list, maintain perspective and connect with my Higher Effective Loving Power.

July 1

One Foot in the Future and One Foot in the Past Makes You Sh-- All Over the Present

A better way of saying this is "The secret of health is not to mourn the past, not to worry about the future, not to anticipate troubles, but to live in the present moment wisely and earnestly." – Buddha. This is what they mean by "One Day at a Time." Don't endlessly grieve over something difficult that may have happened to you. Don't worry about whether some goal you have will work out exactly the way you want. Just make sure your goal is pure, unselfish and loving and do what you can today to head in the direction of the goal.

TO DO: Redirect any thoughts of worry (won't get my way in the future) and regret (didn't get my way in past) to thinking and doing in the NOW. The way you redirect your thoughts is to visualize a big red stop sign, then say to yourself, "STOP!" Then, ask your Higher Power or Higher Self to, "Please let me focus on the now." You can also call a support person and share what is bothering you and ask the support person for advice on how to focus on doing the next reasonable thing.

July 2

Resentment Is Like Drinking Poison Expecting That the Other Person Will Die

The person we resent probably isn't thinking about that resentment. We are not hurting him. But we are hurting ourselves by carrying that negative baggage. The Big Book says resentment is the "number one offender." It causes stress, spiritual bankruptcy, emotional paralysis, and relapse. We need to change from resentful people to forgiving people. In cases where we seek justice or act in self-defense, resentment only serves to cloud our judgment and interfere with our ability to act effectively. At the end of the day, in all situations, resentment only hurts the one holding the resentment.

TO DO: Today I will remember to let go of resentment because it is like drinking poison. Letting go of resentment can be accomplished in various ways. Sometimes forgiveness and understanding help to relieve resentment. Sometimes perspective and a sense of humor help. Sometimes praying for the other person's healing or well-being helps. Sometimes I need to seek guidance from a mentor, sponsor or therapist for assistance in finding the right way to let go of resentment. Today, I will also remember that if I choose to seek justice, act in self-defense, or create a healthy boundary, I will do so only if motivated by love, purity, unselfishness and honesty, rather than resentment.

July 3

Sometimes It Takes a Storm to See How Much Time Has Been Wasted Worrying About the Squalls

The pandemic of 2020! The Great Famine of 1845! The Great Depressions of 1929 and 2008! Hurricanes and War! During these crises, our attention seems to be diverted from our petty indifferences and oversensitivities. Crises can serve as a reminder to not let little things shock, overwhelm, or stress us out. Crises remind us to have perspective and to not "sweat the small stuff." This reminder is important to serenity because it's the little things that usually make us lose our serenity like what somebody says about our physique, or losing a game of monopoly, or not getting the very best deal.

TO DO: Keep remembering all things pass. Both storms and squalls end eventually. Don't let them ruin your serenity. Forget about the little things that bother you because if you let them add up, they will seem like a storm. Part of keeping things small involves remembering how grateful you are to have survived the crises in your life. Another way is to try to remember what was bothering you a week ago. Usually you can't. Keep perspective by asking yourself: "How important is it really?" Think about a real storm that occurred in your life (like the crisis that may have motivated you to reprioritize your life to practice serenity principles rather than materialism) and compare that crisis to the insignificant things you may still be allowing to bother you. Finally, whatever the size of the problem today, don't hesitate to ask for HELP particularly if you feel like it is serenity threatening because sometimes it takes HELP for us to gain perspective.

July 4

Why Do Bad Things Keep Happening to Me?

Life contains suffering regardless of how well you are working your serenity program. There are pandemics, friends die, family gets sick, you will make painful mistakes, etc. It's all part of life. These things are not only happening to you. They are happening to everyone. However, you don't have to make things worse by having a depressed attitude. If you remember the terrible consequences that you had before you made serenity practice a vital part of your life, you may feel gratitude simply due to your personal growth. If you practice good spiritual principles (like mindfulness, love, compassion, and forgiveness) you will thrive during hardship. If you live one day at a time and make the best of this moment, you will not worry about the future or regret the past. If you apply the four steps to challenging situations, you will be at peace and best able to support not only yourself but also others. For example, Step 1 encourages you to accept that you can't change, say, a pandemic. Step 2 suggests that you focus on the fact that your basic needs, though perhaps threatened, are being taken care of due to your own resilience, hard work, and faith. Step 3 encourages you to live by higher principles through a Higher Effective Loving Power. And finally, step 4 suggests that whenever things seem to be overwhelming or troubling, you fix your attitude before you attempt to change other people, places, or things. The result of applying the steps to challenging times is a newfound freedom and calm in the midst of the storm.

TO DO: Today, I will accept the truth of suffering. I won't get depressed over hard times. I will try applying the four steps to difficult situations so that I may become a positive force for myself and others. I may even ask a mentor, friend, or therapist to help me work through the steps regarding a particularly challenging situation. Today, we are not alone.

July 5

If You Do What You Did,
You'll Get What You Got

The person I was will be miserable again. Therefore, I must
change. The first time I heard this I was offended. I didn't want to
be brainwashed, but a good washing was what I needed. Changing
meant doing things differently. For example, to change I had to try to
practice the four steps. I had to accept what I could not control and
learn to adapt to life rather than demanding that life adapt to me. I
had to be grateful for needs fulfilled instead of ungrateful for wants
unfulfilled. I had to connect more to spiritual principles and less to
ego defense mechanisms. I had to fix myself, not others. The result
was peace and enlightenment rather than misery.

TO DO: Don't fear change. You will be keeping the best of your
current self and getting rid of the baggage that has been bringing
you down. Embrace change today by applying the four steps when
dealing with difficulties.

July 6

"The miracle is not to walk on water.
The miracle is walking on earth."
– Thich Nhat Hanh

So many of us try to do the impossible. We have no conception
of "what we can't change" so we force things to the point of
stress. Working toward goals and attempting to influence others
are wonderful only if we do not think that we have to control the
outcome or that catastrophe will result if we fail. Learning how to
let go and accept situations gracefully is the miracle of walking on
earth. This will relieve stress and frustration.

TO DO: Set a healthy goal and head in that direction living
each moment according to the four absolutes: Honesty, Purity,
Unselfishness, and Love. If you have a tendency to overcontrol,
consider doing a personal inventory of issues you need to fix about
yourself (per Step 4) to discover why you tend to overcontrol. Then
let go! Care about you!

July 7

KISS: Keep It Simple Silly

Serenity is a simple process for complicated people. It is a program of unlearning self-defeating habits developed by our imbalanced egos. Kindergarten principles like "Concentrate on what you are doing," "Mind your own business," and, "Tell the truth," are serenity inducing. Stress dissipates as we live a simpler life by following these principles. Our ego doesn't have to work as hard when we keep it simple. As a result, we are pushed further from bad feelings and other self-defeating behaviors.

TO DO: Today I am going to repeat to myself K.I.S.S. throughout the day. Keep It Simple Someone I love (which is me). Instead of trying to control others, I am going to concentrate on what I am doing and mind my own business.

July 8

Today I Don't Have to, I Get To

Before I made serenity practice my priority, I HAD to go to work, run from authority, and suffer all the other consequences of having a bad attitude. Today, I perceive things differently. I am thankful to have a job. I respect others while maintaining personal dignity, and I enjoy all the other privileges of having a positive attitude. I am grateful, have perspective, and am flexible. The result is a peace I never experienced when selfishness, jealousy, and negativity guarded my sensitive ego. Even when I feel distressed, the pain passes more quickly than when I used to bathe in depression.

TO DO: Repeat the phrase, "I don't have to, I get to" especially when you are feeling overwhelmed or sorry for yourself for having responsibilities. This will give you peace of mind even during tough times.

July 9

Things Don't Change, We Do

Problems will always occur. That is life. That doesn't change. As one problem dissipates, another replaces it. However, we can change how we respond to problems. Reading daily messages helps us change so we don't turn problems into trouble.

Examples of daily PROBLEMS:
(a)My neighbor hates my dog.
(b)My eyesight weakens.
(c)The internet connection fails.

How I turn PROBLEMS into TROUBLE:
(a)I let my RESENTMENT at my neighbor cause me to yell at my neighbor.
(b)I let my STUBBORNNESS and DENIAL keep me from getting glasses.
(c)I let my ANGER at the internet provider cause me to throw a chair at the router and get drunk.

SOLUTION: Changing my responses from resentment to understanding, stubbornness to acceptance, and anger to calmness helps me solve problems, not create trouble. Recognizing that there will always be problems allows me to take healthy steps to adjust my attitude to become a healthier, happier person. Changing myself before I address external issues keeps me peaceful. HOW do I change my attitude?

Examples:
(a) I focus on the fact that my neighbor may have been bitten by a dog or is sensitive to my dog barking. This leads to UNDERSTANDING and relieves my bad feelings of resentment.
(b) I get PERSPECTIVE focusing on the fact that at least I have eyes to see. This leads to ACCEPTANCE and relieves my bad feelings of stubbornness and denial.

(c) I become GRATEFUL that the internet usually works and makes my life more convenient. This leads to CALMNESS by relieving my bad feeling of anger.

TO DO: Today I won't let problems become trouble because I won't let my character defects (like anger, resentment and denial) interfere. If I feel a character defect begin to pop up, I will pause, breathe, and remember that character defects only turn problems into trouble. I will also remember that character defects make me feel bad and I do not want bad feelings to interfere with my life. I will try to remember to SIMPLY AND QUICKLY REFOCUS MY THOUGHTS FROM BAD ATTITUDES TO POSITIVE ATTITUDES WHEN CONFRONTED BY A PROBLEM. I will focus on understanding, perspective and gratitude when confronted with resentment, stubbornness, and anger. I will have perspective that my problems are not worse. I will try to have gratitude for what I have. AND WHEN THINGS SEEM COMPLETELY BEYOND MY ABILITY TO HANDLE, I will have FAITH that I can FOCUS ON A LOVING FORCE that has helped me endure everything to this moment the proof being I am here writing this. I will have FAITH that this LOVING POWER will not let me DROWN...and that the overwhelming difficulties will pass as they always have.

July 10

Turn Resentment Into Spinach

People can treat you like dirt, but you are not dirt. I look at challenging people like I look at spinach. I don't like spinach, but I don't get angry at spinach. I simply don't like spinach because I find its taste to be disagreeable. Nevertheless, sometimes I eat spinach for the health benefits. Anyone remember the cartoon character, Popeye? He was famous for eating spinach to get those eye popping muscles. When I look at mean people like they are spinach, mean people don't bother me. They may be distasteful, but they give my character muscles! The more character I have, the further away I am from becoming like them...and the further away I am from losing my serenity.

TO DO: Today my attitude about mean people will change from hatred to distaste. I will look at them like spinach, grateful that they help me to develop character muscles which actually strengthen my serenity. I refuse to treat disagreeable people with contempt because that would make me like them.

July 11

The Sailor Who Has Been in the Dark Is the Best Guide for Other Sailors

If you are someone who has had many struggles in your life, don't despair. By pulling yourself up, you will positively affect others. You are uniquely useful. You have a great purpose and meaning. You can be a model for other struggling individuals. You have the highest calling. By developing patience, resilience, and traits necessary for you to become serene, you can pass along those characteristics by example to those you meet.

TO DO: Today I will rejoice in my progress. I will make it a point to be the best person I can be knowing that I have a great purpose to help myself and be a good example for others. No matter how dark my life has been, I will practice spiritual principles so that I may be a faithful guide should I chance to meet someone who is mired in the darkness that once consumed me.

July 12

Let Go Absolutely

Too long I have been running the show and where did it get me? Lost again. I have trouble giving up control over just about anything, including my parents, children, plans, and results. Maybe if I just let go this time, I will receive some information that will help. It is worth a try. I will try being the RECEIVER rather than the DIRECTOR. Perhaps the main obstacle to letting go is my self-centered fear. Perhaps it is my overactive mind trying to make me miserable again. Perhaps it is just my ego telling me that I know better than they do even though they are professionals or successful or happy or trouble free and I am not a professional, not happy, not successful and certainly not trouble free. For now, I will try to quiet my fear, ego and mind and give myself the day off.

TO DO: Today I am going to listen to what someone else (like my Sponsor, counselor, or competent friend) suggests and not try to overrule their opinion with what I want to do. I am going to relax and give myself a much needed break.

July 13

Don't Sweat the Big Stuff

You know how they say, "Don't sweat the small stuff?" Well, it's even more important, "Not to sweat the BIG stuff." The more important something seems to be, the more important it is for you to act upon it with calm. Astronauts seems to have a sense of calm and good humor even during life threatening situations. You want your doctor to be calm. Allowing things to ruffle you does not help. But you intuitively know this. The hard part is staying calm during stress.

TO DO: Take the four steps to stress reduction:

(1)Accept what is going on and don't try to escape or fight because "flight or fight" is usually useless.

(2)Assess the importance of the situation. Sometimes a "need" may be threatened, but sometimes we magnify situations such that what we think is a "need" may really only be a "want."

(3)Breathe slowly. Control your breath through the inhale and exhale, and connect to a Higher Power. This Higher Power could be music, exercise, art, nature, a God, a trusted friend, a Sponsor, a spouse, a parent, a therapist, a minister, or a combination of many things, etc.

(4) Fix your stress by detaching emotionally and look at what you have to do as "tasks" like any other non-emotionally charged event.

July 14

"Everything is Broken" - Bob Dylan

Say "Everything is broken and that's O.K." when you are discouraged about things being imperfect in your life. Remember that there will always be, for everyone, something wrong or imperfect. It's an impossibility to have everything the way you want it in your life. If you are waiting for everything to be right in your life before you allow yourself to be happy or at peace, you are never going to be happy or at peace.

Money can't do it. Rich people are not immune to broken faucets, fraudulent sales pitches, diseases, etc. Often managing money and things causes more difficulties than predicted.

Healthy people have broken lives too. Computers break, roofs leak. Children and parents hurt.

Serenity practice teaches us to be at peace even though everything (and everyone) is broken. The more we practice serenity principles, the less the broken things get us into trouble.

TO DO: Tell yourself: "Everything is broken, but if I practice the Four Steps to Serenity, the broken things won't be an interference to the basic necessities of my life."

July 15

Step 1

I am miserable and not accepting Life On Life's terms when I am saying phrases like "I should not have to be going through this....I do not deserve this.... Why is the world this way?.... I am so unlucky.... Life isn't fair."

This morning I became miserable because I had to do what I considered duties that were beneath me. I had to do maid work. First, I had to clean up the dog's poop. Second, when I opened the door, all of the Christmas gifts which were in the way of the door got knocked over. Third, I had to change toilet paper, then brushed my teeth only to find there were no tiny cups to wash my mouth out after brushing them. I could not accept the fact that all of these things were happening to someone as important as myself. I thought about the pandemic and how unfair that was to everyone. I blamed my wife, muttering to myself, "Why doesn't she do all of this instead of going out for a bike ride." "Why doesn't she agree to hire a maid?" (even though we both agreed that doing these little chores was less of an inconvenience and expense then having a maid come over once a week).

I became miserable until I finally realized that I simply was not practicing the Four Steps to Serenity. I was not exercising acceptance of Life On Life's terms. I was not being grateful for having the ability to afford toilet paper. I was looking at my dog as a burden rather than a source of love and affection and fun. I was not exercising perspective. My ego was trying to tell me that I was too good for all of this and that life was not fair and therefore not even worth living. I even told myself why go on living if life is going to always be like this. I am convinced that this is my addiction trying to get me to relapse. I am convinced that this is my clinical depression trying to get me to suffer its ugly effects. I am so grateful that I am aware of when I am heading down this rabbit hole, that I can practice the four steps and apply them to accept Life On Life's terms and bring me back to reality and restore the gratitude, perspective and flexibility I need to stay serene. Now, after writing this, I actually feel serene because I am using the coping skill of journaling.

TO DO: If you ever find yourself saying the phrases that I mentioned in my first paragraph above, you need to catch yourself and exercise acceptance. This will begin to change your attitude from misery to serenity. Acceptance is the beginning of positive change. If we change our attitudes, all those things that make us miserable will lose their power. That is the secret of happy people. Once we accept life on life's terms, we can do things to change our attitude.

July 16

Happiness Is an Inside Job

I know someone is experiencing a gift of recovery when despite all the turmoil, he or she says, "You know, I am really still pretty happy." Recently, a patient of mine who had been reading these daily messages for 90 days and consistently practicing the four steps, told me that despite losing his job he felt really happy. He expressed gratitude for therapy and new friends. He said his daily prayer and practice of trying to connect with his Higher Power gave him a sense of peace, hope, confidence and joy. On the same day, another new patient told me that he made one hundred thousand dollars because a business deal closed in his favor. He looked at me sadly saying, "I don't know why I feel this emptiness." He said he was confused because he had lots of money and things but that they never seemed to give him the serenity he thought they should.

TO DO: Happiness comes from within not from the outside World. Today, I will practice the four steps to develop the inner joy that the outside world cannot provide. I will not depend on the World and its things and inhabitants to conform to my desires in order to give me happiness.

July 17

It's Gone but I'm Not Sad,
for Having Had It I Am Glad

When I am grieving over having lost something, it's good for me to remember that I was lucky or blessed to have had it. After suffering the loss of a loved one, it's important for me to remember the joys of that relationship. Whatever it is (a dog, a fun vacation, a beloved car, a friend, youth), I need to accept the loss and feel the sadness, but also as quickly as possible substitute the sadness of the loss with gratitude for having had what I have lost. It's even okay for me to remember that many people have not had the blessings that I have had. By changing from sorrow to perspective, I move further away from depression.

TO DO: To change from sadness to feeling better, remember the good things that you have had even though you have lost it. Remember them with gratitude, not with sorrow.

July 18

It's Normal to Always Have
Something Hard Going On

I have found that no matter how many difficulties I overcome, there is always something challenging remaining. Money doesn't solve difficulties. Things certainly don't. Accomplishments and accolades don't seem to do it. I used to despair over this conundrum. Today, I do the four steps: accept, am grateful for having what I need, trust HELP, and try to fix my attitude. This process usually leads to the peace I erroneously believed money, things, and control could bring.

TO DO: Today I will be happy in the face of trials. I will not depend on the resolution of problems as a prerequisite for my serenity.

July 19

Just Because Daddy and Mommy Said So Doesn't Make It Right

Many of us come from dysfunctional families. As a result, we have a difficult time breaking free from the (1) behaviors which seemed to help us survive childhood but are causing us trouble as adults, and (2) the prejudices that our parents have instilled in us. A computer analogy may help. Our bodies are akin to "hardware" and our personalities are akin to "software." Our software needs reprogramming when it interferes with our life, manageability, and serenity. The oldest and most harmful software malfunctions were created by parental programming. We need to look at that programming. This is done in great depth as a part of therapy and step 4 character inventory. This search is not to create resentment against our parents. Rather, it is to rid ourselves of our own long-standing insane coping skills that now interfere with our lives. For example, drinking alcohol may have worked with regard to coping with our dysfunctional family, but it is causing us trouble in the real world. A more subtle example is the "jokester". Perhaps making jokes may have worked as a coping skill to reduce family stress, but making jokes at work may be causing the jokester problems. Another example is the family "hero" who took control of all of the family responsibilities to cope with her parents' irresponsibility or sickness. This same hero's over controlling attitude may be causing her problems in the real world. Yet another example may be the child who ran and hid as family tension mounted. This behavior may be causing this person to withdraw and miss out on life.

The second problem is that we may have developed prejudices that our parents have instilled in us. Examples include attitudes about race, money, politics, morality, abuse and even concepts of what is right and wrong. Attitudes that may have worked for our parents may not be working for us.

TO DO: Today, without shame, try to notice one of your longstanding behaviors which may be interfering with your serenity. Tell yourself it is okay to change even though your parents would probably think it would be wrong to change. Also, what is a coping skill you learned to deal with your family? Is that coping skill causing you problems today? Don't let this investigation be a cause for resentment against your parents. None of us are perfect. Rather, let this investigation lead to a more liberated you!

July 20

Keep Putting the Plug Back in the Socket

We are either connected or disconnected to our Higher Power
(our program that keeps us serene). When we're connected, we're
heading in the right direction. We tend to feel good. When we're
disconnected, we tend to feel lost.

How do we disconnect? Our lust for security and power are two
ways. When we are ruthlessly seeking security and power, our
selfishness overwhelms us. Our selfishness causes us to fear the
brokers, doctors, contractors, news shows, money issues, health
issues, family responsibilities, etc.

How do we put the plug back in the socket to reconnect? We simply
do step 3 by turning our life and will over to the care of our Higher
Power. We then tend to return to a state of love, gratitude, good
humor, acceptance, and harmony with life. We then stop trying to
over control situations. We do what we can, then we let go of results.
We accept being unable to be responsible for everything. Like a
guitar that naturally falls out of tune, we tune our attitude to stay
connected to the force which is keeping us serene. Momentarily
disconnecting is not a reason to give up and fall into despair. It is a
reason to reconnect.

TO DO: It is natural for the plug to fall out of the socket. Don't
despair about that. The key is to plug it back in. One way to
reconnect is to do a loving act like reaching out to a lonely person.
This act will reduce our loneliness and reconnect us with our loving
Higher Power: our serenity program.

July 21

Making Amends Doesn't Just Mean Saying You're Sorry

Amends are changes. If you only say you're sorry, and do the same act again, you have not made amends. How many times did you say you were sorry when bad motivations like greed, jealousy, resentment and fear ruled your life? Saying you're sorry may be the beginning of an amends. But saying you are sorry means little (and may actually hurt the other person more) unless you change. The fourth step (about fixing yourself) helps you make the amends necessary to avoid reenacting misbehaviors. When you change how you deal with others, you will find that you are less stressed around them and you don't create problems in your own life due to how you treat them. Treating others better helps you treat yourself better because you have to let go of character defects that weigh you down in order to make amends to others. Finally, making amends is not a one time action. It requires continuous progress.

TO DO: Today, think of someone you tend to harm as a result of one of your behaviors. Try to label the behavior. Examples may be impatience, procrastination, selfishness, self-righteousness, perfectionism, etc. When you encounter that person, make a conscious effort not to allow your long standing behavior to rear its ugly head. One way to do this is to make sure you have taken care of your Five Natures (mind, body, emotions, social, and spirit) before you deal with the person.

July 22

Move Two Feet Down From Your Brain

Get out of your head and into your heart. We lose our serenity when we spend too much time manipulating, rationalizing, minimizing, worrying, intellectualizing, and trying to feel good by using our brains and not our hearts. All of this brain usage tends to fuel despair. It's better to trust your heart, which is your good spirit, your childlike acceptance and your trust mechanisms. Your brain tends to create ego defenses. Your heart creates the humility which is necessary for serenity. An obstacle to trusting your heart is fear. A bit of caution does not threaten one's peace, but worry and paranoia can turn caution into fear and panic. It's usually better not to get the best deal than to obsess over the deal. It's often better to trust someone so long as reasonable due diligence has been undertaken. We must remember that serenity practice takes little intellectual energy. The key is to move from your head into your heart.

TO DO: Today, I will meditate on the cute little saying, "I've never known anyone too stupid for serenity, but I have known people to be too smart." Today, I will let my heart lead me, move two feet down from my brain, and feel the freedom!

July 23

See Yourself Doing It First

According to the great philosopher, Neville, the power of your imagination is even more powerful than your own will power. If you imagine yourself doing or accomplishing something before you actually try to do it, the likelihood that you will succeed is greatly enhanced. The great batter visualizes himself hitting the home run before he does it. Not only is it helpful to imagine success, but to imagine it in as specific detail as possible. If you cannot see yourself succeeding, your negative vision will permeate your attempt to succeed. This use of imagination is vital to your serenity.

TO DO: Today, see yourself as a serene person. Envision yourself dealing with life's challenges gracefully and with patience. See yourself accepting life on life's terms and handling situations with calm, honesty, purity, unselfishness, and love. If you are going to be in situations which tempt you to despair, see yourself saying "no" calmly. If you are going to be around challenging people, see yourself as being free of resentment and acting the way someone who you respect would act under the same circumstances.

July 24

The Tow Truck Driver Was Kind

Oh no! The other car wiped out the entire right side of my car. My right arm might be broken. The tow truck arrives. The tow truck driver gets out, looks in my eyes and gives me a gentle smile. He says, "It'll work out." Some good things are going to happen to you today. Even during the midst of turmoil, look for the little good things. They may not be many. They may take a little effort to find. But they are there. Sometimes we tend to be pessimistic or grandiose. Things are too bad or things are too good. We need to keep an even keel to stay serene. If you are feeling sad or that bad things are piling up, remember some good things are happening. The key is to notice them.

TO DO: Tempered with low expectations, start each day knowing good things will happen. You can start your day over anytime.

July 25

Keep an Even Keel

When we were not practicing the four steps, we were imbalanced and everything seemed either too high or too low. Our goal today is to live peacefully and not subject ourselves to extremes. Being angry or even too excited is unpleasant. It's OK to have fun and excitement, but the constant living on the edge only stresses us out and ruins our serenity.

TO DO: Today, I will remember, without shame, the consequences I have experienced for getting too manic and too depressed. Perhaps I will listen to some music. Perhaps I will meditate. I will do whatever it takes to keep an even keel.

July 26

There Is Something More Important Than What You Think Is So Important

Don't allow life to make you angry or depressed. What you think is the end of the world now may really be a wake up call to something better. There may have been a time when you thought that you could never be happy again, but now you are progressing in your serenity practice and things are getting better. Still, you may have moments when you can't understand why there seem to be so many challenges and important things going wrong. One solution is to believe there is something more important happening than what you think is so important. If you think this way, you will connect with a greater purpose which will enable you to turn hardship into victory. Perhaps it is more important for you to learn patience than it is for the red light to change to green immediately. Perhaps it is more important for you to learn to ask for help than it is for you to know the answer to a problem easily. Perhaps it is more important that you learn how to overcome resentment than it is for you to work with colleagues who always agree with you. **Remember that if you don't believe in something more important, then you will never find it. If you do believe in something more important, you have a chance to live a better life.**

TO DO: Think about how there is something more important than what you were originally thinking is so important. Find something positive about your hardship. As the second half of the serenity prayer says, "Accept hardship as the pathway to peace."

July 27

Getting Things Done
Doesn't Mean You're Done

If you are overwhelmed, you need to remember that there will always be something left to do. So don't count on getting things done to make you feel less overwhelmed. Rather, you need to balance your Five Natures and get peace with connecting to your Higher Power. That Higher Power can be anything that restores you to serenity without hurting yourself or others. It could be a Spiritual force, therapy, recovery meetings, your Sponsor, or a combination of these or anything else that restores you to serenity.

TO DO: Don't count on getting things done to make you feel like life is done. There always will be something to do. Rather, connect to your Higher Power now to find peace. You connect to your Higher Power by surrendering (letting go) and living in the moment where you can do the next reasonable thing.

July 28

What Screws Us up Most in Life
Is the Picture in Our Head of
How It's Supposed to Be

Life always turns out differently than we picture. Two kids, two TV's, two computers, two cars, one loving spouse, all healthy, all good students, all interested in what we like, and all loving of us (whoops I forgot the picket fence).

Or your ideal may be different. It doesn't matter. I don't know anybody whose ideal works out.

So don't let that tempt you to feel worthless or eat excessively or anything else. Don't let reality get you depressed.

TO DO: Practice "acceptance" and "doing the next reasonable thing." It's OK and necessary that things work out differently than you planned. You certainly don't have to feel guilty or ashamed about that..

July 29

There's Always Yard Work to Do

If you feel overwhelmed because you feel like you can't get
everything done, remember that you can't get everything done. The
grass grows again. Your hair grows back. Even if you complete
a project, something different will pop up. So if you are feeling
overwhelmed, it might help to realize that it is irrational to condition
serenity on getting everything finished. Realizing this will also help
you overcome procrastination because you won't put off starting
tasks because you feel like you will never finish them.

TO DO: Today, set a time limit to do each task rather than forcing
yourself to finish a task. Tackle the most difficult task first. This
will ease your sense of being overwhelmed and help you stop
procrastinating.

July 30

Maybe It's the Right Way - for Them

Just because it isn't the way you would handle the situation does not mean it's the wrong way. Anger and resentment are fueled when we say, "What a lousy way to do something." For example, a woman did not want to date my patient who was a recovering addict. The woman responded to the addict's second request for a date by texting, "I'm busy." This response, coupled with the woman's attitude and other comments, caused the recovering addict to reasonably infer that the woman wanted nothing to do with him. He felt confused over whether or not she rejected him just because he was a recovering addict or for some other reason. Instead of letting his initial anger cause him to relapse, he discussed the situation with me and his Sponsor, accepted that his feelings were hurt, and concluded that he would have preferred a more direct response from the woman but that he did not need a more direct response. He didn't jump to conclusions. He didn't become paranoid. He didn't have to know why she didn't want to date him. He also realized that her response was right for her even though it was wrong for him. He was freed from the perilous chain reaction that anger, confusion, and resentment cause. Most importantly, he did not allow the woman's behavior to throw him off course in his recovery. He stayed sober and later formed a healthy relationship with another person. Particularly with regard to family interactions, feelings can be easily hurt because one family member perceives the right way to do something differently than how another family member views what is right. Can you think of ways in your life where something seemed right to someone else but wrong to you? Remember that we cannot control other people. However, we can create healthy boundaries to not allow another's sick behavior to control us. Furthermore, we can exercise unselfishness and understanding to allow others to be themselves. This keeps us from overcontrolling and losing our serenity.

TO DO: Don't judge situations as being right or wrong just because you would handle it differently than someone else. Today, make a mental list of the angels that have helped you in your life.

July 31

You Don't Have to Name Your God

Many of us tend to have mental committee meetings. As soon as
we feel we know something, we debate that knowledge in our own
minds. It seems two people live in our brains: the faithful person and
the doubtful person. As soon as the faithful one says something, the
doubter tells us the opposite. One issue that plagues us is the image
or name of a Higher Power. As soon as we resolve what our Higher
Power is to us, the doubter in us tries to convince us that we are
wrong. This conflict can cause distress. The key to end this debate
is to give up on an exact image or "name" for your Higher Power.
Peace results when we surrender to our conflicting selves and be still
and just know that we are at peace without compulsions or a restless
brain. That feeling can be our Higher Power in the moment. Of
course, if it helps you to name your Higher Power, then that's great
too. The steps emphasize that the Higher Power can be anything
that keeps us serene without creating harm. Music, love, a calming
breath, and more can be the God of your own understanding. A
Higher Power can be Higher Powers depending upon the situation.
For example, sometimes music works, sometimes meditation, works,
sometimes a support person works. Sometimes just searching for
HELP works.

TO DO: Today, stop the mental quibbling about a name and image
for your Higher Power and take a deep breath and perhaps you will
know peace. Most importantly, don't rely on your own will power to
become serene; seek HELP.

August 1

It Doesn't Matter Who Is Right,
It Matters Who Is – Left

Sometimes we become frustrated and even resentful when other people do not agree with our opinions. We feel like it is more important to be respected philosophically, than it is to be serene. As we focus on serenity prioritization, we gradually learn not to let these things bother us. We learn to let go of having our serenity depend on convincing others that we are right politically or religiously. We let go of the need to have our opinions accepted and followed. We learn to let go of trying to control others. We learn to keep our eye on the prize. That prize is peace of mind. We truly learn that it doesn't matter whose opinion is right, it only matters that we are left with our serenity.

TO DO: Try not to convince anyone today that your opinion is right. You don't need to defend your ego.

August 2

Beware of the Pitcher Plant

The pitcher plant is a real plant, that is a tempting, insidious trap for insects. Like the venus flytrap, it loves to eat bugs, particularly flies. As the name implies, it is shaped like a pitcher. Inside the pitcher is sweet, sticky nectar that is delicious and aromatic to flies. They land on the lip of the plant, and soon begin to feast on this amazing delicacy. As the fly eats, a very interesting thing begins to happen. It slowly descends deeper and deeper into the pitcher, legs becoming sticky and belly becoming full. Indeed, the fly may see yet another fly, or several flies, positioned deeper or at the bottom of the pitcher plant. The fly, instead of sensing immediate danger, keeps eating. It probably thinks that it can take flight at any time, and what has happened to the other flies – well, that simply won't happen to him.

TO DO: Don't get trapped by the Pitcher Plant of negative thinking. Take warning from the misery that negativity has caused in others. Open your eyes now and see exactly what negative thinking is doing to you. Don't let negative thoughts make you dive deeper into the pitcher plant. Especially during turbulent times, a great way to redirect any negative thoughts is to be grateful for what you have and perspective that your situation could be worse. also, today make sure that you are paying attention to your Five Natures. A balanced life helps alleviate negative thinking.

August 3

You Don't Always Have to Hit the Tennis Ball Back Over the Net

Sometimes you don't have to argue. Sometimes silence is the best answer. Letting go may be the best thing to do when confronted with a person or situation that will not change. When annoyed, confused or irritated, sometimes we are better served by waiting rather than reacting. Living peacefully means acting upon situations not reacting to them.

TO DO: Today, pause when agitated. Remember that self-restraint is the first step to acting upon a situation. Remember that we control ourselves, not them.

August 4

I Don't Care What Anybody Says, Life Is Good

There is a person at our emotional support meeting that says this phrase at the end of every comment he makes. It seems to remind everyone in the room, including him, that it feels good to be positive. It seems to suggest that despite all of the negative philosophies and life's problems, if one can just focus one's mind on goodness, better feelings can arise. Attitude is important, and to have faith that life is good is a great way to improve one's attitude.

TO DO: Today, I will focus on the good things in life rather than the things I wish were different, I will notice how this focus seems to improve my life. I will not let others' negativity bring me down. I will have a positive attitude regardless of the difficulties I must face. I will repeat this phrase a few times today: "I don't care what anybody says, life is good." (Just typing it here makes me feel better.)

August 5

You Learn to Be Less Resentful by Being Exposed to People You Could Resent

Next time you are exposed to someone you could resent, look at the situation differently. Instead of being upset about it, be happy about it. Welcome the situation because this is an opportunity for you to grow. Without being exposed to people you could resent, you will never have an opportunity to improve how you handle resentment. This attitude of welcoming difficult situations will improve your recovery program because you will have an opportunity to practice serenity skills.

TO DO: If you are exposed to someone you could resent, welcome the situation, don't dread it. Use tools like patience, compassion, and the positive thought that no one can drive your bus because you have a serenity program to deal with difficult people, places, and things.

August 6

Want Not, Suffer Not

Since suffering is the difference between what we crave and what we get, we need to eliminate craving because we can't control what we get. Want not, suffer not.

Emotional pain starts with wanting something to be different. Want not and you will suffer not. This is the first step toward serenity, known as **acceptance**. Pain comes from craving. All painful moments start with craving. But, you say, how will I succeed in life if I don't have desire. You will succeed because you will be as happy and useful as possible (not attached to results) by simply working toward a goal and doing the next reasonable thing guided by good spiritual principles. Of course, we cannot always escape afflictive diseases and certain abuses, but we do not have to make them worse by adding the mental obsessions caused by craving. We eliminate craving by working an effective serenity program, minute by minute, day by day. Doing this, you will eventually reach your higher purpose as opposed to your egotistical ambition.

TO DO: Throughout this day, repeat the phrase "Want not, suffer not." Catch yourself when you start wanting something by saying to yourself, "Want not, suffer not."

August 7

Turn Humiliation Into Humility

Many of us have suffered lots of humiliation. We find that we can regain our serenity by turning that humiliation into humility. Humiliation is degrading. Humility is empowering. Humiliation is ego suffering. Humility is freedom. Humiliation involves self-blame. Humility involves the realization that we are not perfect and that we have certain self-defeating behaviors that warrant change. One part of this change may involve finding and following our Higher Power's direction. This process can be joyously empowering. Remember that our Higher Power can be defined as Help, Higher Self, our Recovery Group, a religious force, a spiritual force, spiritual concepts like love, kindness, integrity, purity, etc., or a set of actions and principles that keep us serene.

TO DO: When humiliated, do what your Higher Power would want you to do. Don't lash out or withdraw. Rather, turn the humiliation into humility by realizing you are human. When things seem to go wrong, remember that hardship causes character growth and is the pathway to peace.

August 8

If You Won't Let Go, Prepare to Be Dragged

Letting go means that you apply the four steps to life. You accept and adapt, you realize your needs are fulfilled, you connect to HELP (Higher Effective Loving Power) by acting according to good spiritual principles, and you fix yourself rather than try to change others. If we don't apply the four steps, we are going to be dragged through mud, stones, fire, and every imaginable pain. If we refuse to accept life on life's terms, endlessly try to get our selfish wants fulfilled, refuse to connect to HELP, and stubbornly try to change people, places, and things, we are not letting go, and we are going to be swimming upstream against a tidal wave.

TO DO: Today, let go by practicing the four steps. This will allow you to do the next reasonable thing governed by the highest principles, and you will consequently be doing the best you can now and for your future. Most importantly, this will allow you to maintain your serenity in the midst of challenges.

August 9

Accept Hardship as the Pathway to Peace - Serenity Prayer (Part Two)

No pain, no gain. Without a crisis, change does not occur. Until I experienced the disaster of a DUI, I did not have the motivation to get sober. Early recovery was hard, but through it I have come to love a new way of life.

Hardship also forces us to grow internally and that growth yields internal peace. We should therefore consider being grateful during hardship because without hardship we don't build the character necessary for peace. A GRATEFUL attitude during hardship makes the hardship LESS PAINFUL and consequently minimizes the harm we would otherwise cause others by our bad attitude.

Suffering is a truth of life. We all experience suffering. Don't expect that everything is going to go smoothly or be easy to accept. If you expect tough times, you will NOT BE SHOCKED when they inevitably arrive. You will not be thrust into a horrible pity party. Without bad weather, you would not know what good weather feels like. Without hardship, you would not be able to feel peace. Unfortunately, everyone faces hardship. But if you don't run from it by using your drug of choice or isolating or acting out, the hardship will pass. Don't become attached to a result. Just accept your hardship and know that there is a way to regain peace.

TO DO: Just keep doing the next reasonable thing according to your Higher Power's guidance. Your Higher Power can be your recovery program, coping skills, good spiritual principles and/or anything that keeps you serene without doing harm. Your current hardship will someday result in peace. Accept positive change. Today's hardship may end up being the best day of your life.

August 10

Leave Mental Committee Meetings

Not only do external circumstances (like the pandemic, racial injustice, financial losses, physical pain, and stressful people) cause distress, but also internal conflicts (like a racing mind) cause misery. A common phrase for a racing mind is a mental committee meeting. Competing camps overanalyze and argue in our own minds during these mental committee meetings. They keep us awake at night; they distract us during the day; they make little things big things. Indeed, it is often hard for many of us to think about one thing.

Instead, we think about how one thing will lead to another thing, which could lead to another thing and to another.

TO DO: Try meditating today. For one minute, just breathe and focus on a distant spot. If a thought arises, just breathe and let it go with the exhale. As you go through your day, if a mental committee meeting starts, take a deep breath and let it go. Focus on just doing what's in front of you.

August 11

It's Not Stupidity, It's an Illness

Some of us, and perhaps many of us, have some kind of mental illness. It is important for us not to beat ourselves up about that or label ourselves as stupid. Mental illness has nothing to do with one's level of intelligence. You did not drive your car into a ditch, you did not commit a felony, you did not neglect your children, you did not waste precious time, you did not spend the morning crying because you are stupid. You suffered painful consequences and perhaps even interfered with others' lives because you have a disease that caused you to do so. Don't waste your time calling yourself stupid and beating yourself up. Instead, be thankful that today you are squarely facing your disease and doing the next reasonable thing. Forgive yourself rather than denying that you have a disease. Calling yourself stupid only inhibits your ability to recover.

TO DO: Today, be aware if you are beating yourself up. Watch for the language that you mutter to yourself about yourself. Use kind language when thinking about yourself. Continue to practice the four steps, get HELP from a therapist if necessary. Perhaps participate in a recovering community. Act according to healthy moral principles to effect the personality change necessary to keep the disease (the insanity) in remission.

August 12

I Can Only Make Some Sense of Life When I Think Something Bigger Is Going On

Pandemics, racism, tornadoes, starvation, war, disease, and injustices abound. Trying to attach meaning to the human condition used to send me into confusion and despair. It triggered my need to quiet my brain. I turned to my addiction to do so. Then, I just became more confused and I got into trouble. Today, I quiet my brain in a different way. Today, when I observe that I am trying to understand that which I cannot, I meditate on the fact that there is something going on behind the scenes. I focus on trusting that my Higher Power has a greater plan with greater objectives that transcend my ability to intellectually conceive. Perhaps it's a character building exercise. Perhaps someone's crisis is an opportunity for that person to make a positive change or for me to unselfishly help. Perhaps it's a lesson in perspective. Or perhaps, whatever it is, it's simply greater than I can understand. In that case, I must simply have faith, and this faith relieves my need to escape.

TO DO: Today observe your thinking. When confused, look behind the obvious. Repeat to yourself that something bigger is happening. Perhaps today's challenges are opportunities to grow or to help someone else.

August 13

Lethargy Plus Perfectionism Equals Paralyzing Procrastination

Lethargy usually causes us to delay doing what we are supposed to do. Perfectionism also causes us to delay because we know that it will be very difficult to live up to our impossibly high standards. If we suffer from both lethargy and perfectionism, we may not only delay, but we may never do what we should do. This deadly combination causes us to miss deadlines, to miss important events, to fail in life. We procrastinate until we are so stressed out that we become paralyzed. To get rid of lethargy and perfectionism, we must first admit that we have these issues. Then we must observe them when they operate in our daily lives. We must then take the drama out of doing things by not catastrophizing that trying to do something will be unbearable. Detaching from expectations, we must view reaching goals as doing tasks and we must take small steps in doing these tasks. We must then gently congratulate ourselves for taking small steps forward without constantly measuring how well we think we are doing. Living a balanced lifestyle and leaving the results to our Higher Power aid greatly.

TO DO: Use your Higher Power to take away your lethargy and perfectionism. Keep expectations low. Without fearing the process or the results, take a few small steps toward doing what you know you should do. Remember that stress will melt away as you slowly head for your goal.

August 14

Scream!

Sometimes you need to let your anger out! Better to curse than to internalize anger thereby falling into depression. The key is to let your rage out without interfering with your life or others'. It is not wrong to feel angry. It is better to own your fury and to let it out in a healthy way. One way: get in a car (so as not to scare others) and scream. Another way: do 50 push-ups. Perhaps even better: do vigorous then relaxing slow yoga.

TO DO: Turn to your higher self, your Sponsor, therapist, or other parts of your Higher Power to help you find a healthy way to deal with anger. Exercise, a healthy meal, a break from work, and occasionally even a loud scream are a few examples.

August 15

Don't Turn Someone Else's Character Defect Into Your Resentment

If you feel resentful, you are the one suffering from it not the person you resent. If you feel angry because of someone else's character defect (their impatience, intolerance, prejudice, ego imbalance, jealousy, anger, fear, etc.), then you are punishing yourself for their problem. Why punish yourself for someone else's toxicity?

TO DO: Today, forgive everyone against whom you hold a resentment. Pray that he or she receives all of the blessings you have received (like freedom from your own character defects and love and forgiveness from others). If you can help the person heal, try. Usually, if not always, you can't do anything and your attempts will only be viewed as nagging. If the person is living or working with you and continues to foist his or her character defects on you and you feel you are being abused, consider creating a healthy boundary. A healthy boundary may come about by seeking a third party (like a marriage counselor) to help you deal with the issue. Healthy boundaries are changes you make to limit toxicity. An example of a healthy boundary is talking to a mean person only after you have eaten a meal so you are physically strong enough to not lose your serenity. Another is taking breaks at work to meditate so that you are peaceful despite an oppressive boss. Where do you need to create healthy boundaries and how can you do it?

August 16

So Nice to Know,
I Don't Have to Run the Show

What a relief to know that I'm not responsible for everybody and everything! If you are feeling impatient or frustrated, you may be taking control of people, places, and things you can't control or direct. You may be slipping back into that old behavior of wanting situations to turn out according to your plans. In serenity practice, we continually learn to let go of running the show. We realize that there is some other force in charge of everything. It is a wonderful feeling to realize that you don't have to have things go your way. If one door closes, another good door will open if you are faithfully practicing the four steps of serenity and giving daily attention to your Five Natures.

TO DO: Stop yourself today if you are trying to control others and outcomes. Practice the four steps: acceptance, appreciation of needs fulfilled, connection to HELP, and self-improvement. Make a decision to be a player, not a director.

August 17

I'm Quite Happy With Who I Am, Thank You

Practicing serenity means being happy in your own skin regardless of what the World throws at you and what others think about you. For example, there's no need to take foolish, unnecessary risks to prove yourself as being worthy to others. In other words, being truly serene means being happy with your self-image. There's no need to compare yourself to anyone else. There is no jealousy, no fear of living up to another's expectations. You can also be happy for others accomplishments without feeling "less than."

TO DO: Today I am going to unconditionally love myself. That means I am going to do healthy loving things for myself. I will not worry about whether or not I am living up to anyone's expectations.

August 18

Everybody Has a Different Bottom

Bottoms are different for everyone. They cause one to cry out that one is lost. Being lost is good because when one feels lost, there is room for a Higher Power to help. There is an opening to follow Good Orderly Direction (G.O.D.). Whether or not one recognizes this "spiritual upheaval" depends on the extent of one's depth of desperation, leveling of one's pride and open-mindedness. Though initially tumultuous, the upheaval will always lead to peace if one follows its lead. For me, my bottom occurred on my last drunk 33 years ago. After an evening of drinking and lying to cover up my drinking, I flipped over my car. I could figure out no explanation for how I got in that position. I was lost. I knew I no longer could trust myself to drink alcohol and I knew I didn't know how to definitely stop drinking. So I was open to listening to others suggestions to go to AA and therapy. Finally I was able to follow Good Orderly Direction.

TO DO: If you feel as if you have hit bottom, don't fear, just experience the sense of powerlessness as the beginning of positive change. Remember that your Higher Power is always with you, but you have to be open to be aware of its presence. Sometimes bottoms are necessary for this awareness. Try to connect today through some form of reaching out like prayer, meditation or calling a friend. If your Higher Power includes a recovery group, reach out to a member of that group to share your experience, strength and hope. Remember that your Higher Power can change and evolve, and that it can be of your own choosing so long as it restores you to sanity and keeps you serene. Peace and Light!

August 19

There Are No Guarantees

When you buy something you might get a warranty but never a guarantee that the product will work. When you tie your shoes, you might expect your shoes to stay tied, but there's never a guarantee they will. When you get married, there may be a contract, but never a guarantee.

So often we don't do something that might be fun, helpful or good for us because we have no guarantee that it will work out as planned. So often we procrastinate or fear making a decision because we have no guarantee. But these reasons don't make sense because guarantees don't exist. Wanting guarantees is a product of fear and causes stress because guarantees are impossible to attain.

TO DO: Don't let the fear of uncertain results control you today. Think and act reasonably, let go of results, and don't blame yourself or others if things don't work out as planned. Stay in the moment, relax and keep trying to do the next reasonable thing. If no one has told you that you are loved today, I want you to know, I do!

August 20

If We Resent Them, They Rule Us

"When we resent someone or something, we unknowingly allow that person or thing to control us." Emotions Anonymous.

Do you want someone who may have wronged you to rule you? Then keep carrying around your hatred for that person. Every moment you resent someone, that person exercises POWER over your mood. They continue to hurt you long after they acted. How do you get rid of resentment? Substitute resentment with FORGIVENESS and UNDERSTANDING. For example, imagine that someone who hates your dog got bitten. Or that the person may be mentally or physically ill. Or that someone who abuses you was abused. Set HEALTHY BOUNDARIES to protect yourself, but don't feed the resentment. Another way to exercise understanding is to remember that we humans are all FLAWED. Instead of dwelling on the other person's flaws, take a look at your own without beating yourself up. If you can't FORGIVE or UNDERSTAND them, at least pray that God or some force heals the person so that the evil act can never be done again, then avoid ENABLING the other person's sick behavior. Even if the person you resent is dead, pray or hope that the person's sickness for power or evil is never perpetuated again. But don't carry the baggage of hatred and anger against the person or that person will just continue to weigh upon you.

TO DO: Use your Higher Power to remove your resentment because you may not be able to do it on your own. Substitute resentment with FORGIVENESS and UNDERSTANDING while setting HEALTHY BOUNDARIES. Look at your flaws instead of theirs. Remember that resentment may be the number one threat to our serenity, so get rid of resentment to be free!

August 21

Low Expectations
Do Not Mean Low Optimism

We should keep expectations low about the material World
providing us with all we want because expectations seem to be
inversely proportional to serenity. Alas, expectations are often
called premeditated resentments. But keeping expectations low does
not mean we cannot be optimistic if we make living according to
spiritual principles more important than the acquisition of material
things. We must remember that spiritual principles will give us
more than the material World ever could. Reliance on materialism
has many pitfalls because we usually do not get all that we want.
Things typically don't end up exactly the way we planned. Even
if we get what we want, we usually will want more because we
have learned to make acquisition of material objects the means for
self-satisfaction. We therefore are constantly in a state of desire or
craving for more, and we become frustrated when our craving is not
satisfied and bored when we have nothing to crave. Additionally,
we are eventually going to be unfulfilled because we will suffer
sickness, old age and death. BUT, if we rely on spiritual principles,
we don't need the attainment of material possessions to make us
happy. We can enjoy life's journey because we are always satisfied
in the knowledge that our loving Higher Power is with us. We are
content with doing good actions regardless of what they yield. We
are content with ourselves because we know we are living according
to unselfishness. We are free of resentment because we rely on a
higher justice not ours. We don't need to be manipulative. And best
of all, we don't experience continual craving for the satisfaction of
our own wants. We can be optimistic that even during sickness we
can be a good example to others. Indeed, in the face of death, we can
be fulfilled and fearless knowing that spirituality can transcend our
material finale.

TO DO: Today, I will keep expectations about the material World low. I will focus on communion with my Higher Power because I know that will result in peace. I will remember that my Higher Power is whatever restores me to serenity. My Higher Power can be art, Jesus, Buddha, Love, Nature, the Ocean, the Gift of Desperation, a combination of powers...anything that keeps me happy, joyous, and free without causing harm.

August 22

A Heart Full of Faith Has No Room for Fear

So you are making a big change. You're wondering what will happen if you quit your job or if you start dating again or if you agree to get that surgery or if you make that investment or if you should stop drinking. Your mind envisions all kinds of frightening results. You see yourself penniless. You see yourself getting brokenhearted again. You see yourself free from pain but physically limited. You see yourself unable to stay clean and sober. You feel fear.

Fear is the feeling that you are not going to get your self-centered way in the future. Fear creeps in when you focus on what your Lower Powers want. Examples of lower powers are excessive materialism, notoriety, endless security, power, limitless pleasure, and lustful relationships. These desires cause fear! The remedy is to want whatever your loving Higher Power wants. (Remember your Higher Power is anything you choose but it usually involves living according to good spiritual principles like kindness, forgiveness, love and unselfishness rather than greed, hate, and jealousy). You align your will with your Higher Power's will by doing what your Higher Power suggests. Foremost, your Higher Power wants you to maintain your serenity. Your Higher Power wants you to act unselfishly, lovingly, and honestly because these actions cause joy. Your Higher Power wants you to use your resources (intellect, courage, and strength) to make plans in accordance with serenity inducing principles and to leave the results to your Higher Power. Your Higher Power does not want you to worry about the future but instead gratefully live in the present. This faithful way of life vanquishes fear. The results will perhaps be a journey with a wonderful meaning you didn't even consider. This journey will often be better than what you originally sought. It will always be a journey that you can handle. If you do what your loving Higher Power wants you to do in this moment, you will be able to act reasonably and you will not be fearful. You will be living intelligently even if you make mistakes or if you encounter oppositional people and struggles. The essence of your being will be full of faith with no room for fear!

TO DO: Today I will enjoy each moment by living according to the principles which keep me serene. I will catch myself if my mind wanders toward fear and repeat the mantra, "Faith, Faith, Faith, My heart is full of faith!"

August 23

EGO Stands for Ease God Out

As our ego loses balance, our Higher Power which some call God (the power which keeps us serene) loses force. How does our ego become out of whack? A few examples: We try to control outcomes through will power alone. We try to control others. We rely on things to please us. We believe we are less or more than a human being who makes mistakes. We judge others and ourselves. We measure our self-worth by money. We become hypersensitive to others' criticism. We rely on our own instincts, rather than on our Higher Power's guidance. We feel we don't need to do serenity practices because we believe we are too busy. We become trapped by the 30 Serenity Killers described in this book. Easing our Higher Power out causes us to feel frustrated, alone, fearful, impatient, and generally discontent.

TO DO: How do you ease your Higher Power out? Today, be mindful when you do. Remember we connect to our Higher Power by PRACTICING THE PRINCIPLES WHICH KEEP US SERENE. Such principles can include helping others, wearing a smile rather than a frown, exercising understanding rather than resentment, and living according to the four steps.

August 24

Issue, Said Slowly, Becomes, "It's You."

Say the word "issue" slowly a few times. Pause slightly between the first and second syllable. Say it until you hear the phrase, "It's you."

Remember when you thought that everyone and everything else was the problem? How easy it was to point the finger at your overbearing parents, your obnoxious sister, the red light that always seemed to appear just as you were reaching that intersection. In recovery, we know that the parents, sister and red light are going to do what they do. We can't change them. But we can change how we "act upon" dealing with them. For example, we can seek to understand that our parents may have had a terrible upbringing such that they have become programmed to lash out. Free of resentment, we can then seek to create healthy boundaries or explore without anger ways we can deal with them. With that red light, we can temper our anger with patience. Whatever the issue is, we need to focus on what we are doing and seek to change that, rather than focus on reasons why they should change.

TO DO: Today, I will remember that an issue requires that I look at what I am doing rather than what the other person, place or thing is doing. I refuse to be impatient, offended, or stressed. Instead, I will cherish the freedom of choosing a response which leads me to peace.

August 25

Sometimes "Good Enough" Is All You Need

Perfectionism is usually not a good thing. It can cause depression. Trying to make the optimal deal...laboring hours to write the best letter while neglecting your family...overwhelming yourself with every detail of a vacation which was supposed to be relaxing... obsessing over why one investment goes south while ignoring the ones that did well...procrastinating and doing nothing because you can't figure out how to do it perfectly...crying because your nose is a bit crooked while ignoring the fact that you are healthy and charming. The list is endless.

TO DO: Today, I resolve to look at the blessings I have. I refuse to get overwhelmed, ashamed, sad, or afraid over the things that are not ideal. I will repeat the phrase "it's good enough" whenever I start to beat myself up over anything that seems imperfect.

August 26

"You add as much harm to the world when you take offense as when you give offense."
- Ken Keyes

The point of this saying is that when we take offense, we may become angry then lash out irresponsibly. It encourages us to avoid letting these emotions dictate our actions resulting in adding more harm to ourselves and others. It does not discourage us from seeking justice, being assertive, creating a healthy boundary, or trying to correct a problem. It helps me not to take offense when I meditate on the following incident. I stupidly left my dog in the car on a hot day. I thought I would be back quickly, but the grocery line was much longer than I predicted. When I came back, I found him under the seat shielding himself from the sun rays. Of course, when I reached for him, the only emotion he exhibited was joy to see me. He had taken no offense at my idiotic mistake. A dog does not take offense. He doesn't even have the capacity for resentment. My dog is always serene.

TO DO: Today I will try to be more like my dog. I will do so because I have learned that anger is a foil to my serenity and has the potential of hurting others. I will not take offense knowing that the potentially offending person may simply be ignorant or may have had life experiences that have caused him to act in such a way. I will try to understand and empathize rather than take offense. On rare occasions and only when my needs are threatened, I may seek justice, try to correct a problem, or create a healthy boundary, but I will not take offense because I have accepted that we are all imperfect humans.

August 27

Peel Away the Onion Skin

We become serene when we do not fear being vulnerable, when we drop the false images and facades that we struggle to show others for fear of not being accepted. Serenity grows as we shed the defenses, fears and resentments we use to protect our egos. We begin positive change when we allow our true selves to emerge and get to the core of who we really are beneath the layers of ego defenses. This takes courage because it can feel risky to peel away the onion skins and to look at our core. But once we do, then we can take the steps to free ourselves from the sickness and baggage that comprise those onion skins. The reward is great because once we shed those facades, fears and resentments, we find liberation.

TO DO: Today I will be honest with myself and make a careful examination of the defenses I use to protect my ego. I will honestly examine what is holding me back from being myself and feeling true feelings. I will open up and share something about myself at a recovery meeting, with a therapist or friend. I will not be worried or afraid. At my core, I will know that I am a fearless, loving, decent person who has nothing to lie about or hide.

August 28

Feel, Deal, Let Go

How I deal with my feelings spells the difference between a good day and a bad day. Denying that my feelings exist or trying to escape from them through drugs or distraction only makes bad feelings worse. It is healthier for me to admit I feel a certain way and allow myself to feel while making sure that I don't let bad feelings control my behavior by making me do something harmful to myself or others. I can then deal with the feelings by sharing them with a friend or some other supportive person. I can attempt to exercise perspective about the trigger of my bad feelings. I can try to be grateful by focusing on what I have rather than what I want. This process of letting go gradually releases the bad feelings and returns me to serenity.

TO DO: Today I will feel, deal and let go of negative feelings. I will recognize that the difference between a good day and a bad day depends on my attitude not on what happens in the world. I will repeat this mantra, "feel deal, and let go" whenever I am triggered to feel some negative emotion.

August 29

"Ain't nobody messin' with you but you."
- Robert Hunter

We may think they are the problem, but really we are the problem.
Our rigidity, intolerance, prejudice, oversensitivity, impulsivity,
self-righteousness mess with us. Not their actions, but our reactions
punish us. Feeling better results not from changing them but from
changing ourselves.

TO DO: Today I will ask myself where I am causing my pain,
not where they are causing my pain. What is my hang up in a
challenging moment? Do I need to be less impatient, less self-
centered, more assertive, less demanding, less controlling of others?
What can I do to change my behavior to make me less stressed?
What core belief or desire is actually weighing me down? Usually
the desire to have things work out as I want them to on my timetable
is the chief culprit.

August 30

The Truth Will Set You Free
but First It Will Anger You

Nobody wants to hear that they should change. Nobody wants to take an honest self-examination. It is far easier to point the finger at someone else than at ourselves. Nobody wants to hear "constructive advice" at first. Nobody wants to be told (or admit) that they are too angry, impatient, or in denial or egotistical. Nobody wants to discover that they have character issues. But until you have the open-mindedness to face the truth, you won't have a chance to be free of the troubles caused by your issues.

TO DO: Today, don't let a natural revulsion to criticism or change stop you from taking an honest self-examination. That examination may save your life. It will certainly help you on your path to serenity.

August 31

Get Grounded

Everything seems out of control. You forgot to save your ten page letter, then the computer crashed! Your significant other is making your head spin! We all experience unwelcome shocks and surprises. We all find ourselves obsessing on mistakes and irritations. One tool to gradually lead us back to peace of mind is called "grounding." Grounding can help when you feel like you have lost all control and are beginning to panic. This is how you safely land that mental airplane that feels like it just lost an engine.

TO DO: Today if something happens that makes your blood begin to boil, get grounded. First, look around you. Find five things, then name each thing to yourself. Then name everything you can hear. Then name one thing you could touch. Breath slowly, then do a task you are supposed to do.

September 1

Life is not a T.V. Show

Problems usually don't resolve in a half hour. Life doesn't always give us a satisfying result. The good guy doesn't always win. The hero doesn't always save the day. Even the pizza doesn't always get delivered on time or hot. Life doesn't always make perfect sense. When we judge whether something worked out badly, we are probably judging in the short term and ignoring the long term lessons and benefits that may actually be of greater importance. For example, when I found out I was an alcoholic, I was crushed at first. But now I realize that I needed to see my powerlessness over alcohol to practice a recovery program that has kept me sober and improved my life better than I could have imagined. Practicing the four steps leads to peace of mind. Imperfect judgmentalism can threaten that peace.

TO DO: Today I will not judge a situation as being good or bad. I will therefore not be anxious or depressed. Instead I will trust that my Higher Power (my recovery program, spiritual principles, God, or whatever I rely on for HELP) has the situation well under control. Thus, I will relax without expecting problems to resolve in a half hour or any set time. I will not expect life to resemble a T.V. show.

September 2

You've Got to Be Really "With It" to Know That You Are Not "With It."

This morning my brain was playing a tennis match between whether I was justified to act in response to a resentment I had against my friend. In my mind, I toyed with the idea of how I was going to treat him: with hateful lecturing, by telling him to change, by asserting my rights, by even telling him I would not speak to him again. I finally realized after applying the four steps that letting a resentment govern my actions was stinking thinking. It was making too big a deal out of a temporary hurt feeling. I finally realized that my attitude was the issue and not my friend. I finally got "with it" enough to know that my stinking thinking was not "with it." And fortunately, I got "with it" before I said something to my friend which would have only damaged our relationship.

TO DO: Today ask yourself if you are thinking or doing something that is out of control. When your brain starts tempting you to react negatively, tell yourself that you are not "with it" and take three slow breaths. Remember that stinking thinking is bad for your serenity and that it is more important to pause and transition to positive thinking.

September 3

Stop Beating Yourself up!

The dice are loaded. The game isn't fair. You are imperfect. You make mistakes and have instincts that make you do strange things. You can't predict the future so you have to make decisions that will not work out. Also, the World is imperfect. From bizarre diseases and strange weather patterns to economic irregularities and conflicting religions (and everything in between), the World moves in uncontrollable patterns. We are confused people in a messed up World.

Admitting this should actually be comforting because YOU ARE NOT TO BLAME AND NEITHER IS ANYONE ELSE. There is simply no reason to drive yourself insane because there is no way for you to arrange things to get exactly what you want when you want it. If you are beating yourself up because someone or something conflicts with you, you are treating yourself unfairly. When we admit this Truth, we can relax. When we admit this Truth, we will lose the need to escape from life, and we can face life serenely.

TO DO: Today I will focus on the fact that I am loved. I will not be discouraged, embarrassed, or depressed. I am not hopeless or worthless just because I make mistakes. Without beating myself up, I will try to get rid of my character defects by doing the 4th step so that I can participate in the healing process that will lead me to be happy, joyous, and free.

September 4

Listen to Learn, Not to Reply

"Most people do not listen with the intent to understand. Most people listen with the intent to reply." - Stephen R. Covey.

Sometimes we have a tendency to want to look smart by making a smart comment because our egos tell us that we need to impress others. But if we are thinking about our comment and ignoring others' comments, we may be failing to learn. We also may be failing to understand what the other person is saying which may render our response irrelevant. Indeed, if we are thinking about how to impose our personal opinions while someone else is talking, we are defeating the purpose of open-minded listening. Knowing that we don't have to impress anyone or calculate a reply is relaxing. Knowing that we don't need to manipulate or persuade anyone is relaxing. Uncalculated comments are borne from listening to understand, not to advance our own theory. Finally, if we truly listen to understand, we can be truly open to needed change and more empathetic to the person sharing.

Too often we fail to let someone else finish. Too often we want to win the argument without being open to what the person is saying. Others can sense this and it alienates them and gives them the impression that we are closed minded. Ultimately, this causes resentment and tension in a relationship rather than harmony. Indeed, a fundamental impediment to relationships occurs when a partner feels like he or she can't be heard.

TO DO: Today, I will listen to understand, not to reply. I will remember that this is a good way to stay on the path of serenity.

September 5

It's OK to be Vulnerable

Vulnerability is hard for all of us. We fear that it opens us up to pain and rejection. When we are vulnerable, we risk allowing others to see our true selves, not our facades. The reward to taking this risk is a sense of freedom. Vulnerability also is a way to honestly connect with someone. And if needed, it may be a way to get help with an issue we may be hiding.

TO DO: Today I will take a chance and be vulnerable. I will not let shame or embarrassment stop me. I will open up with a safe person. I will do so because I know that vulnerability will help me lose some of the baggage that may be interfering with my peace of mind.

September 6

You Are NOT Such a Special Snow Flake

You are not terminally unique. You are not the only one who catches the flu or has to put up with difficult customers, parents, and children. You aren't the only one who has to wait in line. When I was sitting alone in a crowded bar, I thought I was the only one who was lonely and ignored. But by practicing the principles of serenity, I learned that there was a way to not feel so unique. When I think I'm the only one who feels overwhelmed, I remember that everyone has problems and that I might not trade mine for theirs.

TO DO: Today I will remember that I am NOT so special or unique and I will end self-pity with perspective and flexibility.

September 7

Look Back but Don't Stare

It's good to remember the consequences from our mistakes but it's bad to feel ashamed or guilty about those consequences. If we spend too much time languishing over our past, we fail to acknowledge our humanity. All we can do about regrets is try not to repeat them. It is better to feel good about the fact that we are doing something right now (like practicing serenity principles) than it is to self-flagellate or feel hopeless due to our past. Today I think it's a good day when I remember the bad consequences I had before I devoted my life to practicing serenity principles. Remembering bad consequences motivates me to stay on the right path and makes me feel grateful I am not doing what I used to do. I am grateful for being a better, though certainly not perfect, person because I am closer to my Higher Powers and have improved my relationships. I would not have been motivated to change had I not had many bad consequences from living my old lifestyle.

TO DO: Today I will not forget the consequences from my old lifestyle. I will look back but not stare. I will remember to be grateful for having had the motivation to change.

September 8

If You Create Peace in Yourself, You Will Create Peace in the World

If you want to improve the World, first look within. Peaceful people don't seem to create disturbances. Rather they tend to provoke love and peace in others. They tend to be more trustworthy and persuasive while angry or depressed people often find themselves ignored. Before we made serenity our priority, many of us were often resentful, impatient, deceitful, and self- centered. We were not trustworthy or approachable. If you want others to trust and listen to you, get rid of your character defects by working step 4. We must get rid of our character defects to become peaceful people. And when we improve ourselves, we become better influences on everything and everyone.

TO DO: Today my goal will be to make peace in myself, not the acquisition of material things or the control of others.

September 9

When You Try to Control Others, They Control You

So you think you want to control people, places and things? You think this will give you power or perhaps peace. You may even think you can help them by controlling them. But what happens is they control you. They make you obsessed. They make you a nag. They even make you a victim. You lose power by controlling others because it takes energy to control. You lose peace and freedom by controlling others because you are imprisoned by your need to control.

TO DO: Today ask yourself if you are trying to control someone to get something for yourself or whether you are trying to help someone who is obviously struggling and needs help to survive. Usually it is best to let go unless the person needs an intervention or wants help. Otherwise, admit to yourself that you are controlled when you attempt to control, particularly if you are trying to control to satisfy your own ego.

September 10

Love but Try Not to Get Screwed

Forgive, don't resent; love, but try not to get abused; but when you do get less than what you think you deserve, don't beat up on yourself because it happens to all of us. We don't have to let others drive our bus (make us feel worthless). We don't have to be a doormat today. We can live our own lives and let others live theirs (live and let live). Therein lies peace.

TO DO: Stop and think about what you are doing. Make honest, pure, loving, unselfish decisions, but don't forget lessons you have learned. Catch yourself if you are letting people, places, and things run you down just because you are afraid to be assertive.

September 11

A Sense of Humor Is a Serious Thing

In a great scene from the classic movie, Butch Cassidy and the Sundance Kid, Butch and Sundance are trapped by bounty hunters at the edge of a cliff. Butch tells Sundance that their only way out is to jump into the flowing river 1000 feet below. Sundance says he'd rather shoot it out. Butch insists that there are hundreds of pursuers and there's no way to shoot it out and win. Sundance finally confesses that he can't swim. Butch breaks into laughter saying, "Hell, the fall will probably kill us." They then jump together and we see them playfully being carried to safety by the mighty river.

When you really feel like you're at the edge of your cliff, a good sense of humor can save you from heartache. When you're worried about whether you made the right decision or when you are fearing the future or ruminating about the past, try to see some humor in your problem. Sometimes it's even a good exercise to speculate as to the worst case scenario (which will probably never happen) and try to make light of it. A good sense of humor is the highest form of acceptance, and acceptance can be the panacea to those menacing perceptions and phantoms that would seek to plague us.

TO DO: Take it easy today and lighten those frightening thoughts into something that makes you laugh. When discouraged, have faith that your mighty river (your loving Higher Power) has not saved you just to let you drown.

September 12

Change "I WANTS" to "DON'T NEEDS"

I used to get depressed because I was frustrated from not getting what I WANTED. It's not more complicated than that. Not getting what I wanted caused me to feel discouraged and even depressed. I isolated and overslept to numb the pain. As I practice serenity principles, I still don't get what I want. But I know that isolating, raging, overeating, and avoiding doing what I am supposed to be doing, will only increase the hurt. So, I adjust my attitude from I WANT to DON'T NEED. For some strange reason, this attitude adjustment relieves the bad feelings and enables me to do something positive and self satisfying.

TO DO: Today, I will repeat the phrase, "DON'T NEED" every time I say or think, "I WANT." Then, I will do an unselfish action like emptying the dishwasher or calling a lonely person. I will enjoy how wonderful doing an unselfish action makes me feel!

September 13

"Shame is a soul eating emotion."
- Carl Jung

For many of us, our obsessive thinking can be inimical to our serenity. Our thinking sometimes causes us to feel ashamed because it creates negative images about who we are. Our thinking suggests that there is something fundamentally wrong with us...that we are losers, idiots or something even indescribably worse. Our connection to HELP (a Higher Effective Loving Power) conquers shame.

TO DO: Today, I will not allow shame to choke my soul. I will nurture my soul by doing loving actions and connecting to HELP. I will try to become OK with who I really am, to forgive myself for perceived wrongs, and to not judge myself. If I do this, I will not feel ashamed. Today, I will repeat to myself, "End the shame game, end the shame game."

September 14

We Are Not Humans Having a Spiritual Experience, We Are Spirits Having a Human Experience

I like to connect with people spiritually. I spend so much time connecting with others in business. So rarely do I allow others to see my GOOD SPIRIT. It's easier for me to show my spirit to my non-judgmental dog. I used to drink to let my guard down. I felt less self-conscious drunk. But I got in trouble and sick from drinking. And it was a false spirituality because it wasn't me. Remembering that I am more spiritual than human alleviates much of the self- flagellation that I used to experience when I made human mistakes. Today, when I make a mistake, I cut myself a break, relax, and just try to do the next right thing guided by love, unselfishness, honesty, and purity (the four absolutes). Ultimately, it is more beneficial today for me to implement spiritual concepts than it is to implement egotistical concepts. Spirituality fulfills, while egotism leaves me unsatisfied and always wanting more and more.

TO DO: Today I will try to let people see my good spirit. I can try this with anyone. Perhaps carrying a smile or a gentle facial expression is a good place to start.

September 15

Scrub the Floor

"If you in your pain call birth an affliction and the support of the flesh a curse written upon your brow, then I answer that naught but the sweat of your brow shall wash away that which is written."
- from the Prophet.

Scrubbing the floor is a great way to pray, meditate, and use up nervous energy. If you are anxious, scrub the floor. I was told to scrub the floor at a 12 step meeting by a CEO of a big corporation when I told him I was overwhelmed by life. He seemed like an intelligent guy, and I was surprised when he told me to do what I then considered to be a stupid, mundane action. But when I tried it, I found that my anxiety melted away.

TO DO: Today I will scrub the floor, paint the wall, do the dishes, start that exercise program, or something else that will allow me to meditate and exhaust anxious energy. I will do it with love in my heart.

September 16

Perfect Is on Mars, You're on Earth

Would I treat someone else as hard as I treat myself? Am I feeling worthless just because a decision I made didn't work out? Did I make a mistake? An oversight? Should I beat myself up and feel worthless just because I'm imperfect? Until I accept the fact that God doesn't make junk, I'm not going to be able to accept myself.

TO DO: Today I will forgive myself and be grateful that my Higher Effective Loving Power does too. I will not use my imperfections as an excuse to feel worthless or to act out.

September 17

"There are no big deals"
- Hogie

Hogie was a very serene guy. He died with forty one years of sobriety. He helped many a newcomer and always was full of wisdom. His favorite saying was, "There are no big deals." He would wink, smile and say that it seems like a big deal on your wedding day, but in no time at all you are just married, which is a lot of little deals. He would say you get a job which seems like a big deal, but then you need to go to work every day which is a bunch of little deals. Hoagie knew that overwhelmed alcoholics tend to relapse. He knew that certain crises like losing a job, getting a divorce, or losing money caused relapse. So his mantra, "There are no big deals" gave many recovering people the perspective they needed to make it through another day sober. We can use Hogie's philosophy to avoid getting stressed, depressed, and overwhelmed and therefore maintain our serenity.

TO DO: Today, no matter what it is, money, health, no matter what, my mantra is going to be "There are no big deals." But I will remember, the one huge deal is maintaining my serenity!

September 18

Joy Comes Not From Getting What You Want; Joy Comes From Living an Effective Serenity Program

Wants never end. They create more wants. Someone wise told me that "Misery is a function of more and next." Depending on fulfilling wants for joy leads to frustration because they never can be finally fulfilled. A friend could not get a husband and children. Instead of letting this want drive her to insanity, she simply applied the four steps every time she thought about her desire. Gradually her serenity returned. She volunteered to help others, and joyously played with her nieces. She became a leader in her volunteer activities and helped many struggling people become mature, self-sufficient individuals. She would often say that participating in the growth of these "children" gave her fulfillment beyond her wildest expectations and that living the four steps changed her sadness into joy, fear into courage, and resentment into love.

TO DO: When I tell myself I won't be happy until I get what I want, today I will simply be grateful for what I have. I will try to use what I have to live in accordance with a good serenity program.

September 19

"The secret of change is to focus all of your energy, not on fighting the old, but on building the new" - Dan Millman

My dog has an instinct to mark objects he finds when I walk him or let him run free. He marks things by raising his leg and peeing on them. I like to let him run free whenever possible especially on the beach. The problem is he marks beach blankets. One would think I would have learned after the first time to put him on a leash anytime he gets near a beach blanket. But I keep thinking I have him trained not to pee on beach blankets, and I have frequently allowed him to run free near them thinking that he will obey me as he usually does and turn around and come back to me when I call him. But he often doesn't obey me, and once again, he pees on a beach blanket. The consequences are terrible. He has peed on a friend's sweater. He has peed on a coat owned by a young man who threatened me with bodily harm. He has peed on a kind lady's beach chair. This has caused me endless regret. But I still allow him to run free on the beach thinking that he won't repeat the same behavior again and thinking that I can control him by verbal commands.

TO DO: Today I will remember that I will get the same results unless I change my behavior. I will remember that the definition of insanity is doing the same actions repeatedly and expecting different results. Like trying to control my dog without a leash, I will accept that my old ways of doing things don't work to give me serenity. I need to build new ways of dealing with life. I need to change my behavior, not just hope that my old way of dealing with life will magically work this time. I need to get out of denial. Knowing that I have a problem amounts to nothing unless I practice new behaviors like the four steps. I will remember half measures avail us nothing. I will remember that KNOWLEDGE of my problem is only half the battle and I need to do a serenity ACTION (change what I do). I simply need to develop new habits.

September 20

Hopelessness Can Be a New Beginning

If you suddenly feel hopeless because you are miserable, you may actually be at the start of something wonderful. Hitting bottom is often a requirement for change. Hitting bottom does not mean that you have to go to jail or a hospital or turn over your car or something else like that. It simply means that you admit hopelessness. Hopelessness means that you don't have the answers anymore about why you can't control your life. Hopelessness means that you finally know you are lost without an idea of what to do to get better.

Though hopelessness sounds frightening, it is actually a blessing because now you are open to the help you need. You can begin the process of change.

I was able to hit bottom when I was laying on my back staring at the ceiling the day after I had flipped my car over because I was drunk. I said to myself, "I have no clue how to change." I remember thinking that I had no hope. I felt completely empty. But that emptiness gave my Higher Power the room it needed to come in.

TO DO: If you feel hopeless, that's a good thing for positive change. It is better to admit that you don't know what to do rather than to think you can help yourself without help from anyone else. Try making a list of consequences resulting from your misery and try to see how you did not want those consequences. This list will help you see how you were out of control. Then, it might be a good time to call someone for help.

September 21

A Truly Miserable Person Won't Give up a Life of Failure Without a Fight

It takes endurance to be miserable. The physical struggle, the lying, the financial losses, the relationship losses, the day to day depression, the painful cravings, the fight to endure one's misery never seems to end even though life just gets worse and worse.

TO DO: It's OK to give up doing things the way you always have done them. Accept change and don't return to your old ways of reacting to life. Don't return to fear, resentment, jealousy, and greed. Instead keep practicing love, kindness, unselfishness, and purity. Accept and adapt rather than deny and force. You will then know the peace and enlightenment you could never find through manipulation and denial.

September 22

An Egomaniac Can Be in the Gutter and Still Look Down on People

Our egos are such dangerous things. Despite suffering self-imposed humiliation after humiliation, our arrogance can still make us think we are better than others. This attitude wreaks havoc on our serenity. We need to be aware as soon as we start comparing ourselves to others. Such comparisons throw our egos out of balance and kill our serenity. We especially need to be on guard for feelings of superiority. When we don't look down on people, we don't isolate, and we actually feel more included in society rather than excluded.

TO DO: If you find yourself judging others or if you find you are adopting an attitude that you are better than anyone else, remember humility, not arrogance, leads us to serenity. Stay grateful today, not proud.

September 23

Are You White Knuckling or
Are You Serene?

If you are struggling, you may be white knuckling. White knuckling is no fun. White knuckling means you are trying not to lose your composure by will power alone. White knuckling causes you to feel stressed and dissatisfied. White knuckling means you are repressed and not serene. Facing life without practicing serenity principles like the four steps makes you repressed and interferes with your joy and freedom. Sooner or later, white knuckling can result in bad consequences like broken relationships and apathy.

TO DO: You will be sad, anxious, and fearful unless you implement a good daily recovery program. Accept, be grateful, have perspective, stay flexible. Connect to a loving force. Sweep your own side of the street and stop trying to control the things you cannot change. This simple discipline, practiced throughout this day, will lead you to peace of mind. Don't deny yourself this joy.

September 24

Don't Pull the Trigger

There can often be people, places, or things which can trigger emotional regression. A trigger can be a visit to our parents who abused us. A trigger can be a television show, certain foods, a cold day, a disgruntled boss, the morning. Yes, a trigger can be anything which has the potential to distance us from our serenity. It is helpful to your serenity to be able to identify triggers and to prepare yourself to deal positively with them. Ways to prepare include making sure you say the serenity prayer or serenity poem before interacting with triggering people, places or things. Other ways are to make sure you are well rested or mindful of the need to apply the four steps if confronted with a trigger. It is important to identify triggers and to prepare for them as best as possible to maintain your serenity.

TO DO: Think about what happened before you last lost your serenity. Take your time and try to remember what events, people, places or things triggered you. Make a list of these triggers and create a plan to avoid having them disturb your peace of mind.

September 25

My Arrogance Gave Me Wings to Fly Then Took Away the Sky

My arrogance (my overblown ego) made me feel high. It masked my fear and destroyed my peace of mind. It gave me wings to fly, but it took away the sky. My arrogance was fueled by trying to control everything, by the ruthless pursuit of trying to fulfill my every selfish desire. I felt that I didn't need anyone's help. I believed that I was always right and the World was at fault for my undoing. Today I know that it is better to practice humility rather than arrogance. It is better to accept and adapt rather than blindly control everyone and everything. I know that connecting to a Higher Effective Loving Force empowers me. I know that I should look at what I can do to change myself rather than blame others.

TO DO: Today I will resist the urge to let my ego run my life. I will follow the urge to be arrogant through to its bitter end by remembering where it ultimately took me. I will enjoy the empowering humility brought about by practicing the four steps.

September 26

The Only Thing That Does Not Change
Is Change

Before I started practicing serenity principles, I thought I could stop things from changing. Ask yourself if you can relate to that? Do you think you can stop your child from growing up? Can you stop your body from aging? Can you stop your favorite sports team from trading players you love? Everything changes, even the air we breathe changes and we cannot control it. You can also look at the benefits of change. Getting older means you probably don't have to take as many final examinations as you used to. Your child's growth means he or she may be more likely to pay for his or her own food and clothing.

TO DO: Don't allow the temptation to stop change make you miserable today. Let go, relax, accept and adapt rather than deny and control. Trying to control change will definitely frustrate you while accepting change gives you the option to laugh along with it and be content.

September 27

Have You Failed Trying Moderation?

To achieve serenity, we may need to eliminate some behaviors. For example, we may have tried to be at peace even though we lie a little or hate just a few people or worry over just one or two things. We may be allowing certain people to whom we are attached (like our parents, children, or spouse) to ruin our serenity because we cannot exercise any assertiveness with them. We may have, for example, tried to control our substance use but found that we cannot use moderately. Serenity involves taking an inventory of our self-defeating behaviors and learning how to resist the temptation to fall prey to them.

TO DO: Today, I will make a list of a few behaviors which I need to eliminate from my life. I will then seek guidance, if appropriate from a professional, on how to implement a strategy to stop allowing them to ruin my serenity.

September 28

It's Not the Caboose That Kills You, It's the Engine That Kills You

We return to misery by doing the first act governed by resentment or fear. That first act is what leads us down the wrong path. That first act is the engine of our troubles. The last act which we think causes us the trouble is really just the natural progression of the first act. That last act is just the caboose being pulled by the engine. Therefore it is critical that we remember to avoid starting to head in the wrong direction.

TO DO: Today, and every day, I will remember to start my day with a meditation on the Four Steps of Serenity. Upon awakening, I will meditate by saying, "Today I will accept and adapt, be grateful for having my needs fulfilled, connect to my Higher sense of being, and fix myself rather than control others." This will keep me from allowing the engine of discontent to interfere with my serenity.

September 29

Look at Change as an Opportunity
Rather Than a Burden

Even though we know that our behaviors are contributing to our misery, we fear change. Perhaps it's because we are uncomfortable trying something unfamiliar. Perhaps we have to have faith in trying a new way of living. Whatever the reason, we have to overcome resistance to change in order to head from misery to serenity. This we know in our hearts.

TO DO: Today, I will have faith in approaching life in a new, positive way. I will nurture my Five Natures. I will avoid Serenity Killers. I will use the four steps rather than my old approach to life. I will look at change as an opportunity for peace rather than a burden.

September 30

FEAR Stands for
False Evidence Appearing Real

So much of what we feel to be threatening simply isn't true. We live with anxiety but most of what we fear never happens. We construct in our minds great walls of fear, but these walls really are of our own perception and nothing actually is threatening.

TO DO: Today, every time I feel fear, I will examine to see if what I fear is really such an awful threat to my needs. I will distinguish intelligent caution from pervasive, irrational fear.

October 1

Helping Is the Sunny Side of Enabling

Sometimes it feels good to help others. We are taught in various religions, for example, to help others. But I learned in Al-Anon that sometimes helping is the sunny side of enabling. In other words, there is a fine line between helping someone and enabling them to continue their self-defeating ways. Take for example the wife who holds a job, takes care of the children, pays all the bills, and covers up for her husband when he can't show up at his job because he had been drinking all night.

There is also a fine line between helping and nagging. It is important to let go sometimes and let someone else experience their own consequences. Unless the person experiences consequences, the person won't change.

TO DO: Today I am going to try to be a good example for other people. I will be careful and mindful about whether helping them is actually enabling them to continue to do harm to themselves. A useful guide is whether I am losing my own serenity in order to help someone else. If I am losing my serenity, it is likely I should just let go and not interfere.

October 2

You Can Control Your Mind

The Serenity Prayer helps us distinguish between what we can control and what we cannot control. The one thing we can control is our mind. We can control what we think about. However, it takes concentration. Meditation helps us control our minds. This mind control allows us to focus on Serenity inducing sayings rather than misery inducing things.

TO DO: Today I am going to meditate for one minute. I am going to gaze at a single spot, and take five relaxing breaths. While gazing, I am going to think only about the word "love." This training will help me control my mind. This mind control, is a powerful tool in giving me serenity especially during challenging times. This mind control will help me avoid allowing triggers to send me spiraling downward.

October 3

When I'm Serene I Can Be a Good Person, When I'm Not Serene I Have to Convince Myself I'm a Good Person

When I was lost in misery, I would spend hours telling myself that I wasn't so bad, that my misery was really everybody else's doing. I would try to defend myself by telling myself that school, taxes, my family, and work were unfair and that I really was doing all that I could but everything was just too much to handle. I would try to convince myself and everyone else that I was a good person. As I practice serenity principles, I am able to do the next reasonable thing. I am able to pay my bills, be kind to others, live decently. I don't have to defend my ego. I don't have to convince myself I am good because I am able to do good things.

TO DO: Take a quick look at the 30 serenity killers listed in this book. Are you doing anything to kill your serenity? Ask yourself if you are a decent person, or whether or not you feel you need to convince someone else that you are a decent person.

October 4

Do the Next Reasonable Thing

No matter what happens, try to do the next reasonable thing by practicing the four steps. Accepting, adapting, being grateful for needs fulfilled, having perspective, being flexible, connecting to a higher power, and fixing ourselves rather than others allows us to do the next reasonable thing. Usually doing the next reasonable thing means that we don't have an endless mental committee meeting about it. For example, unless it is clearly someone else's responsibility, wash the dishes, don't think about it, just wash them. If you make a mistake, don't worry about it, just learn from it and do the next reasonable thing. The reasonable thing is not the perfect thing or the thing that you may want to do. But it is the thing to do if serenity is your priority.

TO DO: Today I am not going to become paralyzed by trying to conjure a perfect solution to every problem. I am not going to overthink. I am going to do the next reasonable thing.

October 5

It Kills My Serenity
When I Forget to Be Grateful

A grateful person is a serene person. Finding reasons to be grateful is a key serenity practice. Especially in the midst of difficulties, especially when life seems to be hard, finding something to be grateful for relieves self-pity and leads us back on a positive path. The first arguably disgusting thing I do each day is clean up my beloved dog's poop. This used to upset me. Then, I changed my attitude about this task. I became grateful that I had a potty bag to clean up the poop. I became grateful for having a loyal friend. I became grateful for being able to practice humility.

TO DO: Today, I will make a list of three things for which I am grateful. I will think of things that give me gratitude if I am headed toward self-pity.

October 6

It's Not Whether Your Glass Is Half Full, It's Whether You Have a Glass at All

Even if I don't have water in my glass, if I have a glass, I can at least have somewhere to put any water I may find. I have hope. I am able to keep a positive attitude knowing I am prepared as I set out on each day's adventure. In life, I need to appreciate what I have and use what I have to meet life's challenges.

TO DO: Today I will have hope. I will be at peace knowing I am heading in the right direction. I will be optimistic about trying to reach goals, and I will congratulate myself for making progress. I will try to find water, but in the meantime, I will be happy to have a glass even if it has no water in it yet.

October 7

A Rich Person Knows He Has Enough

True wealth is freedom from cravings. For example, today I was thinking about getting a new television when I realized I already had a television. I realized that I did not think about getting a new television when I was enjoying watching the television I have. It occurred to me that I am truly wealthy and fulfilled when I know I have what I need. This type of thinking frees me from fears about what I think I don't have.

TO DO: Today I will be grateful for the fulfillment of my needs. I will be grateful for the air I breathe, the love I have, and the food and shelter that sustains me. As soon as a craving creeps into my thinking, I will feel the wealth of thinking about how my needs are fulfilled.

October 8

"Before you diagnose yourself with depression or low self-esteem, first make sure that you are not, in fact, just surrounding yourself with assholes."
- William Gibson

Healthy boundaries are a bigger deal than most of us (especially codependents) are willing to admit. We tend to allow others to victimize us and all we do is submit to the endless cycle of complaining and suffering, complaining and suffering. Many of us even blame ourselves for other peoples' oppression. Indeed, we cannot change, control, or cure other people but we can set limits as to our exposure to them. If we have to be exposed to them, we can create personal sanity habits to deal serenely with their toxicity.

TO DO: All toxic relationships must be dealt with on a case by case basis. But the first step is to list your toxic relationships and then commit to seeking guidance on each. Sometimes professional guidance is necessary.

October 9

Serenity Is What We Get When We Quit Hoping for a Better Past

This saying reminds us that we can't control what has happened and that we must live in the now. Recently I sold my house. After the closing, I kept thinking why didn't I negotiate harder for a better deal. How many examples in every day life can you think of where you hoped for a better past? We lose our peace of mind when we think like this, when we dwell on the past. We must remember that we made decisions based on the facts before us at the time and that it was impossible for us to predict exactly how those decisions would work out. So often we blame ourselves for things we did. All this does is feed our shame and destroy our self-image. Our past was simply part of our journey and letting go of things we regret puts us on the path of serenity.

TO DO: Today, I will be aware if I am regretting things that have happened. I will let them go each time they pop into my mind and substitute thinking about them with thoughts of living fully and happily in the present.

October 10

Everything Will Be Perfect Once I...

Everything will be perfect once I get into Stanford...

Everything will be just perfect when I sell my house...

Everything will be perfect once my wife loses 10 lb...

Everything will just be perfect once I lose 10 lbs...

The list is endless. If you find yourself saying "everything will be perfect when something happens," you need to appreciate what you have right now and realize that nothing will ever be exactly perfect.

TO DO: Today I will not say "everything will be perfect when..." Instead I will accept the perfect serenity of appreciating what I have in this moment.

October 11

If You Think Repetition Is Bad,
Feel Your Pulse

This saying applies to everything! It reminds us that we need to read similar messages every day in this daily message book. Practice helps us break through our long standing, steadfast self-defeating behaviors. Like our pulse, repetitive serenity lessons are life enhancing. Also, as we change, the things that we read previously take on new and more important meanings when we study them again.

TO DO: If you feel like you are getting bored with serenity practice, remember that all of us need to hear the same messages over and over again for them to keep us on the right path.

October 12

Misery Is Not Cured, Only Arrested

The path to serenity does not end. We must stay on the path by daily practice or we will return to our less fulfilling life. We are not cured of self-defeating behaviors. They are arrested each day as we practice the four steps and give adequate attention to each of our Five Natures. One effective daily ritual is to start your day by saying a quick prayer or some kind of focused recitation in which you commit to applying the four steps and to giving balanced attention to your Five Natures.

TO DO: Today, and everyday henceforth, I will say the following immediately after I read the daily message. "Loving power, please let me fearlessly face each challenge today by accepting and adapting, by being grateful for my needs fulfilled, by having perspective, by being flexible, by connecting with a Higher Effective Loving Power, and by seeking to change my character defects rather than those of others. Let me strengthen my physical, mental, emotional, social and spiritual Natures so that I may be of maximum service to myself and others."

October 13

Don't Let Conflict Cause You Resentment

You want to go sunbathing but its a cloudy day. You need to drive to work on time, but first you must stop for gas. You want to use the computer, but the internet is down. You want to sell your product for one price, but potential buyers want to pay less. The list is endless. Don't let natural conflict fuel resentment or other negative thoughts and feelings. Conflict is inevitable.

TO DO: Today, be aware when you are letting natural conflict fuel negative thoughts and feelings. Practice acceptance, separate desires from needs, connect to loving thoughts, and stay flexible. Keep remembering that conflict is acceptable. Meditate on this concept throughout this day.

October 14

Money Is Just a Bunch of Dead Presidents on Dirty Paper

Money can't get you serene. Money actually allows miserable people to continue being miserable because they think (1) having money must mean they are happy even though they know they are not, and (2) they can't be afraid even though they fear they will lose their money. It is far more difficult for people with money to change. Far more valuable than money is knowing how money can't make you happy, knowing that good relationships and positive thinking create true wealth, how freedom from relying on money creates independence, and how hope for eternal peace rather than daily fear yields peace and enlightenment.

TO DO: Today, regardless of how much I have, I will not rely on money for serenity. I will focus instead on staying on the right path by implementing effective serenity principles like the four steps and the balancing of my Five Natures.

October 15

Woulda, Coulda, Shoulda

If only I woulda gotten into law school. If only she couda seen that I was a good guitarist. I shoulda taken that trip to Spain. Whatever you tag on to wouldas, couldas, and shouldas, you are only going to make yourself feel bad over things you cannot change. Wouldas, couldas, and shouldas are vestiges of the past. We are learning each day to live in today for that is all we truly have. We are learning to let go of shame, blame, and guilt by correcting our thinking every time we hear ourselves think what we woulda, coulda, or shoulda done.

TO DO: Today, I will be on guard each time I say or think "woulda, coulda, or shoulda." I will accept my past and be grateful for the chance to live on the path of serenity now.

October 16

Don't Worry About Getting Your Way

This is perhaps the most challenging of all the serenity killing habits to forgo. Our egos and self image tend to be inextricably tied to getting our own way. With the best of intentions, we struggle to get our way. Yet, things seldom turn out exactly the way we want them to. More often, there is some curve in the road, and those curves can threaten our serenity. Even if we do get our way, what we thought we wanted may not give us the serenity we had envisioned it would. It is far better for our peace of mind to set goals and stay flexible as things change. It is far better to keep perspective when things don't turn out exactly as planned. It is far more fulfilling to stay grateful rather than to be in a constant state of wanting more.

TO DO: Today, I will not worry about getting my way. I will try to do the next reasonable thing as I head in the direction of compassion, good work, and love rather than egotistical accomplishments.

October 17

"Care About People's Approval, and You Will Always Be Their Prisoner"
- Lao Tzu

Yet, another serenity killer is "people pleasing". People pleasing actually comes from being our own toughest critic. We beat ourselves up if we feel like we are not living up to others' expectations. We have allowed our desire to be accepted to interfere with our ability to have our own opinions, be original, and be ourselves. This does not mean that we should ignore criticism and guidance to change and improve, but when we are doing so only to please others we become their prisoner.

TO DO: Today, I will not beat myself up if I feel like I am different from others. I will not even worry about what I think others are thinking about me. I will enjoy this freedom. So long as I am not hurting anyone, including myself, I will actually congratulate myself for being different and original!

October 18

"Great Spirits Have Always Encountered Violent Opposition From Mediocre Minds" - Albert Einstein

You ask, "Why am I the only one trying to learn how to surf? Why am I the only one who enjoys figuring out a complex math problem? Why am I the only one befriending the alienated?" Albert Einstein answers, "Because you have a great spirit! You have the ability to see beauty in something that most cannot. You are willing to face a challenge where most will not. You enjoy something that most find frightening."

TO DO: Today whenever I am tempted to give up trying something or when I find myself criticizing myself because I feel different from others, I will instead congratulate myself and carry on free from the need to fall into the pack of mediocrity.

October 19

I Put the "Pro" in Procrastination

Nothing creates as much anxiety as procrastination. It usually comes from fear of failing. Some of us don't want to try to do what we should because we are perfectionists. Others may simply put things off because the tasks are difficult. Still others may not want conflict. Yet another reason for procrastination is that there are too many things to do. Disorganization is also a common reason for procrastination. It is important for you to explore why you procrastinate and then address those issues because procrastination is a serenity killer par excellence.

TO DO: Today, I will not be a professional (pro) at procrastination. I will list what I need to get done and tackle the most time sensitive and difficult tasks as early in the day as possible. I will commit to not being perfect, to not caring if I fail, and to not fearing conflict because conflict is normal and unavoidable.

October 20

Enjoy the Fight!

It's not whether you win or lose. It's whether or not you enjoy the struggle. And you will have struggles whether or not you are looking for it. Life has conflict. Regardless of your wealth, race, gender, or age, challenges arise. To run from the fight, only makes it worse so don't escape by hiding in your bedroom or turning to a bad habit. Accept life on life's terms and adapt your attitude to one which enjoys the struggle rather than dreads it. Of course, if you are struggling for something you know in your heart is wrong, solely for ego satisfaction, to nurture a resentment or other self-defeating behavior, or something that is simply not worth the time or effort, it is better for your serenity to let it go. If you feel like life is a constant struggle, cut yourself a break and let go of fighting everything and everybody. However, if you are avoiding facing the natural challenges that life throws you, do not fear the struggle.

TO DO: Today I am not going to fear the struggle. I am going to enjoy the adventure. I am not going to run from the fight. I am going to enjoy it and not judge myself if things don't work out as I want them to. My motto will be "Bring it on!"

October 21

Whatever You Do Today, Let It Be Enough

We are all subject to conflict, and we all need to courageously struggle by accepting and adapting. We all need to fight the good fight and not run from it. However, many of us drive ourselves insane because we feel we need to constantly conquer the World. We view life as a continual struggle. When we inevitably fall short, we feel as if there is something wrong with us. We find we are constantly measuring ourselves. Questions overwhelm us: "Do we have enough money for our age? Are our grades as good as they should be?" We also second guess ourselves: "Did we handle that problem correctly?" We also worry about things we can't change, "Are our noses too big or too small?" All of this leads to a sense of shame that destroys our serenity. Indeed, we need to be concerned about ridding ourselves of character defects like laziness, greed, hatred, and fear. Sure, we can sometimes be a bit more organized or thoughtful. But obsessively measuring and driving ourselves only leads to anxiety. Some days, perhaps today, we need to accept ourselves and give ourselves a break. We do not have to worry about falling short.

TO DO: Relax. Stop endlessly pushing yourself. Stop with the continual measuring of yourself. Quit comparing. Enjoy the adventure and be flexible. Simply do the next reasonable thing with as much love and kindness that you can muster. Whatever you do today, don't let it keep you from accepting and loving yourself. Like the serenity poem says, "Not all good, not all bad. Judgment only makes me mad."

October 22

Stay in Your Own Lane

Correct yourself, not others. Adjust your own attitude, not everyone else's. The saying, "Stay in your own lane" reminds us to practice the 4th step, to fix ourselves, to clean our own doorstep, to sweep our own side of the street. When we keep our car in our own lane, we have the best chance of not causing an accident. When we drive our car into someone else's lane, all kinds of trouble can occur.

TO DO: Today I am going to stay in my own lane and mind my own business. I am not going to worry about what others are doing. If someone is driving into my lane, I will set up a healthy boundary. I may try to help someone else who asks for help. But I am going to remember to fix myself first to enjoy the freedom that results.

October 23

Just Get on the Bus and Ride

Sometimes the road is bumpy,

Sometimes it has unexpected stops and starts,

Sometimes there's a detour,

Sometimes somebody farts.

The key is to ride it out. Accept that you cannot take over the driver's seat. Know that fussing and trying to escape through some bad habit will only add to your own pity party and make everyone else want to avoid you.

TO DO: Just get on the bus and ride. Sooner or later, it will take you somewhere near where you wanted to go (maybe even some place better). Be patient, stay positive, look out the window and choose to see the beauty. Enjoy the ride!

October 24

Sweep Your Own Side of the Street

When I was miserable, I knew what was best for everyone else and I either told them so or bottled up my anger because they wouldn't do what I wanted. The result usually only caused others to resent me. Today, I have learned that everybody makes mistakes, that everybody has character issues, and that everyone else has their own Higher Power which I certainly cannot control. I have learned that conflict is not something that only I am subjected to, and that maybe, just maybe, I don't know what's best for everyone (including myself sometimes). This new attitude gives me a wonderful peace of mind.

TO DO: Today, I am going to sweep my own side of the street, not everyone else's. I will enjoy the peace and freedom from unnecessary responsibility. I will trust that the universe will supply my needs along the way.

October 25

Not All Good, Not All Bad
Judgment Only Makes Me Mad

"My neighbor hates my dog. She is just mean that's all. She is unfair and doesn't understand how fantastic my little puppy is," I think as images of the Wicked Witch of the West stuffing Toto into her basket to be taken to the pound fill my head. Another example is the overwhelmed post office clerk who curtly dismisses my questions about different mailing options. Self-righteous anger results when I judge others as a Wicked Witch. Better I try to live within the law, keep from black and white thinking, and judge not. My judgment on whether or not someone is wicked has no effect on who I judge; judgment only affects my attitude. Better I remember that people aren't bad, they just may be in a bad situation.

TO DO: Today, I will repeat the phrase, "Not all good, not all bad, judgment only makes me mad." I will remember to positively affect situations with a good and loving attitude rather than labeling everything or everyone as good or bad.

October 26

God Give Me Patience and Give It to Me Now

This classic recovery statement reminds me that I can even be impatient and demanding with my Higher Power. I can forget that perhaps the lesson is in the waiting, not the getting…that I am perhaps selfish and puerile if I think I deserve anything right now and that TIME stands for Things I Must Earn (even the ability to have patience). For example, I must meditate and practice the four steps to slowly develop patience. Today I know that nothing operates on my timetable, that any progress I make takes time and practice. Best of all, I know that if I am in the moment, there is no waiting and thus no need for patience.

TO DO: Today, I will remember to enjoy this moment rather than dwell on why I am not getting my way now. I will repeat the phrase from the Serenity poem, "Not my will, not my way, My Higher Power saves my day." I will remember to be flexible.

October 27

TIME Stands for Things I Must Earn

So many of us feel that we will never be trusted by our family and friends because we haven't been trustworthy in the past. Others can't seem to understand why they are not trusted. For example, they complain, "Can't my wife trust me now that I am no longer drinking?" For those of us who are in the process of making living amends by changing problematic character issues, the saying "TIME stands for things I must earn" is of great importance. Repeating this phrase will give you patience and understanding as you make the daily small steps to change for the better without becoming resentful because others naturally may still be cautious about fully trusting you.

TO DO: Today, I will remember that nothing has the potential to destroy my serenity faster than the feeling of impatience coupled with the sense of not being trusted. I will say that "TIME stands for things I must earn" each time impatience manifests its ugly head. I won't try to force anyone to trust me. Rather, I will simply do trustworthy actions knowing that the result will be immediate peace of mind and eventually perhaps the reemergence of trust others place in me.

October 28

The Only Thing That Doesn't Change Is Change

Serenity killer number 6 is refusing to accept change. To refuse to accept change is to refuse to accept reality. Yet we stubbornly cling to our old ways of dealing with things. Living serenely requires us to change old self-defeating habits. It requires us to unlearn steadfast beliefs that are making it impossible for us to be at peace. Nevertheless, most of us so abhor change that we won't try to change unless we are afraid that failing to do so will threaten something we feel we can't live without. In other words, often a crisis is necessary for someone to change. In addiction recovery, people rarely stop using their drug of choice unless they have actually "hit bottom." Hitting bottom is different for everyone, but suffice it to say that it is a place where drugs (including alcohol) have taken the addict to a state where the addict feels he can never stand returning. So, if you are miserable, hopeless, and feel you have hit an emotional bottom, you are actually in a good place because now you finally may be in the right state of mind to find serenity.

TO DO: Today, I will cherish change, rather than fight it. I will accept that change is inevitable even with things I don't want to change. I will seek to apply step 1 of the four steps by exercising acceptance and adaption, faithful in the belief that eventually serenity will be the reward.

October 29

LeBron James Missed the Game Winning Foul Shot

On February 23, 2021, Lebron James stepped to the foul line with the score tied at the end of the game. His shot bounced off the front of the rim. He missed the game winning shot and his team went on to lose. He calmly walked off the court after missing. He didn't seem distraught. LeBron, arguably the greatest player ever, is a professional who knows missing game winning foul shots is part of the game. He doesn't dramatize it or allow it to crush him. He is a good example of what we all go through. We all miss the game winning shot, probably many times in life. The key is to accept our humanity to stay serene. The key is to remember that if LeBron can miss the game winning shot, then ordinary folks like us can do it to, not be devastated, and move on to the next game. The way LeBron handled missing the shot made me appreciate his true greatness even more than if he had made the shot.

TO DO: Today, I will accept my missed shots. I will accept myself unconditionally and instead of beating myself up, I will move on and do the next reasonable thing.

October 30

It's Not What You're Eating,
It's Who You Eat With That Counts

I was mentally debating over whether I should just be simple and get a pizza for my friend or whether I should take him out to a complicated expensive dinner. It occurred to me, that the expensive, complicated dinner was going to be a pain in the neck, and that it was motivated by my ego wanting to impress him. I then remembered that I chose this person to be my friend because he was not involved in ego games. I opted to keep it simple and get the pizza. I am always happier when I keep it simple, not let my ego interfere, and remember that it's serenity inducing to have a true friend rather than someone I need to impress.

TO DO: Today I am going to keep things simple and not allow my ego to interfere with my peace of mind. I will remember to value relationships over ego gratification. I will repeat often that it is not what I eat, but who I eat it with that matters.

October 31

Am I Evil?

Don't worry, you are not. At some point in our lives, we all wonder if we are good or bad, and many of us, at some point, believe we are bad, evil, sociopathic even. We ask ourselves how we could have done this or that. We are shocked at our capacity to be callous, selfish, hateful, perverse. We mourn about how we thought certain behaviors, which we once thought were reserved only for the depraved, have now become our behaviors. We feel guilty, ashamed, sickened by our own character issues. Take solace. Since we all seem to question ourselves in this way at some point, perhaps this questioning is not so out of the ordinary. Perhaps a sudden strain of our conscience is normal human behavior. Nevertheless, we should look at periods of shame as a wake up call to perhaps enlist aid in addressing behaviors that make us feel ashamed.

TO DO: Today, I refuse to label myself as evil. At the same time, I refuse to sweep under the rug behaviors which I need to examine. I will take a quick personal moral inventory and where I feel I am falling short, I will ask a safe advisor to suggest where I might be able to find help in addressing possible changes. I will not do this to please anyone else. Rather I will do this as a means to maintain my own peace of mind.

November 1

Are You Fretting Over Luxury Problems?

The lights on my Christmas tree won't light. My golf swing seems irreparable. I got the middle seat in the airplane. I was served pinto beans rather than the black beans I ordered. I got stuck in a traffic jam. You can easily add to this list of so-called luxury problems: the typical issues that we all face from day to day. These are the small stuff which can throw us into momentary fits of anger, which can trigger us into thinking that life is not fair, which can add up to ruining our day.

TO DO: Today, I will practice the four steps, particularly step 2 (separating wants from needs). I will not let luxury problems ruin my day.

November 2

Think Happy Thoughts

More important than doing things that we think will make us happy is to think happy thoughts. Negative thinkers worry, ruminate, and overanalyze. If you tend to default to negativity, try forcing yourself to think happy thoughts instead. Some examples of happy thoughts: "I helped someone today." "I had something good to eat." "Someone was kind to me." "I enjoyed playing guitar." "The tree was beautiful." The list can be endless. This concept does not mean that we should deny our true range of human emotions. For example, sometimes we need to grieve and we cannot ignore suffering or mask painful feelings. To do so, would be toxic. But for those of us who chronically ruminate and tend toward negativity, thinking happy thoughts could prove to be beneficial. The difference that "thinking happy" makes to one's day is truly amazing!

TO DO: Today, I will observe my thoughts. As soon as I discover that I am worrying, regretting, or overanalyzing, I am going to substitute those thoughts with happy thoughts.

November 3

Don't Stop Doing It Just Because It Works

Many of us don't like to follow orders. We prefer suggestions. Also
we tend to stop doing things that work well. We say to ourselves,
"OK. I got it. No need to do that anymore." This may be the biggest
mistake we could make. It is important to look at serenity as
something we could lose if we stop practicing. We should remember
that misery is "doing push-ups in the parking lot" and getting
stronger even if we are not miserable. Therefore we must stay one
step ahead of it by continuing to do what works.

TO DO: Today, I will remember to deal with life by using the four
steps and by devoting time to each of my Five Natures. Even if
I think I understand the recovery process, I must keep doing the
recovery process because knowledge avails us nothing. Serenity is
all about action.

November 4

You Can't Stay Clean On Yesterday's Shower

If you think you can stay serene by relying on what you did for your serenity in the past, you are in danger. Misery is still out there, waiting, even if you are feeling serene today. To avoid falling back, you must do something serenity oriented today. That could be calling a friend, reading your serenity literature, or attending a support meeting. It could also be living the right way now by making an amend to someone you have harmed. It could be making a decision to turn your will and life over to the care of your Higher Power (which can be your recovery program, spiritual force, holistic approach, or a combination of whatever restores you to sanity without causing harm).

TO DO: Refuse to be lazy or depressed! Refuse to procrastinate! What can you do right now to practice your serenity program?

November 5

Are You Suffering From Analysis Paralysis?

Hamlet was suffering from analysis paralysis. Always questioning ("To be or not to be..."), never doing. Analysis Paralysis is described as the state of being addicted to thinking. It is a compulsive and unhealthy relationship with one's own thinking. It makes it difficult to focus on work, school, or personal relationships. It makes one procrastinate. It can cause panic attacks and high blood pressure. It therefore interferes with peace of mind and life.

TO DO: Today, I will be aware if I have analysis paralysis. I refuse to let my thinking cause me anxiety. I will set time limits on decision making. I will accept myself unconditionally even if something I do does not turn out as planned. I will use kind language when I talk to myself. I will remind myself not to be a perfectionist. I will accept and be comfortable with uncertainty. I will take a break and do something else (exercise, healthy eating, reading a book) if I find I am obsessively thinking and come back to the problem later. I will remember that there is no such thing as the perfect decision and that there is always a good alternative even if things don't seem to come to the result I intended.

November 6

Over the Long-Term
Everything Will Be Okay

Even if you make mistakes and things don't work out in the short-term, over the long-term everything will be okay, and likely better than you expected, if you concentrate on serenity principles. Even if it is only soul-strengthening that results, you will benefit because soul-strengthening is what leads to the serenity that perhaps you have been seeking erroneously through other means like material acquisition, pain avoidance, bad habits, etc. So don't be so concerned about the short-term results. Don't blame yourself or others if things don't immediately work out. Over the long-term, you will be better off because you will have learned how to experience true serenity.

TO DO: Today I will be less concerned about the short-term results related to things I wish would work out my way. I will have faith that by practicing the principles of Serenity, I will gain long-term peace.

November 7

The George Costanza Principle

There was a character on the classic comedy show, "Seinfeld" named George Costanza, who always did everything wrong. His fundamental flaw was that he always opted to tell lies that were eventually revealed. One day, he decided to shed his ego defenses, and chose to do the opposite of everything that he always did. He mustered the courage to approach an attractive woman. He introduced himself not with some fake opening line, but by saying, "My name is George, I'm 30 years old, unemployed, and I live with my parents." The woman was quite intrigued, obviously attracted to his honesty, and they ultimately had a fantastic romantic interlude.

Applying the George Costanza principle to attaining Serenity is simple. When we get into a pity party, we think about the opposite: what we are grateful for. When we think about how we are not getting our way, we focus on unselfishness. When we have to do something difficult, we tell ourselves that we are going to make this difficult chore fun by having a sense of humor, making a game out of it and being kind. When afraid, we have courage. When doubtful, we have faith. When impatient, we wait. When we feel like we need to tell a lie in order to protect our ego, we tell the truth. We simply do the George Costanza principle of thinking and doing the opposite. This gives us unconditional self-acceptance and joy.

TO DO: Today I am going to exercise the George Costanza principle. If I think negatively, I am going to substitute it with a positive thought borne from gratitude, perspective and flexibility. If I am tempted to defend my ego, I will risk being vulnerable without shame and with a sense of being absolutely OK with who I am.

November 8

Pink Clouds Won't Last,
But That's OK

One of the many benefits of practicing serenity principles is the
GREAT FEELINGS you will have. This elation/ecstasy is sometimes
referred to as the PINK CLOUD! Pink clouds will float away, but
may come back another day.

Pink clouds appear at different times for different people. Sometimes
they occur soon after we make serenity the priority, sometimes a bit
later. ENJOY THEM. Just don't let their appearance make you think
you are cured so that you can stop practicing serenity principles.
Know that you may come down from the pink cloud and that's OK.
In other words, you may feel down again after experiencing the pink
cloud, but that is perfectly normal. Don't let that make you think
your serenity program is failing. Stick with it. Staying serene means
that you are going to experience a range of human emotions and we
don't have to escape from those feelings.

TO DO: Today, I will enjoy any pink clouds and I will not fear
coming down from them because I know I will land on my feet so
long as I stick with my serenity program.

November 9

The Best Way to Be Patient?

When I was drinking, I was always halfway there. I was never there. I was always waiting or struggling. I never made it anywhere. I had such big plans. Always looking forward with arrogance and grandiosity, but living with such low self-esteem that I really had no chance to accomplish anything. In recovery, I have learned to simply take it one day at a time...to make reasonable plans, but not worry about the results...and best of all to appreciate the beauty of this moment. Even if the moment is challenging, I am able to face it. And soon the challenges pass. I am never struggling to be patient because I am no longer waiting for anything to happen. Rather I am living in this moment. Rather than being impatient and being miserable over not yet getting what I want, I feel grateful I have all that I need right now.

TO DO: Today, I will defeat the agony of impatience and any other stinking thinking by simply living in this moment by doing whatever I am supposed to do that is right in front of me. What a relief!

November 10

Are You Self Sabotaging?

Self-sabotaging occurs when someone cannot tolerate stress. Even though that person may want to achieve a goal, the stress of trying to attain that goal is so severe that the person will unconsciously do whatever is possible to end the stress, including that which will destroy the possibility of attaining the goal.

For example, the law student who studies endlessly to pass the bar exam then convinces himself that one drink of alcohol well ease the stress but ends up getting drunk on the eve of the bar exam. Or someone who wants something so desperately that he sends a reactive email which alienates the person who is in control of whether or not he gets it. Or the tennis player who gets into an argument with the referee late in the match and gets penalized for his behavior thereby hurting his chances to win. All of these examples seem to involve someone whose self-esteem is so low that he can't stand the feeling of winning. So the person unconsciously does something uncharacteristically stupid to ensure he cannot succeed.

TO DO: Today ask yourself if you are self-sabotaging? Are you stressed because you desperately want something to happen? Do you feel as if you are unworthy of success so you opt to do something to fail? Are you attaching too much importance to something? Are you reacting with emotions rather than considered thought? Make a plan to live the four steps rather than self-sabotage and return to a state of peace of mind. Serene people are less likely to self- sabotage.

November 11

What Gives You a Sense of Self-Worth?

Some people get a sense of self-worth when they get things. For example, the acquisition of a car, an antique or a painting gives them a sense of self-worth. Some people get a sense of self-worth by creating things i.e. creating an app or a song. Some get a sense of self-worth by giving to others.

For purposes of Serenity, it is important to align your sense of self-worth with serenity inducing principles. For example, you may get a sense of self-worth from acquiring things, but are the consequences of acquisitions assisting you in serenity? For example, do you discover that after you get that boat, the management of it causes stress. You may get a sense of self-worth by producing things, but the work is exhausting. You may get a sense of Serenity by giving, but is your giving enabling someone else to victimize you and wear you out?

TO DO: Today, I will notice what gives me a sense of self-worth. I will also notice the consequences. I will try to rebalance my life to align my sense of self-worth with serenity.

November 12

STOP
(Stay calm, Think, Observe, Plan)

On your knees, you ask her to be your bride, but she says not until you get a better job...You stumble off a cliff and are hanging by one hand...You get an offensive email...You get rejected from that job you so desperately wanted....

TO DO: When confronted with a shocking challenge avoid frantic knee jerk reactions. Practice STOP. Take a few breaths, think realistically about your situation, observe what options you have, and plan a solution. This will make the challenge endurable and give you the best chance to deal with it peacefully and to your best advantage. Today, I refuse to panic or act out when stressed. I will practice STOP!

November 13

Step 1 Does Not Put You Where You Want to Be, but Rescues You From Where You Were

We take step 1 when we refuse to keep trying to control things we cannot. We surrender to win. We are no longer willing to beat ourselves up. We accept and adapt. Sometimes that means we accept that we have a problem that calls for help. Sometimes we accept that we are in a toxic relationship that calls for a healthy boundary. We accept the problem and attempt to do what is in our control to deal with it rather than deny there is a problem, We don't sweep problems under the rug. Adaptation may seem like a subtle difference from taking control but it is in reality a difference that is a wide as the Atlantic Ocean. It is the difference between trying to change people and changing how we deal with them. It is the difference between trying to change unalterable situations and how we adapt to them. It is knowing that we cannot stop the waves of an ocean, but that we can learn how to ride those waves. This is a great lesson which is the first step on the path to serenity. But remember step 1 does not put you where you want to be, it only takes you out of where you have been. The remaining steps remove the fear, obsession, aggression, anxiety, anger and numerous other character defects that ultimately bring a peace and serenity you never imagined existed. But it's not a single dose vaccine. It requires constant practice. It requires separating wants from needs, connecting to HELP, and changing ourselves. Daily recovery disciplines - like emotional reconstruction, rational thinking, therapy, and connectedness to others - strengthen us and even keep us from forgetting where we've been and where we don't want to return. Serenity practice gives us the opportunity to maintain gratitude, perspective, and flexibility. All this reverberates in energy and peace so that we keep balance day to day to face reality.

TO DO: Today, I will remember to accept and adapt. I will also keep applying the remaining steps to stay serene.

347

November 14

Our Actions, Not Our Words, Define Us

He who calls himself a Christian but truly worships money. She who says her career comes first, but doesn't do the work. He who says sobriety is the most important thing, but fails to practice a daily recovery program. All, inside, feel the emptiness that comes from actions not living up to proclamations: a disturbed conscience.

TO DO: Today, I will do what I say I will do. I will enjoy the peace that comes from knowing that I don't have to cover up any lies or make up any excuses.

November 15

You Don't Get Punished for Being Angry, You Get Punished by Being Angry

Sometimes we get punished by society for angry actions, but we always punish ourselves by being angry because anger is a painful, negative emotion that drains energy. Anger, whether righteous or not, is the feeling that we are not getting your way now. From a bad haircut to a disabled car to a pen that runs out of ink, little things can send us in a negative direction that ruins our day. The problem with anger is that "it comes on so suddenly." This is why daily practice to deal with anger is so critical.

TO DO: Today live by your highest principles. For example, exercise understanding rather than resentment. Accept that conflict exists and that you don't have to get angry about this unavoidable reality. This alignment with your highest principles removes stress induced by our small minded, egotistically imbalanced desires. Don't need to have things work out exactly as planned. Reduce needs to preferences. Also, take breaks every few hours to breathe slowly. This reduces the stress associated with living life like an overwhelmed juggernaut.

November 16

Okay When It's Not Okay

The doctor gives me a frightening diagnosis. The accountant tells me I owe more tax than I can afford. I get rejected from the college I want to attend. I fail to make the baseball team. What can I do to maintain serenity during tough times?

Self-acceptance and self-love allow me to be okay when the world is in a shambles. This fundamental inner peace gives me serenity even when things are not going my way – even in the midst of conflict.

TO DO: Today I will be okay even if things are not okay. I will remember to value and care about myself knowing that my inner peace is the key to serenity. I will not condition my serenity on what happens to me but rather on the fact that I am living according to my highest principles of unselfishness, kindness and love. I will give myself positive affirmations like "I unconditionally love myself…I am a good person and that's what counts!"

November 17

"No one who puts a hand to the plow and looks back is fit for service in the kingdom of God." - Luke

This saying is of universal truth whether or not you believe in the Bible, whether or not you are religious or atheistic. This saying tells us that we lose serenity (described in the Bible as the Kingdom of God) if we refuse to try something that is within our physical limitations because we think we are starting too late. Have no regrets! Go for it! You CAN learn to ice skate, play the guitar, sculpt, go to law school, write a book, get sober, mend character issues, and any myriad of other things even though you are starting late in life or have a sketchy history. Simply put, "It's never too late." Don't worry about how you look or whether you are any good. Put on that wetsuit and get out there and surf!

TO DO: Today, I am going to enjoy life. I am not going to lament on my past. I will live robustly and make the changes that will lead me to Serenity!

November 18

If You Have Nothing to Be Grateful For, Check Your Pulse

Everything seems to be going wrong. I lost my wallet. The baseball game got rained out. I even had to go to the emergency ward because I slipped and broke my ankle. Life is so unfair. Why does all of this have to happen to me? When everything seems to be going wrong, lowering the bar to being grateful just to be alive puts us on the path to serenity. I have learned that gratitude for the simplest of things such as having what I need to survive is better for my serenity than wanting things to go my way.

TO DO: Today I will simply be grateful for being alive. I will be grateful for the simplest of necessities when life throws me curveballs.

November 19

Gratitude, Love, and Flexibility
Are My Three Main Higher Powers

When the roof starts to leak, and the wind begins to howl, when all seems lost, when all seems foul, I look to gratitude, love, and flexibility. They become my God, they become my Higher Power, they become the forces to which I kneel, pray, and divine. Atheists, Muslims, Christians, etc., regardless, these Higher Powers can be reached by anyone who prioritizes peace and serenity.

TO DO: Today, my Higher Powers will be gratitude, love, and flexibility. As soon as I feel as if life isn't fair or if it is too hard, I will mentally connect to something I am grateful for (breathing counts), I will be flexible with my time and plans, and most importantly, I will act courageously, facing problems directly without fear and full of love.

November 20

Not All Wrong, Not All Right,
Life Is Rarely Black or White

"How could I have let that person take advantage of me!...Why couldn't I see that buying that house was stupid?... How could I have been such a fool!" Labeling a person or situation as being one way without taking into account all of the other possible characteristics, lessons, features, and shades of gray inherent in that person or situation can be disastrous for our perception and attitude. Everything has shades of gray. This is also true with decisions. There is no such thing as the perfect decision. We treat ourselves unfairly when we judge ourselves as having made a blunder when we tried our best to make a reasonable decision based on the facts at the time we made the decision. Labeling and judgment destroy our serenity.

TO DO: Today I will change my thinking whenever I label someone or some situation as being all wrong or all right. I will enjoy the peace that comes from freeing myself from extreme thinking. I will simply do the best I can in each moment guided by rational principles.

November 21

How to Tell If You Are Worrying or Making a Decision

Worrying involves emotions. Mental self talk like, "Oh no, this will never work out," or "I pray and pray that will happen!" is worry. Rational decisions involve detachment and calm. They are not hurried. You simply give yourself time to reflect on options. You may go back to something during a period of meditation and think of options and if nothing seems to make sense or feels correct, you move on to another task and return to the decision-making process later. Worrying involves drama; appropriate decision-making involves calm and patience.

TO DO: Today I will distinguish between worrying and appropriate decision making each time an issue arises. I will remember to breathe calmly and not rush into any decisions.

November 22

In the Now, On We Go, Fearing Not Win, Place or Show

We win some, we lose some. We cannot always control results. Sometimes we make mistakes. Sometimes, our adversaries play better than we do. Sometimes the unforeseeable avails itself. Sometimes we do everything right, but it was just not meant to be. So how do we maintain our serenity in the face of losing? We stay in this moment; we do the next right thing. We are humble and don't make our self image dependent on winning. We do not fear losing and so we put our best foot forward knowing that we can live with defeat. This attitude actually allows us to play the game of life without stress, and stress free performers perform best. Most importantly, this fearlessness of how things will work out in the end increases our peace of mind and serenity.

TO DO: Today, I will give reasonable efforts to reach the next step in whatever good goal I seek. I will stay in the now, fearing not win, place or show.

November 23

A Fresh Start to Each Day

"Write it on your heart that every day is the best day in the year.
He is rich who owns the day,
and no one owns the day who allows it to be invaded
with fret and anxiety.
Finish every day and be done with it.
You have done what you could.
Some blunders and absurdities, no doubt crept in.
Forget them as soon as you can, tomorrow is a new day;
begin it well and serenely,
with too high a spirit to be cumbered with your old nonsense.
This new day is too dear, with its hopes and invitations,
to waste a moment on the yesterdays."

–Ralph Waldo Emerson

One of the worst things we can do for our serenity is to carry
yesterday's mistakes with us today. Shame, which is perhaps the
greatest threat to our serenity, results when we let our "blunders
and absurdities" invade our hearts. Obsessing over our inevitable
mistakes ruins our peace of mind and opens the door to shame.

TO DO: Cherish this day! Live and make changes shamelessly and
fearlessly guided by love, unselfishness, purity, and kindness.

November 24

Act Out of Gratitude, Not Shame, Guilt or the Need to Earn Salvation

Serenity comes from actions motivated by gratitude. When we act out of gratitude, we are not trying to earn something, pay an obligation or trying to atone for guilty feelings. We are free of all that forced motivation when we try to do something out of gratitude. For example, writing this book can be hard work if I am focused on earning notoriety or God's love or money. It even gets harder if I focus on the fact that I am trying to do something good because I am working off some kind of shameful past behavior. But if I am grateful for having the ability to do it, for having been saved from my self-defeating behaviors, and for the ability to serve, writing becomes easier and more flowing. It becomes an act of love and joy.

TO DO: Today, especially when confronted with hard work, I am going to find a reason to have a grateful attitude for being able to do it.

November 25

Loving Detachment Lets Me Be; Understanding, Not Resentment, Sets Me Free

Attachment can be very misleading. We think because we are attached to someone (a child, a spouse), we love them so much that we will do anything for them. But in reality, attachment means we are dependent on their acting a certain way according to our expectations. Attachment means our serenity is controlled by their behavior. It makes us nag them and try to control them. It causes resistance from those we are trying to control. Loving detachment is far healthier. It means we can let others be free of satisfying our needs. It means we care about their freedom. We still love them, but don't need them to be anything but themselves. It also keeps us from becoming victims of others' behavior because we can set up healthy boundaries and not feel forced to sacrifice ourselves to protect others' misbehaviors. When we let others experience the consequences of their own sick behaviors, they have the best chance of trying to change. We can also be attached to a project or certain things. If they don't work out according to our expectations, we become miserable. Far better to love a project or thing but realize that our serenity does not depend on our expectations about them. Expectations are resentments waiting to happen. When one's expectations are not met, be it with people, the weather, a new car, a movie, etc., resentment and disappointment are quick to follow. By detaching from expectations, we are freed from resentment. An effective way to rid ourselves of expectations is to let go rather than control. "Letting go" creates loving detachment rather than painful attachment.

TO DO: Today, I will not let others behavior control my emotions. I will understand rather than resent. I will love but not attach.

November 26

What CAN I Control?

It was a beautiful day and I had tickets to the baseball game. But I was trapped in a traffic jam and could not make it until late in the game. Because serenity was my priority, I took care of myself. I did not become miserable about what I missed. I did not get depressed over the traffic jam. I enjoyed what I could of the game. I therefore was able to separate what I could control and what I could not.

Serenity practice seems to involve a lot about what we cannot control (outcomes, other people, our own diseases, etc.) But what is it that we can control? We can learn to maintain our serene attitude so long as we practice the four steps and nurture our Five Natures.

TO DO: Today, I will have the courage to change the things I can by focusing on what needs to be changed in me and my attitude rather than focusing on changing the rest of the World.

November 27

True Serenity Doesn't Depend on Life Satisfying Your Desires

You know you are truly serene when you are truly happy even when things don't seem to go your way. For example, I really wanted to go surfing. The waves for the first time in a month were perfect. My best friend was out surfing and I wanted to be with him. But, I had to go to a doctor's appointment for a check up. At first I felt disgruntled. Then I applied the four steps and ultimately I felt happy for my friend and grateful that I could take care of my responsibility. I was truly happy even though I could not do what I wanted to do. I have learned that happiness is an inside job. I have learned that many things each day do not work out the way I want them to and it is great to have the four steps as an insurance policy which gives me serenity regardless.

Similarly, serenity does not depend on whether or not others like me. Rather, serenity results when I know I will be fine even if they don't like me.

I also don't self-sabotage. I don't give up trying to do something because I feel I don't deserve to win or think I will be disappointed if things don't work out as planned. It seems that the key is to try reasonably to do something in the moment and be able to not beat myself up regardless of the result.

TO DO: Today I will remember to be happy even when things don't work out the way I want them to. I will simply focus on gratitude, perspective and flexible plans.

November 28

Never Perfect, Not All Knowing,
Little by Little Constantly Growing

I missed the game winning shot. Ouch. How do I deal with it?

I stare dumbfounded at the professor after he calls on me in front of the whole class, and I don't have a clue what the correct answer is even though I had studied all night and thought I was fully prepared.

My ego can tell me I have to be perfect, that I know it all. These misconceptions stress me out and fill me with regret. Far better to be humble and look at slow personal growth measured by increasing time of peace of mind. Far better to accept my fallibilities and learn a little at a time.

TO DO: Today I am going to give myself a break and not beat myself up over mistakes. I am going to unconditionally like and respect myself.

November 29

It May Be Too Late to Put the Oxygen Mask on You First

You can't give away what you don't have. You can't help someone else unless you are strong. When the plane is starting to crash, everyone knows we need to put the oxygen mask on ourselves first so that we can help others put theirs on. But why wait to help yourself until the situation is desperate? At that point it may be too late…at that point you may have already lost a significant amount of serenity. Serenity is a daily practice. Nourishing habits like eating well, taking a relaxing walk, connecting with friends, getting rid of burdensome stuff, even watching a silly TV show, keep us from reaching the desperate state where we have to put on the oxygen mask. We also need to value ourselves and not ruin our peace of mind and serenity because we are constantly slaving for others, especially if we are doing for them what they should be doing for themselves.

TO DO: Today I will remember that I can't help others until I help myself. I will remember to incorporate in this day, and every day, something self- nourishing. I will try to give balanced attention to each of my Five Natures. I will also be aware if my helping others is actually weakening them, for example, if I am enabling someone else to be lazy because I am doing what that person should be doing. I will be aware of my own need to rest and have fun.

November 30

Not Better Than, Not Worse;
Constantly Comparing Is a Curse

He's a better golfer than I am. She's a better gardener. Why can't I catch a fish? Everyone else is. My car is better than his. On and on... What was the last comparison you made?

List here: _____

Comparisons trouble our ego and self-image. They rarely lead to serenity. But how do we stop comparing? We must remember that everything changes and everyone is different...that it simply doesn't matter whether I am better or worse than someone else because better or worse is subjective and not important. What is important is how much I value myself and whether or not I am doing my best to do that which maintains that value according to good spiritual concepts like love, fearlessness and self-caring.

TO DO: Today, I am going to accept myself for who I am. I will be aware if I compare. Then I will tell myself to stop this nonsense and repeat to myself: I have individual attributes which I like!

December 1

I Used to HAVE to, Today I GET To

Before I started my path toward peace and light, it seemed like my life was full of burdens I had to do. Common tasks like being on hold while on the phone or going to the store or working a challenging job, weighed me down. I had to take care of what seemed like overwhelming, endless responsibilities. Now that I am on the path toward serenity, my problems seem more like opportunities – even privileges. I feel like I get to work, I get to pay bills, I get to see a smile on my spouse's face, I get to be at peace with myself.

TO DO: Today whenever I feel sorry for myself for having to do anything, I am going to use the suggestions I have learned daily from this book to change my attitude. As I move toward the light, I will feel that it is in fact a privilege to get to do what I am doing today. And for that I am so grateful.

December 2

Privilege, Not Obligation

I have to go to the dentist to get a filling. First thoughts: "Poor me. It will hurt. What a loss of time. The dentist will try to sell me a package of cleanings and x rays that will cost a lot." Then I connected with a Forum that I use for support. I check it every morning as part of Step 3 of my Serenity practice. My forum happens to be called the SoberTool Forum. There are many Forums on line and in person groups for any kind of issue. Another recovery group is Emotions Anonymous (EA). EA is a support group for people with emotional conditions such as depression, anxiety, and stress. On my forum, someone posts how grateful he is to be able to go to a dentist, how many people struggle to find or afford a dentist. This reminder helps my attitude. Suddenly, this chore becomes a privilege, not an obligation.

TO DO: Today, every time I think of a task I have to do, I will substitute my thought with: "Not an obligation, rather a privilege."

December 3

Don't Worry About Eternity

Refusing to believe that your actions cannot have some eternal meaning can be a serenity killer if you are trying to do good things. In other words, it usually makes us feel good if we do something good that we think will have a lasting impact on others. However, believing that everything you do has eternal meaning can also destroy your serenity. For example, I will be miserable if I believe I am damned because I mistakenly hurt someone. I can also be stressed out if I attach too much importance to what I do. Worrying about eternal meaning can therefore be problematic in our quest for serenity because we all do some good and some bad, some right and some wrong, and lots in between.

TO DO: Today I will live in this day and not worry about eternity. I will simply try to do the next reasonable thing according to good spiritual principles like love and unselfishness.

December 4

Not My Will, Not My Way,
My Higher Power Saves My Day

If I condition my serenity on getting things to go in a way that fulfills my selfish desires or makes life always easier for me, I am setting myself up for misery. "Self will run riot" is a particularly debilitating state of mind. Serenity practice teaches us to align our will with the will of our Higher Effective Loving Power (HELP). HELP gives us principles and support to do actions which lead us toward serenity. One example of HELP can be a self-help group. The purpose of a self-help group is to share suggestions to deal with a particular self-defeating behavior. Additionally, the self-help group consists of others who are dealing with the same particular self-defeating behavior, and they can provide support and accountability. Even if you think you don't have an overwhelming self-defeating behavior, it is helpful to serenity to participate in some kind of group (as simple as a stamp club or bicycle club or a group focused on a problem such as a 12 step group, etc.).

TO DO: Today, I will try to find a group of individuals who share a common problem or interest that I may have. If I already participate in such a group, I will try to improve my participation. I will remember that no person is an island, and we all need HELP from others.

December 5

Controlling Others Feels Like
I Am Walking on a Melting Glacier

I used to think that I wanted to control other people because I thought I knew what was best for them. But the truth is that I wanted to control them because I thought that somehow they affected my life. Examples: socializing with people who were a source of money for me; being kind to my neighbor so that he did not complain about my barking dog. The list is endless. All of these things involve my own ego and my own selfishness. Being serene involves constantly trying to treat people with respect and compassion sometimes for fairness and compromise and sometimes for their benefit, not only mine. Fairness and compromise may involve vigorously defending a good moral principle. Helping others may be appropriate so long as I am not enabling them to avoid doing what they can do for themselves. More often than not, I simply need to let go (stop trying to control or influence others). Letting go can be difficult. To do so, I need to recognize how I am feeling when dealing with others and stop trying to help as soon I am feeling uneasy or overwhelmed…I need to let go when I begin feeling like I am walking on a glacier that is melting before my eyes lest I drown. Perhaps a little uneasiness is necessary in trying to influence others, but if I feel as if my serenity is disappearing as a result of trying to influence others, I likely am making a mistake.

TO DO: Today I will be aware of my feelings and let go of others before I become overwhelmed. I will not let my desire to control others destroy my serenity. I will not let others control my peace of mind. I will turn back and seek solid ground if the glacier begins to melt.

December 6

Little Sacrifices Beget Momentous Rewards

"I just wish I could have a few drinks with my friends. I just wish I could have one cigarette with breakfast..." These are the thoughts which destroy serenity. Magical thinking is wishful thinking that can't happen. It leads alcoholics back to drinking, overeaters back to cake, and serene people back to misery. To maintain serenity, make no doubt about it, we need to make little sacrifices. But, take heart! Those little sacrifices will not seem like sacrifices soon. For example, you will enjoy your friends without needing to drink, you will love the taste of your morning eggs even more when you don't have a cigarette. Although you might find practicing the four steps challenging at first, you will soon experience the joys of acceptance, gratitude, connection and shameless self-improvement! Your initial little sacrifices will beget momentous rewards of peace and serenity!

TO DO: Today I will remember that serenity results from little changes I make. Even though all changes involve some initial discomfort, I will not let that discomfort knock me off the path to peace and enlightenment.

December 7

Don't Conquer the Mountain, Become One With the Mountain

Experience life while letting go of the results. Don't live to win, There is no good step or bad step, only the best possible foothold brought about by unencumbered focus. There is no past or future, anticipation or regret, worry or remorse, success or failure. All that is when becoming one with the mountain is fully engaged beauty. We don't struggle to the top. There is no "if only I can keep going, I can reach the top." There is only this moment. .. No end...No how will I make it back down the mountain or what will I do then... No that was great or that was terrible. Perfect serenity is being fully engaged, at one with the mountain, with each other, with the car ride, with each breath. There are no chores or tasks, no expectations or resentments, no better than or worse. Just serenity.

TO DO: Right now, I will not conquer the moment, I will become one with the moment.

December 8

This Is What I Am Supposed to Be Doing Right Now

When I am disturbed, it is because I want some person, place or thing to be different than it is right now. I use phrases like, it "OUGHT" to be different. He "SHOULD" not be doing that. The computer, "SHOULD" be connected to the internet. My dog "OUGHT" to be better potty trained. Far better for me to remember to use oughts and shoulds sparingly. They are cautionary words for my not accepting this moment, and when I am not accepting this moment I tend to lose my peace of mind. Oughts and shoulds interfere with my concentration on doing what is in front of me such that it takes me longer to do what I am supposed to be doing. Life is full of unexpected twists and turns, and my serenity is enhanced when I flow rather than fight. I also need to remember that sometimes I have to do things that my ego tells me are beneath me. I need to stay humble and flexible.

TO DO: Today, I refuse to become overwhelmed, rageful or depressed over life's continual unexpected interferences. I will stay patient by doing what I am supposed to be doing now. I will watch out if I start using phrases like "OUGHT" and "SHOULD."

December 9

The Deeper the Ignorance, the Greater the Awakening

Don't worry if you feel as if you have dug a hole so deep it seems impossible to get out. Don't despair if you don't know how to dig yourself out. You are in an enviable position for your awakening can be greater than someone who has not fallen to such depths. If you are totally clueless as to how to help yourself, you have a completely open mind, desperate enough to try principles that can lead you to an awesome serenity. It is easier for you to try what works than it is for someone who still thinks he is not ignorant but is living a life unfulfilled.

TO DO: Today, be aware of that which gives you peace and begin to nurture it. Try doing a compassionate act. Accept, connect, be grateful and let go of character defects like selfishness, fear and impatience. Your awakening is beginning.

December 10

It Is Too Soon to Tell

That was good. That was bad. I definitely made a mistake. That sure didn't work out. I lost. I won.

All of the above are erroneous thoughts. You are still alive. You are still breathing. Nothing is over yet. Conditions are constantly changing. People in your life are constantly changing. You are constantly changing. The snow ends only to start again. People come and go. Nothing is permanent. They don't make me happy or unhappy. They just make my life interesting.

TO DO: Today I will practice the phrase: "It's too soon to tell." I will remember that everything changes. I will immerse myself in the present moment and not perceive things as good or bad, but simply interesting.

December 11

Stick With the Winners

Creating healthy boundaries and minimizing contact with toxic people enhance serenity. But then the question becomes: who do we socialize with? Who do we go to for support? Stick with the winners! Associate with positive people who share your interests and goals, who maintain a healthy lifestyle, who seem to be on the path that you want to take toward serenity. "We are who we hang with" is a favorite saying of actor Will Smith. If we hang with depressed, drug abusing, malicious people, we become depressed, drug abusing, malicious people. If we hang with compassionate people, we become compassionate.

TO DO: Today I am going to stick with the winners. I will connect with an individual or a group that nurtures my serenity.

December 12

Meeting Makers Make It

We all have a private self and a social self. Sharing as much as we can about our private selves with others can be therapeutic and serenity inducing. However, we need to feel safe to share our private selves. The safest social place to do this is in a group of like-minded people who are there for a similar reason. Whatever your interests, whatever your concerns, there is a group available that will take away the blues of feeling isolated and terminally unique. There is a place where you can connect with others.

TO DO: If I know of a group that has a good history of providing support for people like me, I will do my best to participate in that group. If I am unfamiliar with a group, I will try to find one. I might google one word that describes some interest or concern I have. After that word I will insert group. Even though I will allow myself to feel any social anxiety I may have, I will still take a chance in finding a group because I know that the benefits of group interaction (mutual, nonjudgmental support) may be well worth some initial uneasiness.

December 13

Progress, Not Perfection

My mentor: "We are not saints. Progress, not perfection."

Regardless of where we are on our Serenity path, we are going to surprise ourselves with self-defeating behaviors. We are going to feel like we are regressing. We are going to feel like we are not changing as quickly as we would like. We will lose our serenity at times. But, if this is happening to you, don't give up. Get back on the path. When you regress, make it as brief as possible. Be grateful you have the insight to know you are off the path. This means you are living consciously and not like the unconscious, brutal juggernaut you used to be.

TO DO: Today I will live consciously. I will be aware if a character defect creeps back into my behaviors. I will not be ashamed, rather I will make amends to improve.

December 14

It's All Gravy

A trigger for me to lose my serenity is to think I am not getting my wants fulfilled, that something important is not coming to fruition, Whenever I feel tempted to lose my serenity, I ask myself ,"How important is it really?" Usually my little crises are just that: little… insignificant. When I am upset I am forgetting that my needs are being taken care of. And what I am upset over is just the gravy not the meat.

TO DO: Today I am going to consciously assess whether or not I am letting unimportant events cloud my vision.

December 15

Life on Life's Terms, Not My Terms

A major source of my unhappiness is my inability to accept life on life's terms. I am unhappy when I want life on my terms. I have to be aware that when I begin a phrase with the words, "I want" that I am being selfish, and selfishness is a serenity killer.

Many of us struggle with the difference between controlling life and accepting and adapting to life. Controlling means I must have life on my terms or I will be miserable and/or refuse to participate, like the child who refuses to play baseball unless he can be the pitcher. Accepting and adapting means that I will be happy if the big picture is attained (playing baseball) even if I have to play another position. If I am cut from the team and can't play at all, I will be OK with either practicing to try to make the team next year or I will try a different sport. When I accept and adapt I will get what I need but I may not get what I want. I will get some kind of activity which challenges my body, but I may not get it exactly the way I WANT it. We can always accept and adapt to get what we need and often when we adapt we find something far better than what we initially wanted. Even though we can't be the star pitcher our ego craved to be, we end up enjoying surfing even more.

All of us are put on hold regularly when we make a call. That is one reason more people text than call. That in and of itself is accepting and adapting rather than stubbornly refusing to correspond with the person. I recently had to set up a dentist appointment and was put on hold. In this case, I accepted that I would be on hold, but I figured one dentist was pretty much the same as another so I tried a different dentist. I didn't just procrastinate or not see a dentist. Often, I need to stay on hold so I find out what my character defect is that is making me want to hang up. Ah ha, of course, it's patience. I then adapt by perhaps calling and staying on hold when I am also doing another task like working on the computer or walking my dog or just meditating on perspective. These activities help me with my impatience.

Sometimes living life on life's terms involves, "Just doing it." Sometimes I just have to go to the dentist or else I will be sacrificing something far greater. in this case, I suck it up and do it. Amazingly, things rarely end up being as bad as I predicted so I use techniques to vanquish the worry, like simply staying mentally focused on living in the NOW.

TO DO: Today I will live life on life's terms. I will not control. Rather I will accept, adapt and marvel at how things often occur that seem better than I could have planned.

December 16

What Is Letting Go?

You've heard the phrase "let go" again and again. But what does it really mean? Step 1 teaches us to accept and adapt. "Let go" tells us to ACCEPT, not go into denial and hide from what is. "Let go" tells us to let go of our wishful thinking – of our desire that something is not so, and accept reality. Then, "let go" tells us to ADAPT in a manner motivated by positive principles, like love and fearlessness. Such adaptation may involve some action on our part, but more often than not, "letting go" involves NO ACTION. Often, choosing to do nothing, letting someone or something be, is the most advantageous way to let go when our serenity is our priority. And isn't serenity what you are ultimately trying to get and maintain?

TO DO: Today, I will meditate on the meaning of "letting go." I will accept and adapt by either doing the next reasonable thing or nothing at all. I will be conscious of my motivations when I adapt. I will be conscious of any character defects of mine which may be interfering with my process of letting go and perhaps connect to a Higher, Effective, Loving Power for help in this process.

December 17

We Are All Dualistic

Even though it's better not to judge ourselves in black-and-white terms, sometimes it is serenity inducing to simply admit that we have good and bad qualities. I need not self-flagellate or waste time making excuses with respect to my bad qualities. My bad qualities range from being a sore loser, to having an explosive temper, to being too cheap. I wish these were not my qualities because they hurt myself and others. Nevertheless, they exist. For me, I need to have faith that my Higher Effective Loving Power (my support group, my philosophy, etc.) forgives me. I also need to remember that I am in a pretty good place internally and externally today, serene most of the time. But my serenity wanes as soon as I start beating myself up over my bad qualities. It's okay for me to be aware of them and admit them. That actually gives me the best chance of some improvement. But it's also serenity inducing for me to remember that I still have very bad, arguably evil characteristics and it's also okay for me to remember that every human being has some bad qualities too and that it is absolutely impossible for me not to have bad qualities. This admission really helps me feel better about who I am.

TO DO: Today I am not going to make excuses over my bad qualities. I am going to just recognize them as they come up, and not beat myself up over them. I will try to improve, but I won't despair over my inadequacies. I will also remember that I have many good qualities, and that all humans are dualistic.

December 18

The Only Person That Disrupts
My Peace of Mind Is Me

The broken computer, the inclement weather; they are all just triggers. How I act upon those triggers is what dictates my peace of mind. If I can be okay with who I am despite the external world, I can maintain my serenity. This is quite a challenge. But I have tools to accept myself today. I can accept my feelings and flaws. I don't have to be judgmental. I don't have to win an argument. I can accept that the external World changes. I can change my attitude by using the four steps to peace of mind. I am empowered. Perhaps my greatest strength is knowing that bad feelings won't kill me, and if I don't do something harmful to deal with them, they will always pass.

TO DO: Today I will remember that ultimately I am empowered in the sense that I can do something about my own peace of mind despite what happens in the external world.

December 19

If I Didn't Know That I Had Already Lost My Mind, I Would Think That I Am Losing My Mind

Sometimes we all do stuff that doesn't make any sense. We forget things, we get distracted, we become disorganized, we eat ice cream even after our doctor tells us not to. The key to serenity is not to take yourself too seriously, especially when personal flaws don't rise to the level of hurting ourselves and others too badly. Recently, I forgot to save an email that a client was supposed to send me. The day after he sent it to me, I asked for the same email again. When he pointed out that he sent it to me, I didn't get defensive. I didn't get embarrassed. I didn't allow my mistake to impact my serenity. I simply made amends to him appropriately and added the phrase, "If I didn't know that I had already lost my mind, I would think that I am losing my mind." Of course, if I keep making the same mistake repeatedly, I need to correct my accountability system. But at the end of the day, life is too short to lose serenity over simple human failings.

TO DO: Today, I am going to be aware if I am taking myself too seriously.

December 20

Focus On the Things You've Accomplished, Not Only on the Things You Regret

Sometimes my mind obsesses on regrets: "Why didn't I make more money?" "Why didn't I sell my car for more?" "Why didn't I spend more time with my children?" "Why did I waste so much hard work on writing a movie script that never sold?" I forget to focus on the lessons learned, the risks I reasonably took, the other priorities I fulfilled, and the many successes I have had. Of course I made mistakes, but I also had some things work out better than expected. Even if I sit today in a jail cell, it is perfectly acceptable for me to remember that I am still alive, that I have had to accomplish something to be alive like overcoming adversities. Focusing on my assets is as important as focusing on my liabilities as I live in this day and try to do the next reasonable thing motivated by spiritual principles like honesty, unselfishness, empathy, and love. None of us are all bad or all good. It's wrong to be too hard on ourselves, ashamed, or defeatist. We can list wonderful things about ourselves, wonderful things we have done, if only we allow ourselves to remember them.

TO DO: Today, if I find myself creating a mental list of regrets, I will also make a list of accomplishments. I will use this list of accomplishments to give me confidence to know that I can nurture my positive behaviors and change my self-defeating behaviors – and to simply feel better about who I am. Most importantly, I will not dwell on the past, but try to make the best of this day by living a balanced life full of good spirituality and maximal physical and mental activity.

December 21

All You Have to Do Is Be Yourself

This sounds simple, doesn't it? How many of us can actually do it. We tend to reflect off of other people, places and things - adjusting and accommodating our behavior depending upon who we are with. Faking our feelings to get what we want, we often have no clue as to who we are. For example, we lose our identity as our job consumes us. "Are you a doctor, a teacher, a truck driver, or are you a person?" We shock ourselves by our own behavior. And perhaps saddest of all, often we don't even like who we are. We escape from our true nature by using drugs and seeking constant distractions like gambling and television. So how do we be ourselves? Meditation and conscious living are two effective ways we get to know ourselves. Meditation gets rid of the distractions. Conscious living helps us to notice how we are behaving throughout the day. If we get to know ourselves a little better, we can appreciate our true nature to keep the things that seem to be working for our peace of mind and change the things that are self-defeating. This is an essential step to serenity. Important side note: don't fret about not perfectly knowing who you are and how to be yourself. None of us ever can arrive at full self- awareness or actualization. We are all constantly changing. Getting to know ourselves is like shooting at a moving target. So we are only going to know ourselves in this moment.

TO DO: Today, I am going to take four deep breaths and if my mind becomes distracted, I am just going to return my concentration to my breathing. I will also be a little more aware of how I am behaving throughout the day rather than just reacting to everything unconsciously. I will particularly try to sense how my personality changes with regard to my environment. I want to get to know myself a bit better because I unconditionally love myself and would like to be the most serene person I can be.

December 22

Own Your Feelings!

All of a sudden, I snapped at my wife just because she walked in the room. As part of my serenity training, I've learned that I tend to lose my peace of mind and act out with anger when I am stuffing my feelings about something else. So, I did a quick scan of what was truly bothering me. It didn't take long for me to acknowledge that I was sad because my 11 year old dog (whom I love, is my best friend) appeared to be dying. I also realized that I was in denial about how sad I felt and that I was also (perhaps irrationally) blaming myself because I could have taken better care of him. As soon as I went through this process, I cried. But I also felt great relief and knew I was not going to act out irrationally with rage again. I then apologized to my wife and told her I believed I was sad because of the dog. She was very understanding. She did not think less of me for being sad and tearful. Incidentally, men frequently tend to not want to appear sad. They tragically think no emotion or anger is more masculine. In any event, the relief I felt by owning my sadness, by acknowledging it and sharing it with another human being gave me back my peace of mind. The cry was well worth the relief of owning my feeling. There was no way I was going to rage again irrationally because my serenity had returned.

TO DO: Today I am going to own my feelings. I am going to reflect upon what I actually am feeling and not be afraid to deal with the feeling by sharing it.

December 23

Keep an Even Keel (Just Breathe)

The computer goblins were at it again. That email I worked so hard
on disappeared. Instead of panicking, I breathed in through my
nose and out through my mouth, slowly. I closed the program and
reopened it. Magically the email reappeared. When confronted with
panic, I acknowledge the feeling then breathe in through my nose
and out through my mouth two times. This returns me to an even
keel. Research shows that slowly breathing in through the nose and
out through the mouth helps to reduce blood pressure and stress.
I also sometimes fall prey to being too happy or excited. I have
learned that it is better for me to simply stay in a mindful state as
much as possible throughout the day. This keeps me on a very nice
plain of serenity.

TO DO: Today, if I feel stress, I am not going to go into a pity party
because of the challenge. Rather I will welcome it. I will own my
feeling, then I will remember the benefits of keeping an even keel as
I slowly breathe in through my nose and out through my mouth.

December 24

Sometimes When We Look Away From Something in the Dark, We Can See It More Clearly

It was the dark of night. This was when the giant sea turtles came from the sea to traverse the beach to make their huge nests to lay their eggs. I scanned the dark beach, hoping to see this miracle: a beautiful sea turtle slowly, with great determination and fortitude pushing its heavy body toward the perfect spot. I noticed a dark spot but wasn't sure if it was a turtle or just a shadow. To see more clearly, I slightly diverted my gaze knowing that in the past by looking away, I could actually discern the spot more clearly. From the corner of my eye, I saw the dark round shape slowly trudging forward.

Later, my mind started obsessing about a life problem. I couldn't see any solution. So I decided to try my sea turtle approach. I meditated by thinking about nothing except my rising and falling stomach as I gently breathed in through my nose on a four count, holding my breath for four seconds, then letting the breath out through my mouth on a six count. I quickly felt refreshed, and the answer to my problem suddenly came to my consciousness.

TO DO: Today, when challenged I will remember that when in the dark, I may see more clearly if I look away. I will restore my peace of mind by meditating, taking a walk or having a good meal rather than continuing to bang my head against the wall struggling over an answer.

December 25

Help Others to Help Yourself,
Not to Hurt Yourself

A classic alcohol recovery saying is "poor me, poor me, pour me another drink." Another is "me, me, me like an opera singer." Helping others takes our focus off of the "poor me's." But we can unconsciously cross the line into codependence if we help others to the point where we are victimizing ourselves. If you are losing balance in your own life by neglecting your body, mind, and spirit because you are so focused on another, then you are slipping into codependence. You are enabling others to do what they should be doing for themselves, so you are not only hurting yourself, you are hurting the person you are trying to help.

TO DO: Today I am going to be generous and kind. If helping others also helps my body, mind and spirit, I will give unselfishly. But I am going to be conscious of whether I am helping or enabling.

December 26

Don't Wait for the World
to Give You Harmony

Create harmony, don't wait for the world to give it to you. One way to create harmony is to have a daily plan – a daily structure. Structure creates harmony because it reduces stressful decision-making. Automatic daily rituals like morning meditation and exercise create harmony. Answering emails at a set time creates harmony. Eating at the same time, going to bed and waking up at the same time create harmony. Some extremists even wear the same colored shirt every day to reduce decision-making. Structure reduces the time and effort needed to think about things that are not important or that would have otherwise required a decision. Of course, unexpected things occur. Flexibility allows us to deal with life's curveballs. But after we swing at the curveball, we should return to structure to stay balanced and serene.

TO DO: Today I will create a list of daily activities to do for the next seven days. I will include activities that nurture my body, mind, emotions, social self, and spirit. I will focus on structure to create harmony.

December 27

You Have Meaning

I felt like it was all over. I was old, retired, and no one needed me. Or, I was young, new, and didn't even know how to read. Then, someone called me and asked for my help. My serenity was restored. I had regained meaning.

TO DO: Today I am going to make sure I have some meaning in my life. Meaning could be as simple and small as giving an encouraging smile to someone. I will not let my past stop me from having a meaningful life. I will remember that so long as I am alive, and no matter how far I have fallen, I can have some meaning so long as I am willing to help others. I will be confident that this meaning will return me to peace of mind.

December 28

It's Okay to Acknowledge
That You Are Good At Something

I may be lousy at tennis, overweight, and have some issues with an explosive temper, but I am pretty good at counseling substance abuse patients. Sure, I am always trying to learn and I don't constantly tell myself how great I am. However, every now and then, it is good that I acknowledge that I'm good at something. It does help restore me to serenity.

TO DO: Today I am going to remember that I am probably good at something. I may not be as good as Rodger Federer is to tennis, Tom Brady is to football or LeBron James is to basketball, but I might be pretty good at something and perhaps I will turn that into my calling so that I may know freedom and happiness.

December 29

A Little Rust Is Beautiful

"Oh no, a spot of rust on my Mercedes!" Before I got into serenity practice, I would only see that rust spot and ignore the rest of the car. I would let that rust spot debilitate my entire self-image. I would allow a tiny dust spot to mar my vision of the glorious cathedral stained glass. I would let a few wrinkles make me see myself as withered.

"Mental filtering" is a serenity killer where you focus exclusively on one negative detail and you let that scratch darken your attitude and reduce your self-image.

TO DO: Today, I will be conscious of mental filtering. I will broaden my vision to see the whole picture. I will exercise perspective. I will acknowledge that everything has some flaws, and I will not let imperfections ruin the beauty; rather I will see the imperfections as a part of the beauty.

December 30

Are You Thinking Love or Hate?

"I took a bite out of a sandwich and that expensive crown fell out of my mouth. I stared at it on my plate as my anger welled. I thought of all of the reasons to despise that dentist. $1,000 for this. I now have to go back to him yet again. How could he do this to me?" I would not let my hatred go. And why should I let it go? I was completely justified in hating him. But as I nurtured my resentment, I only felt worse. The dentist was of course not being affected at all.

Another example: "While playing a recreational tennis game without a referee, the opposing player calls my shot out. It was clearly in. Anyone could tell! What a cheat! How could someone treat me like that?" I am so distracted by my hate I cannot concentrate on the game, and I allow the "cheater" to come back to beat me.

Yet another example: "The hurricane missed every house but mine. Now I have to clean up all the damage."

The list of life's injustices is endless and so are the reasons to have justifiable resentment. However, resentment, even when it is justifiable, only causes the resenter to lose serenity. Thinking and acting out of love restores us to serenity. The four steps lead us to thinking and acting out of love. Change your hateful thoughts to loving thoughts because you love yourself and want to stay serene.

TO DO: Own the feeling of anger, but as quickly as possible, practice the Four Steps to Serenity:

1. Accept and adapt.

2. Be grateful that you can do something to satisfy your needs even if you have to do something that you prefer not to do.

3. Share your feelings of anger by calling a friend or reach out to someone who needs help so that you can exercise love.

4. Look at the character issues that are causing you resentment like impatience, expectations that others should be perfect, your need to have your plans workout the way you want them to without any divergences, your inability to forgive. Today, think love, not hate.

December 31

What We Can Control: Our Attitude

So much in life is out of our control. The list is endless. We cannot control people, places or things. The weather, outcomes, technology, aging, diseases, on and on this infinite list goes. So how can we make peace with powerlessness? Finding little things we can control, like choosing today's clothing, seems to give us some semblance of stability. Trying to have some structure seems to help. But at the end of the day, the most important thing we seem to be able to control is our attitude. And how do we control our attitude to be serene in the face of all this powerlessness? How do we attain peace of mind rather than despair? We can ask ourselves, "Why must we choose to be upset if we can't control it?" Why not let this lack of control let us relax in knowing there is nothing we can do to definitely control an outcome. We can resolve to accept, give thanks for needs satisfied, connect with a Higher Effective Loving Power to act in accordance with good spiritual principles, and seek to change our own self-defeating behaviors rather than trying to change others. These are the Four Steps to Serenity.

TO DO: Today, I am going to make controlling my attitude the priority in my life. Before I try to do the next reasonable thing, I am going to invest the necessary time and energy to do the four step process. I will then be confident that I am handling situations and making decisions out of peace of mind rather than cognitive dissonance and despair.

Troubled?

I. DEALING WITH
HARMFUL TEMPTATIONS?

II. WANT TO FEEL BETTER?

III. WANT TO FIX A
SELF DEFEATING BEHAVIOR?

IV. HAVING DIFFICULTY MAKING A DECISION?

V. NEED MOTIVATION?

VI. WANT SOME HELPFUL CONCEPTS TO GROW BY?

SERENITY

Serenity is peace and enlightenment. The simplest notion of enlightenment is the knowledge that you are on the right path, that you are in tune with the universe, correctly following the great compass. Serenity sometimes is a blissful, carefree state. However, sometimes it refers to the ability to manage challenges and crises in a functional, realistic manner. Sometimes it involves a strong, resilient attitude. Sometimes it involves a sense of humor.

It does not always mean one is happy or joyous, but it does mean that one possesses the skills to return to a content attitude when confronted with difficulties. Serenity means we can respond to life's challenges without our own self-defeating behaviors causing harm to ourselves or others. No human is perfect in maintaining serenity. It is a continual journey of progress not perfection.

Serenity can also be described as being true to one's feelings or "owning" one's feelings and not being in denial about their existence. Serenity does not mean one never experiences hurt, frustration, anger, fear, or sadness. However, serene people are able to deal appropriately with such negative emotions so that these emotions do not harm their lives or extinguish their hope. Serene people may feel anger occasionally, but they do not allow that anger to interfere with their lives by, say, using drugs or acting out. A serene person is able to recover, usually quite quickly, from negativity. A serene person is able to recognize that things change and that there are also good things in life even during hardships. A serene person, whether consciously or unconsciously, practices the Four Steps to Serenity.

THE FOUR STEPS TO SERENITY

When you start each day, say the four steps to yourself. If you feel negative during the day, apply one or more.

1. We choose to accept and adapt rather than control.

2. We distinguish between wants and needs as we focus on gratitude, perspective, and flexibility.

3. We connect to HELP (Higher Effective Loving Power).

4. We choose to fix ourselves, not others, then do the next reasonable thing.

Note: Step 1 is the choice we make to be serene. It is the first thing we consider when confronted with any situation. Steps 2 through 4 help us to accept and adapt. The result is serenity when we also take care of our Five Natures. This is a daily process. We can apply the four steps to all of life's situations.

STEP 1

We choose to accept and adapt rather than control.

ACCEPTANCE: Acceptance is the opposite of denial. Until one accepts a problem, one cannot address the problem. Until one exercises acceptance, one cannot begin to be serene. A bad team has to accept it is bad. A troubled marriage has to accept it is troubled. An ill person has to accept that he is ill. A successful warrior must accept the strengths and weaknesses of his adversary.

Much of what we sometimes fail to accept are things that have already happened. Yet we are still upset over them. The only thing we can change is being upset. We also waste too much time worrying about things that might happen even when we have done all that we can to prepare reasonably for them. Living in the present moment is fundamental to avoiding regrets about the past and worry about the future.

ADAPTATION: Adaptation means that we change what is possible to be changed. We adapt by changing how we cope with situations and people. The focus is more on our own behavior rather than others. For example, we avoid drowning by becoming buoyant not by making the water buoyant. To adapt, we practice Steps 2 through 4. According to Charles Darwin, the law of adaptation is a fundamental law of nature, survival, and evolution. It is also the fundamental law for serenity.

Adaptation is not acquiescence. Serenity can be enhanced when we refuse to acquiesce to abuse. Healthy boundaries, sometimes by decisive even confrontational means, help. Sometimes adaptation means we have to fight or struggle. But the struggle requires us to change ourselves first so that we are strong enough to give it our best fight. Creating healthy boundaries and refusing to enable others who abuse us are ways we can respond positively to others who are beyond our control. Typically we change our responses to their abuse and don't waste our time and energy trying to change them. How liberating it is to adapt rather than control things we cannot control!

CONTROL: Controlling others can be very counterproductive and thereby serenity threatening. Controlling often causes resentment, anger, fear, and resistance. The illusion of control is the greatest threat to our sanity. We are not in charge of people, places, things, and even our own destiny. We cannot control the internet, our friend getting sober, our car breaking down, the weather, a pandemic, the government, health, doctors, the police, the ocean, or outcomes. We may be able to influence people, places, and things, but we cannot control them. We can try different means to solve problems and work toward goals, but we have to learn when to stop and when to attempt alternatives in order to maintain our serenity. We must also bear in mind that often our attempts to influence or control others cause unintended consequences and resistance.

We know we are controlling when we are losing our serenity. Some signs that we need to stop controlling are:
1. A palpable risk of doing harm.
2. When we are thinking obsessively about something.
3. When nothing more can be done within the limits of good moral or spiritual principles.
4. When H.A.L.T. (hunger, anger, loneliness and tiredness) appears.
5. When we can no longer exercise common sense solutions.
6. When we are being an annoyance.
7. When we are using negative language and negative self talk.

David Foster Wallace may have said it best when he observed that most people stop controlling as a matter of fatigue more than anything else. Step 1 encourages us not to wait until we are fatigued to stop controlling, but rather to avoid controlling altogether to maintain our peace of mind.

STEP 2

We distinguish between wants and needs as we focus on gratitude, perspective, and flexibility.

WANTS VS. NEEDS: Often it is painful to exercise acceptance because we don't get what we want. We can feel better if we do step 2 to realize that we get what we need, not what we want. This makes us realize we are fundamentally OK even if we did not get what we wanted.

This recognition of needs being fulfilled gives us the gratitude, perspective, and flexibility which makes the continually changing world a manageable, even joyous place. Of course, needs are food, water, shelter, air, etc. The more we appreciate the simplest and most fundamental fulfilled needs, the more serene we tend to be.

Ironically, sometimes we get want we want, and discover that we are disappointed. For example, we may want and get that Lexus RX whatever, but it may not fulfill what we are really seeking like self-worth, ego fulfillment, or love which is truly why we are paying so much more for it than a comparable Chevrolet. We may want and get drugs, but what we really want is peace of mind or exhilaration.

Separating what we want and need can sometimes be simple and sometimes not so simple. Doing steps 3 and 4 can assist us in clarifying our wants and needs. It also helps our serenity to reduce or eliminate wants because wants can actually cause unnecessary stress.

GRATITUDE: Gratitude is a prerequisite for serenity. A grateful person typically is not a miserable person. Gratitude typically arises when we focus on our fulfilled needs rather than our wants.

PERSPECTIVE: Perspective is also a happy consequence of distinguishing between wants and needs. For example, when we realize that we are upset over losing a game of monopoly while others have no food to eat, we question whether we really should be so upset about losing at Monopoly.

FLEXIBILITY: Flexibility also results by distinguishing between wants and needs. For example, if we lose a cherished job, we can remember that we still have the ability to search for another. This may not be what we want, but we still have what we need. Flexibility gives us the power to live for the adventure, not the result. Flexibility helps remove the worry associated with wanting things to turn out a certain way. We spend 99 percent of our time living the journey, and often the journey's end is far different than what we were seeking initially. Flexibility allows us to be content because we are in the journey. Flexibility allows us to go with the flow, have a sense of humor, stay positive, accept conflict and changing circumstances, and to work toward achieving good, disciplined principles rather than set goals. We all win some and lose some. Serenity results from enjoying the daily adventures. This makes us unafraid to try challenging, new things. Each day, we live little adventures. From going to the store to doing our jobs, we need to congratulate ourselves for our participation regardless of the outcome. We must remember that we can exert effort, but we cannot control outcomes. So flexibility prevents outcomes from destroying serenity.

Inflexibility causes stress. Unexpected things happen to everyone. Expecting things to happen differently than we plan (being flexible), aids in the relief of emotional suffering. Being prepared for unavoidable conflict enhances our ability to gracefully manage our emotional responses to trauma and life's "little difficulties." Expecting things to change also increases our ability to prepare for alternatives. Everything changes. We cannot predict the future. And if we are alive and living fully in this moment, our needs are being fulfilled and we can be flexible.

STEP 3

We connect to HELP
(Higher Effective Loving Power).

HELP is anything that works without harming ourselves or others. HELP stands for Higher Effective Loving Power. Higher means greater competence. Effective means purposely relevant to your situation. Loving means caring for your whole being. Power stands for support. HELP is a force you can believe in to carry the burden with you and sometimes for you. Depending upon the level of pain involved with your situation, your HELP could be as simple as a quick refreshing breath or as extreme as going to a physician. HELP can be a combination of powers. It can be connecting to a friend, a religious God, a purely spiritual God, higher values, a Big Sister, group support, spiritual principles, this Book, creativity, art, music, work, nature, hobbies, etc. Some find HELP in the loving eyes of a dog. Connection to HELP occurs through prayer, meditation, attendance, service, and often accountability. As the level of suffering increases due to what we need to accept (an abusive spouse, an addiction, a mental illness, death, etc.) an increased level of HELP, i.e. that provided by a professional or group, may be in order.

HELP usually involves something that we know will unconditionally accept us. Sometimes that can be a professional therapist. Sometimes HELP can be someone who has successfully dealt with the same challenges that we are currently experiencing like a mentor or sponsor. Such people tend to unconditionally love and accept us because they can personally relate to what we are experiencing. They can share with us their strategies for dealing with our challenges.

HELP also provides us with a sense of stability and the confidence that we are fundamentally O.K. especially during trying times. In short, HELP is anything that restores us to serenity without harming ourselves or others.

It is important to remember that HELP usually is not self-reliance or our own willpower. Perhaps the reason self-reliance and willpower don't work is because we tend to try the same failing methods we always used. A definition of insanity is doing the same thing over and over again and expecting different results. It is better to reach out and try something new.

In my 33 years of addiction recovery and my 20 years of being a therapist, it seems that people who can tap into a loving force through some kind of prayer and meditation seem to have an advantage at achieving and maintaining serenity. Perhaps this is so because there will be occasions where one is suddenly thrust into an extremely challenging situation, unable to find any other form of HELP, or unable to intellectually apply any other coping skills. HELP also always involves, as best as possible, daily attention to our Five Natures (more about our Five Natures later). Such attention gives us a certain balance that supports serenity.

It cannot be emphasized enough that one must be careful not to connect to NONHELP! Connecting to addiction and toxic people are our biggest culprits. These forms of NONHELP provide paths to misery. Solitude can be described as connecting to one's Higher Self, and it can be an effective path to serenity. Solitude gives us an opportunity to get to know ourselves without the influence of others on our behavior. However, a purely isolated existence does not seem to work well for serenity. John Donne perhaps said it best: "No man is an island."

We all have a social self and a private self and one goal of serenity is to allow the private self to emerge safely in social situations. "Safely" means without breaking too many laws of course, but more importantly, "safely" means without the fear of self-consciousness, social anxiety, or self-judgment combined with self-flagellation.

Learning to be who we are, wonderful individuals, free from societal opinions, restrictions and judgments, can often best be accomplished in solitude. Solitude relieves us of any need to appear a certain way to please anyone else.

It keeps others' character defects from interfering with our peace of mind. Solitude holds at bay the natural conflicts caused by society like traffic jams, crowded elevators, and long lines. Solitude gives us a break from societal stressors. Refreshed we can better adapt to the World. Too often our self develops in relation to others, rather than in relation to our own mind, body, and soul. Solitude can be a useful Higher Effective Loving Power. Psychologists often distinguish between the "authentic self" and the "false self." They posit that we look to other people to construct our self-perception. Others therefore construct our identity, not us. When we're alone, when others' judgments, standards, and ideals are no longer there to mold our self- conception, the "false self" tends to diminish. That can be frightening, but it also can be wonderfully enlightening and blissful. When the false self disappears, the authentic self reveals itself – without fear, guilt, or shame. The next step is to nurture that authentic self in our relationships. Helpful ways to do this is to find a group that is interested in the same thing that we are' i.e. a stamp club, a softball team, a self-support recovery group (like a 12 step meeting), a gym, a temple, a LGBT group…any group that may accept our authentic self and support us non-judgmentally…any group where it is OK TO BE US.

STEP 4

We choose to fix ourselves, not others, then do the next reasonable thing.

FIXING OURSELVES: The process of fixing ourselves begins with changing our focus from what others are doing to us to what we are doing to ourselves. We come to realize that what others do may trigger emotions in us but that the duration and severity of our emotional responses depend on our own character attributes. The more defective our attributes, the greater the severity and duration our emotional suffering tends to be. Therefore, part of the process of ending emotional suffering seems to be in changing ourselves, not others. Examples of defective character attributes include impatience, resentment, fear, jealousy, selfishness, and of course a host of many more. Listing our personal character defects (perhaps the top five), then substituting each with the opposite character attributes is a method of fixing ourselves. For example, we can substitute resentment with empathy and understanding. Another method also involves finding the defect, then questioning what utility it has. Usually, if not always, character defects are not useful and they only make us feel bad. This method leaves us no other reasonable alternative but to discard the defect. The happy result is greater serenity. It is liberating to know that no one can make us feel a certain way for very long, that we commandeer our own emotional destiny.

Another reason to focus on fixing ourselves rather than attempting to fix others is simple: WE CANNOT CHANGE OTHERS. We cannot fix others' defects no matter how hard we try. Helpful sayings like, "We can only sweep our own side of the street" and "clean our own doorstep" remind us to do what is possible.

Fixing ourselves is critical to adaptation and consequently survival, but it is often overlooked. We must remember that we must adapt psychologically as well as physically. Perhaps it is difficult to adapt psychologically because we cannot see the psyche. But if we allow maladaptive psychological patterns to persist, we tend to compensate maladaptively by, for example, abusing drugs, ourselves, and others. We tend to cope by being more resentful, blaming others, even committing suicide. Perhaps the most harmful defect is shame. Shame is thinking that there is something wrong and unalterable about ourselves. Although shame can be an initial wake up call to change, it does not mean we are hopeless. As we practice the four steps and give daily attention to the Five Natures, we find that shame tends to dissipate because we see that we can make positive change.

Two other common character defects are fear and regret. An effective way to calm fear and regret is by keeping our mind in the present moment. Fear is the feeling that we are not going to get our way in the future. Regret is the feeling that we did not get our way in the past. So, to eliminate fear and regret, we focus on the moment. We can make plans in the moment without fearing the future so long as we remember that it is impossible to predict the future. We can learn from our mistakes in the moment without regret so long as we do not dwell on the past. Sometimes though, this moment is difficult. We handle difficulties by accepting what is, and knowing that the painful moments will pass because all things change. They will change as painlessly possible if we do not make them worse due to our own self-defeating behaviors.

As we focus on fixing ourselves, we learn to take care of our business, not everyone else's. We no longer feel so angry or deflated when someone else stands us up or cuts us off. We no longer feel defeated due to other people's shortcomings. We care less about what they do because we know we cannot control them and we have rid ourselves of our self-defeating thoughts and behaviors which really were the cause of our misery. We do not waste time and energy pointing out their defects (taking their inventory).

We suit up (be at our best), show up (be where we are supposed to be in heart and mind), and sweep our side of the street (change ourselves). It's such a relief trying to do something possible (improving ourselves) rather than banging our heads against the wall trying to do something impossible (changing them).

But what if we are in a relationship where we are continually being abused? In such a case, we consult with a counselor about what we can do to change how we handle the relationship, not about what the other person can do to change the relationship. Usually what a victim can do is to stop enabling the other person. We enable someone to abuse us when we think we need an abusive person - or when we think we can help, save, or fix an abusive person. Interestingly, when we stop enabling, other people often have a better chance of changing themselves.

DOING THE REASONABLE VS. THE BEST NEXT THING:
Doing the next right thing means doing the next reasonable thing. The next reasonable thing is choosing to act or not to act after applying the four steps to the situation. Doing reasonably is quite different from doing our best. We do not do the "next best thing" because we realize that we can only be reasonable, that we are imperfect, that we cannot predict the future, that we may have other matters that require more attention than the present matter. "Good enough is good enough." We don't want to belabor or endlessly overanalyze a situation and thereby procrastinate. For example, due to time constraints, sometimes it is better to send the email rather than make it grammatically perfect. We know we did not do our best, but we acted reasonably. Doing our best opens the door to judgment in hindsight. Doing our best can lead to unrealistic expectations which is a precursor to resentment. Doing our best can make us fearful for making too great an investment in what we could do simply. Doing our best can lead to the dangers of overcontrolling. Doing our best often causes us to compare ourselves to others. Thus, seeking serenity can often be summed up in the phrases, "Easy does it" and "Keep it simple."

Doing our best risks overdoing it and actually makes us perform worse. For example, a good wrestler knows when to pace himself. I have had many patients end up back in mental hospitals because they were doing their best trying to take care of aging parents, careers, children, etc. without taking reasonable breaks. Doing one's best often requires extreme aggression which can tip over into rage. Just ask tennis world number one, Novak Djokovic, after his aggressiveness became rage as he smashed a tennis ball which hit a referee, and caused his disqualification from the US Open. Again, serenity is not about winning all the time. We all win some and lose some. Serenity is about surviving and thriving in the face of all of life's challenges by adaptation. Charles Darwin would indeed be pleased.

Doing reasonably implies that we will not beat ourselves up over mistakes which we will inevitably make because we are human. Sometimes doing the next reasonable thing is to do nothing or to stop doing what we are doing. Doing reasonably implies doing actions or inactions based on perhaps weighing pros and cons, thought motivated, rather than full of character defects that veer us off course. Step 4 suggests we first fix ourselves so that we can act reasonably. Doing reasonably is relaxing while doing our best is often unduly stressful. Interestingly, people who do reasonably tend to be far more successful than people who are hell bent on doing their best. People who do reasonably tend to outlast people who are always stressing themselves out by living at full throttle. We must remember that the turtle wins the race. We don't want to burn out. We keep an even keel. Again, "Easy does it... Keep it simple." In serenity practice, we realize we may not know what is best and we are relieved of the bondage of having to do so. But we also realize that we can act reasonably when we apply the four steps and give daily attention to our Five Natures.

HIGHER POWER AND SPIRITUALITY

A WORD ABOUT HIGHER POWER:

A higher power is any force you use to restore you to serenity. A good higher power does not cause harm to you or others. A bad higher power eventually leads to suffering. A higher power can be a religious god, but it does not have to be. A higher power can be anything. It can be more than one thing and it can change.

Spiritual principles are different than religious principles. Agnostics and atheists can be spiritual. Spirituality is a connection to a greater power which makes you more likely to deal successfully with a challenge. For example, playing a basketball game with Lebron James on your team is a spiritual experience. Doing an agility trial with my brilliant dog Blitzen is a spiritual experience. For many, participating in an AA meeting is a connection to a greater power which helps an alcoholic stay sober. Nothing is more misinterpreted than the term higher power or god. Nothing seems to be more misunderstood than the difference between religion and spirituality. Spirituality is not a worldly emotion. It is a nature of humans in and of itself that can be used to produce a better way to deal with a problem. For example, "understanding" is a spiritual concept that defeats the harm caused by resentment. Love is a spiritual concept that defeats the harmful concept of fear. The point of this book is not to get you to believe in a religious god. The point is to help you to be serene.

THE FIVE NATURES

Daily devotion to each of the following greatly assists Serenity.

1. MIND: A healthy mind knows how to focus on what the individual wants it to focus on rather than wandering uncontrollably. It knows how to replace irrational, self-defeating thoughts with rational, healthy thoughts. Cognitive restructuring and meditation help. Being involved in mentally stimulating activities also help. Common thinking distortions include magnification (making problems more critical than they really are), catastrophizing (thinking the worst will happen), personalization (thinking everything that happens is mostly about you).

2. BODY: A healthy body is functional, vibrant, and well rested. It is not lethargic or too fidgety. Proper nutrition, exercise and rest contribute to a serene body. Posture is critical to serenity. Science has proved that slumping bodies with neck forward and drooping pressure adversely affect the spine and actually weigh on the internal organs. The most important physical exercise – the first one that should be considered – involves finding the specific muscles that need to be improved for one's specific posture. These exercises differ for each individual so it is necessary to consult with an expert. For maintenance, daily exercise, which stimulates cardiovascular fitness and tunes all of the body, assists serenity.

3. EMOTIONS: Healthy emotions tend to span the human range of feelings without those feelings causing harm to oneself or others. Daily stimulation and freedom from repression or escape through bad habits help with being in a healthy emotional state. Healthy emotions improve performance and serenity. Dealing appropriately with challenging emotions like grief and anger as well as enjoying happiness are all goals of emotional training.

4. SPIRIT: A healthy spirit connects with others and powers which keep it strong particularly in the face of crises and challenges. Living spiritual principles like humility, love, and compassion engages the Spirit. Powers include anything that helps the individual regain serenity without hurting that individual or others.

5. SOCIAL: A serene social self engages with others without sacrificing individuality and with an open mind to understanding differing opinions. This social self can assimilate and apply others' influences to nurture and improve one's individuality. For the serene individual, engaging in healthy social activities are a source of joy rather than embarrassment or self-consciousness. This social self acknowledges that there is some measure of fitting in allowed without falling prey to herd mentality. Engaging socially allows one to exercise empathy and other spiritual principles. It can also assist in developing the other Natures. The saying that no person is an island unto oneself applies regardless of the extent one gains or loses energy when one is in a social setting.

CASE SCENARIOS

Examples of how to apply the four steps

A. Someone I dated once won't return my call.

Step 1. We choose to accept and adapt, rather than control.
I accept I cannot force the person to return my call. I ask myself how can I adapt?

Step 2. We distinguish between wants and needs as we focus on gratitude, perspective, and flexibility.
Having her respond to me does not affect my basic needs. I'm still able to eat, etc. I am still healthy. I am grateful for having important needs fulfilled. I am grateful to have adventures in my life without the need for particular outcomes. I focus on perspective by contemplating on how my status may be different from others who lack basic necessities like food and shelter. I resolve to be flexible in my dating strategies.

Step 3. We connect to HELP (Higher Effective Loving Power).
Fortunately, there are many choices to connect to HELP.
(i.) I take a deep breath and take a walk.
(ii.) I practice a spiritual principle like helping someone else.
(iii.) I call a friend who I know will support me in my decision not to control but to accept and adapt – someone who seems to apply the ideas conceptualized by the four steps in his or her life.
(iv.) I listen to some music.
(v.) I play with my dog.

Step 4. We choose to fix ourselves, not others, then do the next reasonable thing.

I focus on myself not the other person. I do not obsess over the other person's personality. Rather, I fix myself by recognizing and dealing with my obsessive thinking. I tell myself obsessive thinking doesn't help anything and that I need to let that kind of thinking go or I might generate harmful resentment. I choose not to obsessively think about what I may or may not have done or said during the date which the other person may or may not have liked. I then do a reasonable action which in this case could be to do nothing. However, it feels like a reasonable next action to (a) test whether or not the call was received, (b) whether or not the person likes someone who tries twice, and (c) to give myself a sense of finality. So I resolve to call or text her one last time. I therefore adapt reasonably, not perfectly. I know I have acted reasonably if my character defect, which in this case is obsessive thought, gradually dissipates. I don't expect to be perfect. I do not need to have any resolution.

I have therefore adapted, not controlled so that I may be serene in knowing I have done all that I can reasonably do and therefore can move on with my life in peace. Also, I know that it is natural if the obsessive thought returns. I simply apply the four steps each time it returns. Each time, the obsessive thinking will lessen until it disappears. Serenity is a process.

Note that I also have to do the Five Natures as my day proceeds. Serenity is a holistic process. So, I take care of my spiritual and social selves by, for example, exercising compassion (in this case I call a friend who is struggling), I dance to some music (physical), I journal (intellectual), and I watch a funny YouTube video (emotional).

B. I am promised delivery of a new dress but it never comes after delay after delay.

Step 1. We choose to accept and adapt, rather than control.
I accept that I cannot control the delivery of the dress, that it could be lost or permanently out of stock, etc. I ask myself how can I adapt?

Step 2. We distinguish between wants and needs as we focus on gratitude, perspective, and flexibility.
I realize that I don't even really need the new dress. I am flexible as I recall that I have a dress in my closet that would work well for the party. I am grateful for the dress I have. I remember the good experience I had wearing it. I get perspective by appreciating my dilemma which does not involve "life or death" but is more akin to what is commonly referred to as a "luxury problem" not worth fighting the delivery person to mail it. I remember that 99% of the time things are delivered timely. Having the new dress does not affect my basic needs. I'm still able to eat, etc. I am still healthy. I am grateful for having important needs fulfilled. I am grateful to have adventures in my life without the need for particular outcomes. I think about how the universe has treated me with lots of lucky breaks and that there have been many angels in my life.

Step 3. We connect to HELP (Higher Effective Loving Power).
As usual, there are many choices to connect to HELP if we are only willing to
look for them.
(i.) I meditate on a principle like unconditional forgiveness.
(ii.) If I am religious, I may read a bible verse.
(iii.) I call a friend who I know will support me in my decision not to control but to accept and adapt – someone who seems to apply the ideas conceptualized by the four steps in his or her life.
(iv.) I paint a picture.
(v.) I scrub the kitchen floor.

Step 4. We choose to fix ourselves, not others, then do the next reasonable thing.

I focus on myself not the other person. I do not obsess over the other person's personality. Rather, I fix myself by recognizing and dealing with my anger over my belief that I have been treated unfairly. I tell myself that such a belief doesn't help anything and that I need to let that kind of thinking go or I might generate harmful resentment. I choose not to spiral into a pity party. I reason that I should not punish myself by letting my thinking depress me, particularly when the fault lies with something or someone else and is completely beyond my control. I reason that I need to take the drama out of the situation so I substitute my seriousness with a sense of humor. Then, I peacefully resolve to do the next reasonable action which could be a number of things or nothing at all. I know I won't be perfect. I know I have to weigh the time and energy on a cost benefit analysis. Ultimately I decide to simply click on My Orders and let the deliverer know to credit back my credit card. I therefore adapt reasonably, not perfectly. I know I have acted reasonably if my character defect, which in this case is my anger over the uncontrollable aspect of life and injustice, lessens.

I have therefore adapted, not controlled so that I may be serene in knowing I have done all that I can reasonably do and therefore can move on with my life in peace. Also, it's natural if my disappointment over the lost dress does not immediately fully disappear. I simply apply the four steps each time it returns. Each time, serenity will gradually return and the lost dress issue will be forgotten. Serenity is a process.

I also remember that I have to do the Five Natures as my day proceeds. Serenity is a holistic process. So, I take care of my Spirit (by saying a prayer of gratitude), and social self by, for example, going to a record store and chatting with a clerk, doing an upper body weight lifting session (physical), reading a novel (intellectual), and watching a soapy, romantic movie (emotional).

C. I am told I have diabetes. I get a second opinion which confirms the diagnosis.

Step 1. We choose to accept and adapt, rather than control.
The first step is simple. I must accept the diagnosis. Even though I may initially dislike the information and the person giving me the information, I have to accept the opinion. I also accept that it is natural for me to have a period of grieving, but that the grief will end in acceptance.

Step 2. We distinguish between wants and needs as we focus on gratitude, perspective, and flexibility.
I certainly don't want to be told I have diabetes. Nevertheless, I can honestly say that I have needs met in this moment despite the severity of the news. I still have food, shelter, and other basic necessities. I can be grateful for what I have like medical technology to treat the disease. I can exercise perspective by looking at the statistics which indicate that the diagnosis is most likely not a death sentence if I am willing to change my lifestyle and accept certain medical treatment. I also know I need to be flexible to accept the diagnosis and the course of dealing with it.

Step 3. We connect to HELP (Higher Effective Loving Power).
As usual, there are many choices to connect to HELP if we are only willing to look for them.
(i.) First, I am having trouble getting over my grief, so I get HELP from a grief counselor.
(ii.) I personally have a Higher Effective Loving Power which I call God. For me, it is a force which I believe strengthens me and all the universe. I say a heartfelt prayer asking for strength and for the ability to deal positively with this diagnosis so that I may not only help myself but also help others who may be similarly suffering.
(iii.) I trust the physician.
(iv.) I seek connectedness with a support group.
(v.) I share the news of the diagnosis with a friend or family member.

Step 4. We choose to fix ourselves, not others, then do the next reasonable thing.

The only thing I can do is change my attitude. From my discussions with supportive people, connection to HELP, and self inquiry of what is bothering me, I resolve that the main character issue I must fix is fear. I have fear of change, fear of the unknown, fear to trust others, and even fear of death. To deal with this fear, I use positive self messaging like "No one knows what is going to happen in the future." I choose to live in today and correct my thinking when my mind wanders into the future. I ask myself "What use is it to worry?" "I find the word "worry" in the index of this book and read a supportive message about worry like "Worry does not change the outcome, it just makes you feel bad in the meantime." I congratulate myself for having the courage to face this fear. I consider how I might be able to help others today as I continue to focus on gratitude, perspective, and flexibility. I do not expect to feel completely serene immediately, but know that if I keep practicing the four steps and pay attention to my Five Natures daily, I will have peace of mind.

D. Sometimes I am overwhelmed by many challenges happening within a very short period of time. For example, in just the first two hours of my day, I have had many situations which I have had to accept that I could not change.

1. A promised pay check was not delivered.
2. Someone failed to show up for an appointment.
3. Five urgent emails were sent to me at once.
4. I was unable to go for a walk due to rain and lightning.
5. A client would not respond to me.
6. My son needed help finding something in the attic.
7. My body was sore from doing yard work yesterday.
8. I needed to feed the dog.
9. A computer issue required me to call I.T. people.

Step 1. We choose to accept and adapt, rather than control.
I want to control each scenario, but realize that I have to accept and adapt to them to return to peace of mind. I tell myself that serenity is the foundation for being able to cope with this sudden flood of problems, and that serenity is my true goal in life today. I therefore consciously choose to accept and adapt. I also do not go into denial about the fact that I feel overwhelmed. I own this feeling.

Step 2. We distinguish between wants and needs as we focus on gratitude, perspective, and flexibility.
Although there are a flood of issues, I keep them "right sized" by recognizing that they present situations that threaten my wants but not my needs. For example, I become grateful for not needing the paycheck today. I gain perspective by realizing that many people don't have savings so that not receiving a paycheck at a needed time would create far more difficult problems. I exercise flexibility by deciding to wait a few days before making a purchase of something I really don't need anyway. I do this analysis quickly with regard to each event and soon I feel my serenity restored.

Step 3. We connect to HELP (Higher Effective Loving Power).
Already feeling better, I call a friend and tell him how I am dealing with my overwhelming morning and to see if I can support the friend in any way. By sharing my experience and strength, I get validation of my serenity practice and also help my friend.

Step 4. We choose to fix ourselves, not others, then do the next reasonable thing.
I tell myself that these events have given me an opportunity to build patience. I substitute any feelings of resentment with empathy and understanding because I know that building resentment will only hurt me. I tell myself that I can only do one thing at a time, that it is the nature of life to have unexpected issues, that everyone has to live through twists and turns, and that it is simply my turn to experience a group of issues at the same time. I then do the next reasonable thing by dealing with what seems to be the most pressing problem first. I don't expect everything to get done immediately or perfectly, but I am confident that in time, these items will resolve with my serenity maintained.

I also make it a point not to neglect my Five Natures even though I have to deal with problems. I take breaks, eat correctly, exercise, visit a friend, and meditate. I tell myself that regardless of what happens with regard to the events, the most important thing has already occurred: the restoration of my serenity.

The next page contains a simple form that you can print out or otherwise download and duplicate as many times as you like. Use it to guide you to applying the four steps as you walk your path of serenity.

Applying the four steps

Describe Situation: _____
_____

_____

Step 1. We choose to accept and adapt, rather than control.

_____

_____

_____

Step 2. We distinguish between wants and needs as we focus on gratitude, perspective, and flexibility.

_____

_____

_____

Step 3. We connect to HELP (Higher Effective Loving Power).

_____

_____

_____

Step 4. We choose to fix ourselves, not others, then do the next reasonable thing.

_____

_____

_____

_____

**REMEMBER TO TAKE CARE OF
MY FIVE NATURES EACH DAY**

IF YOU ARE FEELING BAD, ASK YOURSELF IF YOU NEED TO STOP DOING ANY OF THE FOLLOWING 30 SERENITY KILLING HABITS

1. Not accepting life on life's terms and worrying about getting your own way.

2. Worrying about what others think about you.

3. Measuring yourself.

4. Comparing yourself with others.

5. Seeing things as all bad.

6. Refusing to accept change.

7. Expecting that life will always be fair.

8. Refusing to forgive yourself.

9. Refusing to believe that you can't influence anything meaningfully.

10. Believing pain will never end.

11. Forgetting to be grateful.

12. Losing perspective.

13. Living fearfully.

14. Trying to control what is impossible to control like other people and outcomes.

15. Allowing others to control you because you fail to create healthy boundaries and engage in toxic relationships.

16. Acting out of hatred, anger and resentment instead of love, understanding and compassion.

17. Procrastinating.

18. Neglecting to do activities that promote physical, mental, spiritual, social, and emotional balance.

19. Being inflexible.

20. Refusing to love yourself unconditionally.

21. Lacking an appropriate sense of humor.

22. Letting your emotions get you into trouble.

23. Failing to distinguish between wants and needs.

24. Letting winning be the most important thing.

25. Neglecting to connect with someone with your heart.

26. Neglecting to connect with a power that helps you maintain serenity.

27. Neglecting to practice spiritual principles like acceptance, truth, forgiveness, unselfishness, love, patience, humility, and understanding rather than ego, resentment, greed, power, fear, and prejudice.

28. Failing to accept that you make mistakes.

29. Ignoring your own character defects and refusing to change yourself.

30. Keeping your mind from wandering into unproductive, self-defeating thoughts which tend to fear the future and regret the past rather than focusing on the present moment.

THE SERENITY POEM

Not all wrong, not all right.
Life is seldom black or white.
In the now, on we go,
Fearing not win, place or show.

Not all good, not all bad.
Judgment only makes me mad.
Never perfect, not all-knowing.
Little by little, constantly growing.

Not better than, not worse.
Constantly comparing is a curse.
Loving detachment lets me be.
Understanding, not resentment, sets me free.

Not my will, not my way,
A balanced life saves my day.
With gratitude, perspective, and flexible plans,
I am at peace in everlasting hands.

January

February

March

April

May

June

July

August

September

October

November

December

About the Author and Acknowledgments

Paul Caimi J.D., LCDC has been sober for 33 years. He received his psychology degree from Harvard where he was a research assistant for B.F. Skinner. He is also a lawyer, licensed chemical dependency counselor, and the creator and author of SoberTool, one of the first and most widely used recovery apps. The Father of two wonderful adult sons, Paul finds much serenity with his wife of 35 years and his dog on an island where he surfs, scuba dives, and observes the great turtles nest before they return to the sea.

Illustrated by A.J. Caimi (ajtoons.com)

Special thanks to John Sandoval for his support and messages: "How can I resist temptation," "Suffering? Become a Lake," "Gratitude, Nothing is trite," "Be Kind to Yourself," "Happy New Child," "As I miss my Grandmother," "The Sundial," "The Dark Night of the Soul," "The Problem is not the Problem," and the message about who you are not on the back cover, all of which are included herein with his permission.

DISCLAIMER: None of the information in this book creates a counselor/ patient relationship or should substitute for any other forms of therapy. This book makes no claims that it will help the Reader, and the Reader waives the right to make any claims of any kind against Author for any injuries or losses claimed from the use of this Book. This Book is not therapy or treatment and does not substitute for therapy or treatment.

Made in the USA
Las Vegas, NV
01 January 2024

83759079R00267